Suicide and the God of Grace

Suicide and the God of Grace

A Collection of Christian Reflection

EDITED BY
MARK KOONZ

Foreword by Christina Baxter

WIPF & STOCK · Eugene, Oregon

SUICIDE AND THE GOD OF GRACE
A collection of Christian reflection

Copyright © 2025 Mark Koonz. All rights reserved. Except for brief quotations in critical publications or reviews, no part of this book may be reproduced in any manner without prior written permission from the publisher. Write: Permissions, Wipf and Stock Publishers, 199 W. 8th Ave., Suite 3, Eugene, OR 97401.

Wipf & Stock
An Imprint of Wipf and Stock Publishers
199 W. 8th Ave., Suite 3
Eugene, OR 97401

www.wipfandstock.com

PAPERBACK ISBN: 979-8-3852-4100-2
HARDCOVER ISBN: 979-8-3852-4101-9
EBOOK ISBN: 979-8-3852-4102-6

08/15/25

Unless otherwise indicated, Scripture quotations are from the (NASB®) New American Standard Bible®, Copyright © 1960, 1971, 1977, 1995, 2020 by The Lockman Foundation. Used by permission. All rights reserved. www.lockman.org.

To the memory of William O. Harris and Brenda J. Hermanson
who were faithful in friendship and gave comfort to others

Contents

Permissions | ix
Foreword by Christina Baxter | xiii
Acknowledgments | xvii

Section One: Christian Reflection on Suicide

1 What God Only Knows | 1
2 For Ministry to Grieving Survivors | 7
3 Questions in Need of Reflection | 13

Section Two: Historical Survey of Christian Reflection

4 The Bible: Key Narratives | 33
5 The Bible: Key Passages | 56
6 Augustine of Hippo (354–430), Thomas Aquinas (1225–1274) | 72
7 Martin Luther (1483–1546) | 91
8 John Calvin (1509–1564) | 101
9 John Donne (1572–1631) | 115
10 John Wesley (1708–1791), Samuel Johnson (1709–1784) | 120
11 Søren Kierkegaard (1813–1855) | 131
12 Two Victorians: George MacDonald (1824–1905), Charles Haddon Spurgeon (1834–1892) | 138
13 G. K. Chesterton (1874–1936) | 146

14 Paul Tillich (1886–1965) | 156

15 Karl Barth (1886–1968) | 169

16 C. S. Lewis (1898–1963) | 177

17 Dietrich Bonhoeffer (1906–1945) | 181

18 Modern Continentals: Jürgen Moltmann (1926–2024), Wolfhart Pannenberg (1928–2014) | 187

19 Diverse North American Evangelicals: J. Vernon McGee (1904–1988), John Warwick Montgomery (1931–2024), R. C. Sproul (1939–2017), Jack Cottrell (1938–2022) | 193

20 Roman Catholic and Eastern Orthodox Views | 200

Section Three:
Contemporary Samples of Christian Reflection

21 Sermon for Michael Foster by Canon Dr. Vigo A. Demant | 213

22 A Suicide, a Funeral, a Sermon by Will Willimon | 223

23 Sermon for a Teenage Boy by Eric Peterson | 232

24 Talking About Suicide in Reference to Societal Issues: a Sermon by Will Willimon | 245

25 Searching for Words on Occasions When People Weep by Mark Koonz | 258

Bibliography | 275

Index | 287

Permissions

I WISH TO THANK the following persons, executors or institutions for granting permission to use copyrighted materials:

1517 Publishing, for permission to quote from *Defending the Faith in a Messy World: A Christian Apologetics Primer*, by John Warwick Montgomery. Used by permission.
Augsburg Fortress Publishers, for permission to quote from *The Large Catechism*, by Martin Luther, translated by Robert H. Fischer. Used by permission.
Augsburg Fortress Publishers, for permission to quote from *Table Talk*, by Martin Luther, translated and edited by Theodore G. Tappert. Used by permission.
Baker Publishing Group, for their fair usage policy allowing 250 words. Used with gratitude.
Bloomsbury Publishing PLC., for permission to quote from Karl Barth, *Church Dogmatics* (T&T Clark is an imprint of the Bloomsbury Publishing PLC.). Used by permission.
James T. Como, for permission to quote from *C. S. Lewis at the Breakfast Table and Other Reminiscences*. Used by permission.
Concordia Publishing House, for permission to quote from *Luther Works Volume 19*, edited by Hilton C. Oswald © 1974, 2002. Used with permission. All rights reserved. cph.org.
Concordia Publishing House, for permission to quote from *What Luther Says*, edited by Ewald M. Plass © 1959, 1987. Used by permission. All rights reserved. cph.org.
Barbara Cottrell, for permission to quote from *The Collected Writings of Jack Cottrell: God's Amazing Salvation*, Volume I, by Jack Cottrell. Used by permission.
William B. Eerdmans Publishing Company, for permission to quote from *A Karl Barth Reader*, edited by Rolf Joachim Erler and Reiner Marquard. Used by permission.
William B. Eerdmans Publishing Company, for permission to quote from *Bioethics*, by Gilbert Meilander. Used by permission.
William B. Eerdmans Publishing Company, for permission to quote from *Christian Reflections*, by C. S. Lewis, edited by Walter Hooper. Used by permission.
Fortress Press, for allowing up to 500 words of *Dietrich Bonhoeffer Works*, Volume 6: *Ethics*.
Fortress Press, for permission to quote from *Ethics of Hope*, by Jürgen Moltmann. Used by permission.

PERMISSIONS

Indiana University Press, for permission to quote from *Journals and Papers, Volume 4*, by Søren Kierkegaard. Used by permission.

InterVarsity Press, for permission to quote from *A Long Obedience in the Same Direction*, by Eugene Peterson. Used by permission.

Deborah Johannesen/Johannesen Printing and Publishing, for permission to quote from *George MacDonald and His Wife*, by Greville MacDonald. Used by permission.

Deborah Johannesen/Johannesen Printing and Publishing, for permission to quote from *Unspoken Sermons*, by George MacDonald. Used by permission.

Kregel Publications, for their fair usage allowance of 300 words per book. Used with gratitude.

Meg Peery McLaughlin and Jarrett McLaughlin, for permission granted Will Willimon to use a major portion of an untitled funeral sermon. Used by permission.

H. C. Erik Midelfort, for permission to quote from "Religious Melancholy and Suicide: On the Reformation Origins of a Sociological Stereotype" in *Madness, Melancholy, and the Limits of the Self: Studies in Culture, Law, and the Sacred*, edited by Andrew D. Weiner, Leonard V. Kaplan, and Sonja Hansard-Weiner.

Paul K. Moser, for permission to quote from *God in Experience: Essays of Hugh Ross Mackintosh*, edited by Paul K. Moser and Benjamin Nasmith. Used by permission.

Penguin Random House, for permission to quote from *The House of Wittgenstein: A Family at War*, by Alexander Waugh. Used by permission.

Princeton University Press, for permission to quote from, *The Sickness unto Death: A Christian Psychological Exposition for Upbuilding and Awakening*, by Søren Kierkegaard, edited and translated by Howard V. Hong and Edna H. Hong. Used by permission.

Princeton University Press, for communication of fair usage policy allowing me to quote from *Stages on Life's Way: Studies by Various Persons*, by Søren Kierkegaard, edited and translated by Howard V. Hong and Edna H. Hong. Princeton: Princeton University Press, 1988. Used with gratitude.

Regent College Publishing, for permission to quote from *Luther: Letters of Spiritual Counsel*, translated and edited by Theodore G. Tappert. Used with permission.

The C. S. Lewis Company Ltd., for permission to quote from *Christian Reflections*, by C. S. Lewis, edited by Walter Hooper, copyright © 1967, 1980 C.S. Lewis Pte. Ltd. Extracts reprinted by permission.

The C. S. Lewis Company Ltd., for permission to quote from *George MacDonald An Anthology*, by C. S. Lewis, copyright © 1946 C. S. Lewis Pte. Ltd. Extracts reprinted by permission.

The C. S. Lewis Company Ltd., for permission to quote from *Mere Christianity*, by C. S. Lewis copyright © 1942, 1943, 1944, 1952 C. S. Lewis Pte. Ltd. Extracts reprinted by permission.

The C. S. Lewis Company Ltd., for permission to quote from *The Problem of Pain*, by C. S. Lewis, copyright © 1940 C. S. Lewis Pte. Ltd. Extracts reprinted by permission.

The C. S. Lewis Company Ltd., for permission to quote from Lewis's letter in *A Severe Mercy*, by Sheldon Vanauken: C. S. Lewis copyright © 1977 C. S. Lewis Pte. Ltd. Extracts reprinted by permission.

The Office of the President of the Lutheran Church—Missouri Synod, for permission to quote from *That They May Have Life*. Used by permission.

The Office of the President of The Lutheran Church—Missouri Synod, for permission to quote from *That They May Live*. Used by permission.

PERMISSIONS

The University of Chicago Press, for permission within their fair usage guidelines to quote from *Systematic Theology, Volume II and Volume III*, by Paul Tillich. Used by permission.

Tyndale House Publishers, for permission to quote some content from *Now, That's a Good Question* by R. C. Sproul. Copyright © 2020. All rights reserved.

Alan Torrance, for permission to quote from *Worship, Community, and the Triune God of Grace*, by James B. Torrance. Used by permission.

Sarah Veblen, for permission to quote from *Suicide: "Biathanatos" Transcribed and Edited for Modern Readers*, edited by William A. Clebsch. Used by permission.

Jeffrey R. Watt, for permission to quote from *Choosing Death: Suicide and Calvinism in Early Modern Geneva*. Used by permission.

Westminster/John Knox for their generous fair usage policy allowing me to quote from *Anthropology in Theological Perspective*, by Wolfhart Pannenberg. Used with gratitude.

Westminster/John Knox for their generous fair usage policy allowing me to quote from *Institutes of the Christian Religion*, edited by John T. McNeill, translated by Ford Lewis Battles. Used with gratitude.

Dana R. Wright, for permission to quote from *Educational Ministry in the Logic of the Spirit*, by James E. Loder Jr., edited by Dana R. Wright. Used by permission.

Yale University Press, for their fair usage policy allowing 300 words. Used with gratitude.

Foreword

FEW PASTORS OR MINISTERS will engage in a lifetime of ministry without encountering suicide at some point in their vocation. I was very glad to have the chance to read this book, as there have been a number of occasions when I have been close to those who were struggling with the idea of suicide, or who had failed in their attempt to bring their own life to an end. Others to whom I was offering pastoral support had lost a dear friend or family member in this way. I had not previously had the chance to read and think at length about the subject, so my ideas were hazy, not informed by the rich resource of theological reflection now available in this publication.

All deaths raise deep challenges for those left behind, but none more so than the death by suicide of those who suddenly decide to take their own lives. Family and friends face agonizing questions as to whether they could have done more to prevent it, but alas too often are left not knowing exactly what caused the tragedy. The finality, mystery and shock, especially if they are the ones who discover the deceased, traumatizes them, leaving an indelible shadow over the rest of their lives. For their sakes, as well as for the sake of those who are themselves contemplating such an action, and who may seek pastoral support as they struggle with their ideation, this book deserves to be read by pastors and ministers everywhere.

In researching this book, the author has been eager to read as widely as possible the work of theologians and ministers on this topic—but has been disappointed to find some serious gaps in primary material. There seem to be few, if any, female theologians who have tackled this subject; even some major theologians who write about ethics or practical theology have been silent on this matter. Recognizing that some readers may not have time to read the whole volume, the author has included discussions from a wide range of viewpoints, and been able to show that there is more overall agreement about Christian theological approaches to suicide than might at first be expected. Perhaps people steer away from a consideration of the subject, not only because it is emotionally challenging, but also because one needs a strong framework of eschatology and the four last things—death, judgement, hell and heaven—as well as a robust understanding of the Christian understanding of sin, salvation and the work of the Holy Spirit if one is to make any thorough attempt at offering a Christian theological approach to understanding suicide, or ministering to those caught up in this loss. This book offers clear access to all of these themes as it traces the way that the greatest theological minds— Augustine, Luther, Calvin, Barth and others—have carved a way through these thickets of complexity.

The lack of female theologians who have tackled this subject is perhaps surprising. A recent report in the UK disclosed that "suicide continues to be the leading cause of [maternal] death between six weeks and twelve months after birth, accounting for a staggering 39 percent of deaths in this period."[1] Whilst not wishing to suggest that only female theologians can tackle this question, it is surely the case that the matter of giving birth, which such a large proportion of women experience, thereby putting themselves at risk, might put them at the forefront of Christian approaches to this subject. There are, of course, some theological reflections to be made on the way that a society fails to treat women adequately in these circumstances. In the UK, there is a growing unease at the way that health policies often disregard regular female experience by normalizing male health patterns. Without diminishing any sense of personal responsibility, it is also possible to argue that women at the time of giving birth are particularly vulnerable because of the way that hormones adjust postpartum. It is important to recognize that even if excellent family and community support is available, it may not be sufficient to enable a woman to cope with herself and her baby at this critical time. At the very least, Christians who believe in the sanctity of every human life have a duty to campaign for better maternal care for all who need it. Modern practices make possible studies that can show which groups of people are most likely to commit suicide, thereby offering the chance for social strategies to be

---

1. Tubb, "Suicide." These statistics remain cause for concern even as they vary slightly from year to year.

developed which can assist and mitigate their risks. Mature charities such as The Samaritans in the UK, who offer 24/7 listening services to anyone in crisis, have a wealth of experience that can guide such strategies. But because suicidal ideation is often hidden, Christians can live their lives without ever really engaging with those who are most desperate or realizing how important some social change could be. The conspiracy of silence on this matter may begin to crumble as we think more rigorously from a theological point of view about suicide. This book will aid this task.

In addition to those most closely related to those who commit suicide, there are also others who may be deeply affected and need not only support and professional assistance but also the tools to think about what they have witnessed. Amongst those are a small group of people who were unwittingly the "cause" of a suicide when people throw themselves off road bridges, or in front of underground trains. And the first responders who have to attend the scene, whilst not the unwitting cause of the death, will also be traumatized. Not all of these will be Christian people or even people of faith, but some will be and they may need help as they not only process their own reactions, but also seek to pray about what they have encountered. Such praying depends on a theological framework which they may not have ever had the chance to explore in their church life.

This raises, as the author indicates, deep questions as to whether local churches ever teach about this subject at moments when it is not an immediate matter, so that Christians are given a basic outline of how they might understand suicide within the framework of their faith and the tools to tackle it when they encounter it themselves. Teachers and preachers in Christian churches will be assisted in ensuring that this topic is addressed by this resource, as it offers careful consideration of matters such as whether God's final judgement of a person depends entirely on their state of mind in the moment of their death. It deals not only with theological complexities, but also offers practical reflections—including sermons written to be preached at the funeral of a suicide victim. Earthed in the realities of contemporary secular life, and churchly challenges, it will also enable ministers to engage with some serious questions as to how to approach the funerals of those whose choice of suicide comes in the painful months of terminal illness, but before natural death might be expected. It is to be welcomed as a significant contribution to Christian ministry and is likely to be a resource to which the reader returns.

Christina Baxter
Ascension Day 2025

CANON DR CHRISTINA BAXTER *was Principal of St John's College Nottingham until her retirement in 2012; much involved in her local church as a lay preacher, and was formerly Lay Chair of the Church of England's governing body, the General Synod and a member of the Archbishops' Council.*

Acknowledgments

For brevity's sake, please forgive the absence of titles. I am deeply grateful to Christina Baxter for writing the foreword to this book. Her work and encouragement has been invaluable these past many years. I am especially grateful to those who allowed their own material to be used in this collection: Meg Peery McLaughlin, Jarrett McLaughlin, Eric Peterson, and Will Willimon.

My thanks also goes to Alan Torrance for permission to quote from his father, James Torrance, and to Stephen Demant for permission to use his grandfather Vigo Demant's sermon. Additional vignettes were provided by Alan Beasley, Scott Keith, and Silouan Thompson. My thanks goes to Barbara Cottrell for permission to quote from her husband, Jack Cottrell, and to Sarah Veblen, for permission to quote from her father, William A. Clebsch.

As this has been an on and off again project for many years, I fear the unintentional absence of some who should be mentioned here. Seventeen years ago in my initial search for essays and sample sermons, phone calls or letters of support came from Ray Anderson, Eugene and Jan Peterson, Haddon Robinson, Rod Rosenbladt, John Stott, Gardner C. Taylor, and Ralph Quere. More than one said there was a gap that needed to be filled. I treasure the letter John Stott sent to Walla Walla, Australia, which then traveled round the globe to reach the other Walla Walla. Roberta Hestenes, Kalman Kaplan, and Earl Palmer each met with me to discuss my project. The interest and encouragement of so many people whom I looked up to stayed in memory, helping me wade through seasons of discouragement. Sadly, given my own pastoral duties that took precedence, I could not finish in time to show them the finished product.

Valuable practical assistance was given by Andrew Bawtree, Carol Ann Buelow, Chuck Cooper, John Jefferson Davis, Paul Kent, Gretchen Passantino, Jen Pope, Greg Smith, and Edward L. Taylor. I am indebted to Kathryn Helmers for her earlier editorial assistance and advocacy, and for the further assistance of the editorial staff at Wipf & Stock. I am grateful to several officials of other publishing houses who discussed their fair usage rules and gave me informal permission to use their material so long as properly cited. Any errors in historical theology, biography, or flaws in communication are my own.

At the outset of my ministry my mentors were John Mark Goerss and Leonard Dale, both of whom were very patient and taught me lessons that helped me navigate difficult moments in ministry. Along the way I have learned much from my friend and discussion partner, Bill Barrett, who convinced me of the importance of bringing this book to completion. I am also grateful to the faithful people of Opheim and Larslan, Montana, and Emmanuel Lutheran Church, Walla Walla, for supporting my efforts in ministry. Overarching this project, the prayers of my family and many friends have been a sustaining blessing.

Section One

Christian Reflection on Suicide

1

What God Only Knows

MANY OF US EXPERIENCE daily living as an exquisite burden—a gift full of hope and promise even if shot through with personal trials, illness, or financial setbacks. But that burden can be rejected. Few things are more shattering than a friend or loved one's suicide. We hear the painful news with horror and perplexity.

The first place our racing thoughts go is usually "Why?" Why did that member of our community despair and choose death over life? Why did my brother not understand how much we cared? Why would my child do something so irrevocably final?

We look for clues that fit a familiar pattern because we strive to understand by finding a core reason. Dan Olsen, a professor of pastoral care, used to remind students preparing for ministry, "We want to think that we, as individual possessors of free will, are unique and unpredictable in the use of our freedom, but at the same time we need other people to be predictable in their behavior."[1]

We need the pattern of other people's behavior to be understandable because explainable behavior makes the world seem reliable, less threatening, something through which we can navigate. Yet we cannot always make another individual's choices fit neatly into our own understanding of human behavior, nor compatible with how we ourselves would have thought, felt, or acted in similar circumstances. Other people can be so confusing.

---

1. Personal class notes from Olsen's course on pastoral counseling, Wartburg Theological Seminary, academic year 1991–1992.

We often say, "I don't know what makes that person tick." Individuals are such a mystery.

When confronted with suicide, we often search for a label or category that makes this frightening, outrageously irrational decision seem more rational and explainable in terms we can understand. It is ironic that we look for reasons in an irrational act. We want the event to seem rational at some point because the irrational scares us. We also look for reasons in order to sympathize and be less severe in our judgment.[2]

It is not wrong to look for reasons, but the search is not always fruitful. This is because the question "Why?" in any given case is the one that cannot be answered with complete certainty. We are motivated to find a reason, or cluster of reasons, because we feel very unsettled when there is no explanation to help us navigate through grief and bewilderment. Yet it is not always possible to find one explanation that tells all we need to know, something accurate as well as comprehensive. The "reasons" we discover may only count as powerful inducements, not necessarily causes. All of us face choices about alternatives, then make choices, on a daily basis. Yet not all motivations behind our choices are obvious.

A man knew that he could rub people the wrong way, so he wore a t-shirt saying, "I don't have stress but I'm a carrier." When it was worn out, his wife and employees got him another one. In our problematic condition we both create new problems and respond improperly to other people's problems. We do not always understand how everyone else thinks and feels about these situations. We like to rate choices and actions as good or bad, wise or foolish. Some a little less so, others a little more so. But that is often starting at the wrong end, coming at the human condition from our own point of view.

Donald Barnhouse grew up when flying in airplanes was a new experience. He illustrated this problem of making comparisons. How large a house seems when you stand next to it. Compare yourself with a tree, a barn, a water tower, or a five story building. We see largeness of size in a relative way, by comparing small and large objects. Looking from the ground up so many things seem tall. Yet when you get high enough in an airplane and look down what do you see? Everything looks flat. And there is a theological truth in this shift of perspective.

We look at our problems, choices, and sins from our limited point of view, not from God's point of view. Some things seem more wrong than

---

2. Caird, *Truth of the Gospel*, 74.

others, like lying and stealing, with murder the most terrible of all. Do not get me wrong, I think God sees these things as wrong too, but this is also the case with the "smaller" sins that do not seem so important to us. The sins of the human race may be more leveled or flattened in God's sight than in ours, because each one represents a bentness that has to be straightened, a poison that has to be cured, something out of kilter. We only know more accurately what God thinks of our sinful condition (and occasional volcanic eruptions) because of the life, death, and resurrection of Jesus. Given the truth of the incarnation, his agony on the cross is the key moment that reveals God's depth of opposition to all human sin and evil. That key moment of atonement (reconciliation) also reveals the depth of God's determination to forgive and renew the human family. This is our starting point.

Only God knows how to redeem those who have failed, if only once or many times, to fully trust in God's providential care and sustaining grace through all tribulations. The circle of God's faithfulness to each one of us must be drawn with a greater circumference, encircling the smaller circle of our inadequate faith. The faithfulness of God is a wider circle that engulfs the smaller circle of our weakness, shabby living, inconsistent gratitude, and incomplete faithfulness. God's faithfulness to us is far greater in commitment than our deficient response to his love. Nothing can separate us from the love of God (Romans 8), including the pain in our souls. That is part of the message of the cross.

I do not have answers for the mystery of despair and suicide. Moreover, God may not allow us to have too many answers. As we take our questions to the One who knows, we open our lives to the ministry of God's Spirit. Even so, it is not easy to entrust our questions to God when living in pain and confusion. Questions continually arise out of our suffering, catching us unprepared and refusing to go away. With or without answers, we can be strengthened in prayer within this relationality.

My Early Experiences

On the week of my fourteenth birthday, my mother Nancy died of heart complications due to a long battle with an autoimmune disease called lupus. In the aftermath of my mother's death, many of the students at my junior high school were very kind to me, not often with direct words but by allowing me the space I needed for my private grief. There were a couple kids, however, who spoke to me about my loss, and some of the ones who expressed sympathy were not kids I had done a lot with previously. This probably made me more receptive to unusual conversations. One day after football practice a boy named Erik, who had recently suffered a sports injury, indicated he wanted to walk home with me. He had never taken much notice of me before, as we were in different grades and had our own circle of friends, yet there was a basic comfort level because we had both gone to the same elementary school. I knew he had one very close friend and they were usually inseparable, but for some reason they were not together that afternoon.

We had a fifteen minute walk together before we parted, and Erik was very friendly but talked a lot about himself. It was the extent to which he suddenly opened up about deeply personal matters that surprised me, all of which I will keep private. In that moment I assumed he could tell me because he knew I was in pain too, which somehow freed him to talk about his own life. As he spoke I sensed his troubled spirit, but did not anticipate where this was heading.

We lived fairly close to each other, only three blocks apart. I went to my home and wondered if our talk could be the start of a new friendship. Erik went home and, within the hour, shot himself. By the time he was found he was beyond all help. When I heard about this at school the next day I was devastated. I was the last person who saw him alive, and he had bared his soul to an extent that was unusual. But he never hinted at what he planned to do, and I never dreamed that any person would choose against life when given an opportunity to live. As soon as I heard the news, the whole day became surreal.

I was unaware that often a person intent on suicide will have one final conversation with a friend, neighbor, or total stranger. This can happen with an unusual degree of intimacy and self-disclosure. In that final conversation the speaker may seem buoyant in spirit, animated, almost on top of the world, or appear very calm. The calmness may come from a sense of relief that a problem has been resolved and a great weight has been lifted.

Teen suicides often involve a cluster of problems, not just one, and bullying and social cruelty remain a serious problem for teens made vulnerable by other personal or family problems, particularly death, divorce, remarriage of a parent, any of these combined with a relocation or sustained tensions. Alcohol or drug use compound negative emotions and mood swings. This is not said to blame parents or peers for any death in a simplistic way, but to recognize that when too many personal supports (inner or social) are taken away, resilience is weakened. When major problems come in clusters, the impact can be overwhelming. If life seems unendurable and no resolution is immediately possible, then the spiritually-wounded person feels like he or she is caught in a trap and seeks a way of escape. Poor decisions, sometimes deadly ones, result.

Erik's death was my baptism into the awareness that other people struggle with great problems without having all the personal, communal, or spiritual resources they need for survival. It is possible for a good person to be overwhelmed by difficulties and go under, just as a strong swimmer can be overwhelmed by the force of a current. The suicidal person may have a final conversation as a way of saying goodbye; the swimmer sometimes raises a groping hand in a final thrust before sinking. Both are endangered and unreachable, dying before help arrives. In so many ways the suicidal person usually struggles out of sight. His or her plight is not readily apparent to other people.

While I never forgot my walk home that day, I was too young to remain preoccupied and did not dwell on it, keeping busy with friends and activities at school. About two years later, while working at my father's shop, dad pulled me aside to tell me that he had just received tragic news. My cousin, Don, had taken his own life. I was sixteen at the time and Don was nineteen. Once again, I was in the shock of disbelief. I could not conceive why anyone would do something like this. Don had been separated from his father by a divorce, living with his mother, though my uncle continued to see him and vacation with him. As a teenager there was a convergence of negative factors at work in his life. Sadly, my uncle's life was never the same after the death of his only child. He held down a demanding job and functioned commendably well until retirement, but the light was gone from his eyes and there was anger under the surface along with emotional distance.

Erik and Don are examples of the fact that young males, once they determine on suicide, generally make sure the attempt is successful and irrevocable. Recognizing calls for help is not easy. It is important for adults or peers to stand by a teen who is temporarily unbalanced by life circumstances or a sudden mood swing, usually made worse by alcohol consumption. In many cases, if a temporary crisis is survived by a teen then it may be unrepeatable, that is, the feeling of being overwhelmed may not return again with the same intensity. There may be ongoing struggles with a sense of inferiority, fear, confusion, shame or guilt, and any of these problematic feelings may not be handled very well, but the suicidal ideation may not be repeated. Even many adults who survive one attempt say they were not tempted again with the same intensity of despair or anger.

My Pastoral Initiation

Several years after Don's death, when I was a young pastor and new to a rural community, I had to plan a funeral service for a teenage boy who committed suicide. The memory of the pain I felt for Erik and Don returned with a vengeance. I was frightened by memories of vivid scenes of people racked with grief, the overflow crowd at Erik's service, of my grandmother whose knees buckled at the cemetery during Don's committal service. I feared all kinds of things, but above all I feared that I would not speak well at the service. For that reason I allowed a Baptist pastor who knew the family to speak, and he did a superb job.

But in the days leading up to the service my initial search for theological resources began. Some veterans in ministry gave me sage advice, but no one knew of a good resource. There are basic funeral handbooks, but many are short on theological reflections that specifically help people think about suicide in relation to the gospel. Sometimes what we need most are not answers, but ways to process our questions until they lead us into the presence of God.

Recommended Reading:

Ray Anderson, *Dancing with Wolves While Feeding the Sheep.*
Michael D. Bush, *This Incomplete One.*
Albert Y. Hsu, *Grieving a Suicide.*
Fleming Rutledge, *Three Hours.*

2

For Ministry to Grieving Survivors

When individuals are overwhelmed by agonizing struggles, as happened with Erik, sometimes suicide seems to be the only way out. Yet losing someone to suicide and receiving the news is so overwhelming that we, too, can feel like a swimmer pulled down by an undertow.

When I first had to plan a suicide funeral, I was struck by my own inadequacy and lack of resources. Why did I never ask my seminary professors how they would have handled something like this?

When I made phone calls to three or four veteran preachers, each one gave me encouragement and prayer support, but none said any printed resource came to mind (that was over thirty years ago—and since then some good material has been published, but there are still gaps that need to be filled). Suicide is difficult to talk about. It makes us feel awful and empty. It disorders our lives with a tragedy we cannot process no matter how hard we try. People in pastoral care are no different in these emotional responses than ordinary people, yet they often have immediate responsibilities towards the family of the victim. Through it all, sadness freezes the spirit and numbs the mind. Yet those who have to prepare a message for a funeral service do not have the luxury of time, needing to harness their energy and focus immediately.

This anthology of Christian reflection is intended to provide resources for clergy who need to think theologically about this tragedy. It is also for surviving loved ones who have wounded hearts and hard questions.

What follows are historical and contemporary reviews along with sample sermons, and pastors can start with those if they choose. I have included biblical reflections as well as insights from prominent theologians and writers, many of whom are older but still read today, and a few from people less well known. Because suicide was never their primary focus, I share whatever I could find, and give brief information to help establish context for the new reader.

You may be interested in one trusted name over others. If so, go directly to St. Thomas Aquinas or Dietrich Bonhoeffer or another theologian. Each are in order of the timeline of their lives, moving from ancient to modern. It is likely that other good reflections need to be brought to light. This is a handbook, not something to be read from cover to cover. Some readers will come to it in haste when preparing for a funeral message, while others may want to explore a specific question when there is more time for reading.

A Word to Preachers

As preachers we do our best to communicate. In doing so, we depend on God's assistance, but also on God's provision for healing graces that do not depend on us. These may be given to a grieving family in various ways. There will be hugs and support from other people. Some may receive a healing dream in answer to prayer. You and I may be part of this, to be sure, but what God graciously uses may not be based on the length of our careful message.

One or two comments may do more good than we can imagine. In many cases, a long sermon is not what grieving people need. I have certainly made mistakes in crafting messages that are too long, plenty of times. There is a great deal of richness in Christian hope and biblical truth, but we cannot tell it all in one sermon. I think we need to make our words and concepts accessible without attempting to say everything at once.

We preach with our spirits, not just our words, a retired preacher once said. But because words are important, we wonder about length. A veteran pastor, who loved theological discussions as much as anyone, warned not to weigh people down with words when they are distressed, not in a time of tragedy. That was wise and helpful counsel.

Guiding our words are theological concepts and biblical interpretations, but there are often alternatives to consider. Because theology matters, the work is never done. Whether you only dip into a few pages or read the entire anthology, I promise you that not every question will be answered. As theology is open-ended, it will be hard for everything to be neatly wrapped up in one package. Some questions cannot be answered by human authority or direct biblical statements, even if there are guideposts for finding answers to other questions. In all our searches regarding questions on sin and grace, hope or despair, we require the guidance of the Holy Spirit.

You do not need to agree with everything said in my reflections and editorial comments. In any important conversation where there is disagreement there is life. Hopefully you will have your own theological ideas stimulated from something said here. You can agree or disagree with Luther or Calvin or Bonhoeffer or Lewis, telling your congregations what you think and why.

The sheer difficulty of ministering to suffering people led me to conceive this project. When any type of tragedy strikes, whether suicide or otherwise, a pastor can be drained of energy from ministering to those who are in shock. When you are weary, it can be hard to think creatively in order to compose a message, and that is why I hope this anthology can help by stimulating ideas and providing reflections on questions that are repeatedly asked. Sometimes all it takes is a comment to trigger one key idea and then a train of thought can develop. If so, this book has served its purpose.

In selecting material for this anthology, I added some of my own thoughts and questions. This is not because I am a gifted thinker but because asking questions of those who served faithfully is meant to honor and assimilate their contributions.

A high number of theologians do not separate the problem of suicide from the general human need for God's forgiveness and renewal. Overall they do not think of the suicidal person as automatically receiving less grace and mercy from God than those who die in accidental deaths or from old age. We all stand in need of the gift of forgiveness, and this has not been lost sight of in the history of Christian thought.

While the preacher is the intended audience, there may be other readers whose needs are different but equally important. For very personal reasons, people will come to this discussion in the aftermath of a tragedy. Their need is not to prepare a sermon but to reflect. They too are seeking answers to hard questions.

In the wake of suicide the bereaved often endure a long-lasting sorrow. Some people are like Frodo in *The Lord of the Rings*. Long after the ring was destroyed and the evil power of Sauron defeated, Frodo was touched by a pain that would never go away, always a present reminder of the old wound. Although we participate in different life stories, old wounds are all around us. For this reason I realize that some of my comments throughout the book are not needed by the pastor, but they are not said to be patronizing. They are included because I anticipate other readers who do not have formal theological training and may need background information along with more general comments. Private readers have a motivation that is not divorced from painful loss. My prayer is for them to find both strength and direction.

A Word to Surviving Loved Ones

To you who have loved and lost more than we can know, where do we begin? I wish that we could sit together in silence as well as in conversation. Silence can include a personal welcome and protect the heart. In such moments silence is not empty. For anyone suffering in the aftermath of a suicide, words seem weak and unhelpful.

This is not a book about remembering or grieving, counseling or surviving. Hopefully you are supported by helpful friends who are near you. Because there are significant counseling resources already, I will not attempt to duplicate that material here.

Suicide troubles all of us. We cannot encourage it and wish no one thought of it. When it happens in the life of someone we know, for whom we had affection, we tend to blame ourselves afterwards even when the event took us by surprise. We recalculate cause and effect in our minds and wonder. If only we could go back in time, would something done or said differently have changed the outcome? When we do reflect, it is not always a major choice that disturbs us. Little ones also fester.

We search for reasons why the final choice was made and cannot be sure to find the right ones. We miss a lot that may have been involved in the runup to suicide. Often there is not just one factor but a cluster of contributing factors. The victim was not thinking or feeling exactly what you or I would have done under similar circumstances. That which happens to a person is one thing to consider, but what meaning did those reactions have?

No two people experience and respond to events, problems, or people exactly the same way. And in the end, looking for a rational explanation for an irrational act is not helpful. What we can pinpoint may not align with another person's response. Part of this terrible grief is that we cannot know what we want to know and have to entrust this person's death to God, including this undiscoverable element.

With heartfelt grief you cannot expose it to just anyone, but carrying it all alone does not bring relief either. If you trust someone, then, when you are ready, a conversation may be restorative. If you want to discuss some aspects of the event or your feelings towards the victim either before or after the suicide, then that may be important to you. There is no right or wrong timing about this, for some people need extra time in solitude and others need more people around them; some are ready to talk sooner than others, and the opposite can be the case.

On one day you may feel numb or exhausted, on another you will feel pain. Later, as you find you can resume your life in various ways, you may even feel guilty if your attention embraces happier thoughts without effort. When you love someone who died there is a part of you that does not want the pain to go away. You always want to care about them and acknowledge their loss as important; but it may be good to have the pain recede in intensity as you carry your grief. For this we pray, because you also live. There are other people who have an important place in your life, and you in theirs.

At any funeral for a suicide (or any other type of death) I come to serve a family from the point of view of a Christian pastor trying to honor the person who died. And also to worship the God who gave the gift of life, in whom we place our hope. In every case, I have been able to honor the person who committed suicide, not for his or her final choice in death, but for qualities in his or her life that were worthy and could be publicly acknowledged. Some act of kindness, compassion, or helpfulness. Or a unique personality trait remembered in specific stories.

When you have a person's name in mind, this is a search for understanding, not a mere academic exercise or spiritual brain teaser. Your own questions and fears for your loved one must be brought to God in prayer. There is no other way than this relational way. No one else can give you what God's Spirit can give you. We pray together for the resources of heaven.

Recommended reading for ministry:

Bryan Chapell, *The Hardest Sermons You'll Ever Have to Preach*.
Scott M. Gibson and Karen Mason, *Preaching Hope in Darkness*.
Warren and David Wiersbe, *Ministering to the Mourning*.

3

Questions in Need of Reflection

BEFORE OUR SURVEY OF historical and contemporary resources, I want to review some common questions that arise around a suicide. As we face tragedy, our sense of order is challenged and we search to understand the event, if that is possible. Usually one or more of these questions is asked around the time of a funeral, often in private conversation. Sometimes a person will get a question out in the open at a Bible study or tea, which may be an indicator of what several people have been wondering about. People have a desire to process what they know about their biblical faith and apply it to the problem of suicide, regarding both the loss of life and the impact that loss has on the survivors.

It is often a good idea not to answer someone's question too quickly, for a genuine hesitation is appropriate and indicates that the question is a good one, not easy to answer, and is taken seriously. You will try your best but you acknowledge your difficulty at the outset. Perhaps the person has been in conversation with others and may be asking on behalf of someone else. There is no set order for a starting place, so we will plunge in.

(1) Is Suicide One of the Worst Possible Sins, with Graver Consequences Than Others?

The gravity of this choice to end life is real. This tragedy bears the heaviest on those who knew and loved the victim. The parents who fed and clothed their child, the brother or sister who teased and played together, the friends with shared memories. Upon hearing the news we recoil. Because we have a deep visceral response to suicide, we may feel it is one of the worst things to do, then rate it as one of the most terrible sins, assuming God must do the same. Yet we cannot probe God's thoughts or speak for God on subjects that are not clearly stated in biblical revelation.

The concept of sin is not primarily about correct or incorrect behavior, but about a condition which carries its own problems. A physician can treat a boil on the surface of the skin, but if there is an infection in the bloodstream that caused the boil then this condition has to be dealt with—or there will be additional trouble because treating surface issues will not clear it up.

Another way to think about sin is to consider the stories of Robin Hood or William Tell. An archer with acute skill can hit the bullseye at a distance. A kid at summer camp aiming for the first time would be fortunate to even strike the edge of the target. Imagine the arrow goes astray. Either the aim is off or the skill is off. The condition of weakness, lack of interest, or lack of training contributes to the result. Sinful acts may not be the same as criminal behavior, but they are like an arrow going astray. If there is a right attitude, a good behavior, an appropriate choice of words, we do not always hit the target. In our relations with God and with one another, something is off. Even the thoughts we think about ourselves can be improperly related to who we actually are. Our current human condition is distorted (think of faces in a fun-house mirror). Sin as a problematic condition is what we mean by the word sinful.

The Reformers taught that our problem with sin is not first and foremost a problem with particular sins, those bad things we say or do. Our chief problem is with sin as condition. It is because we are sinful that we say unkind words, do wrong things, or omit helpful responses to those in need. Sinful deeds are wrong, but we do not become sinful by doing them. We merely exhibit what we already are as radically self-centered persons. This condition results in many confusions and wrong turns.[1]

Why does sin as condition matter? Because who we are needs redemption, not just what we do. Hugh Ross Mackintosh said that we need to be forgiven less for what we have done than for what we are.[2] This

---

1. In a class I once attended at Princeton Theological Seminary, lecturer Diogenes Allen distinguished between sin and evil by standing in front of his class and turn his back to them. "Sin is turning your back on God," he told them before walking away. "Evil is walking farther away. All are equally sinful. Not all are equally evil."

2. Mackintosh, *God In Experience*, 108.

insight applies both to the person who commits suicide and to the person who never does. The total person is in need of redemption, regardless of how we live or die. In this way we have much common ground with those who commit suicide even if we are never tempted to do the same. We have a spiritual need for grace and renewal, as they do.

Family and close friends suffer tremendous anguish following a suicide. A life is lost and we will never know what small part of the world was lost as a consequence. This is a tragedy, but a chosen one.[3] Is that choice not a terrible sin? Well, yes, terrible in the inability to receive or accept help prior to death, whether from other humans or from God's spiritual resources. And terrible in its consequences. But how do we rate this choice? Automobile wrecks generally follow from reckless driving. Suppose we rate these forms of death based on both intentions and outcomes, moving from bad to worse. If so, where on the spectrum is the passenger who distracted the driver? Where on the spectrum is the road crew that delayed fixing a pothole? Where on the spectrum is the single vehicle or the two vehicle wreck?

We can try to rank human motives and behavior, but do our thoughts line up with God's evaluation? To quote again from H. R. Mackintosh, "Only at stray moments do we catch sight of sin as it must look to God."[4] This caution reminds me that I cannot say exactly how suicide looks to God. That has not been shown to us. It is not that I want us to think lightly of suicide, for it generally brings intense pain to one's family. But many other things are not right either, and we do not know enough to say that this one sin ranks as more offensive to God than other sins. It is a very final way to end life, and I have never seen it bring good in its wake. For this reason I oppose it in my heart and counsel people against it whenever given the opportunity, but not because I know how God weighs this sin in comparison with other types of sin.

---

3. Some contemporary counselors do not want to call suicide a choice, saying instead that the victim really had no choice about what he or she did. This is a problematic interpretation. Accidentally touching a live electrical current is not the same as intentionally touching it while anticipating the result. Such counselors likely have a motivation to help the family cope with their loss and be free of casting blame, but when a "no choice was involved" interpretation does not accurately reflect what happened it can give false comfort that does not last.

4. Mackintosh, *Experience*, 91.

(2) If We're Supposed to Repent of Our Sinful Choices, How Can Suicide Be Forgiven If there Is No Opportunity to Ask for God's Forgiveness?

This is a question of primary concern with Christians all around the world. They are right to think one's relationality with God matters in life and in death, and the loss of salvific opportunity is a genuine concern.

What if the person had survived and was given the opportunity to repent? We do not know what he or she would have chosen next. Only God knows what they would have done next, and only God knows the original motivation for the suicide attempt. Not all intentions are the same even when the outcome is the same. For example, not all suicides are impulsive, but some are. Not all suicides can be properly judged to be a rejection of God's offer of grace, yet perhaps some are. However we probe these issues, we have limitations. We cannot guess at God's ultimate judgment concerning any particular person. We cannot place all the weight on the final moment of life, which is not the same as saying it is unimportant. There is certainly good precedence for this caution.

Dietrich Bonhoeffer said that many people die other forms of death without being properly prepared by timely prayers of repentance. A skiing or mountain climbing accident can happen suddenly, as can an automobile wreck or plane crash, to say nothing of a stroke or heart attack. What if that person had a relationality with God but did not properly repent of something by that final day? Does the emphasis belong with God's provision of grace or with the unworthy human who needs forgiveness? Bonhoeffer does not place the emphasis on the ability of humans to repent of all their sins on their last day. "This is setting too much store on the last moment."[5] To do so is to remove the atonement's reality from the center of our hope. By atonement we mean the reconciliation which God provided in Christ and cannot turn away from, because this is wedded to God's life and being forever. The work of Christ is not made more or less efficacious based on the constancy or thoroughness of human repentance, for if that were the case we would all be in trouble. What I mean to say is that repentance is always good if we need to turn away from bad things, but it is never fulfilled unless we also turn towards God. None of us turn towards God at all times in the right way, so our hope must be based on God's faithfulness rather than our own.

---

5. This is a paraphrase of Bonhoeffer, *Ethics* (1962), 124.

(3) Is a Suicidal Person's Action in the Final Moment of Life Their Most Definitive Act for Or Against God?

We see the final moment of life in the context of the fallen process of death, which does not necessarily mean the final moment of a human life is the all-determinative factor as far as God's judgment is concerned. Just as the breakdown of the physical body participates in the process of death and eventually leads to the moment of death, so can the breakdown of the mind slowly lead up to the moment of death. Physical, emotional, or mental breakdowns participate in the outworking of death in its corrupted form under the power of sin.

Kidney failure or diabetes can lead to heart failure, examples of a long but slow weakening of health. It is the same with suicide. The choice of the final moment may be based on an inner pain and confusion that was long in the making. In such a case, everything that went into it over the years–the breakdown of inner strength and balance, the removal of support from within the human community–was a participation in a process leading to death. In multiple scenarios, suicide was about more than the victim's state of mind in the final moment. There were contributing factors that put great strain on inner resources prior to the end.

Matters that touch the soul can fester and disease the inner life, weakening strength. The final crisis may not come yet, but the inner resources to deal with it have been steadily diminished or removed. This puts some people on dangerous ground. The weakening of one's spirit over time may not seem like the ultimate crisis, but whenever the human spirit is weakened that individual may then be left without adequate strength, hope, and creative energy to face the next crisis. The compounding of despair, confusion, and inner pain may be an invisible process which builds momentum over time, giving impetus to thoughts of self-destruction.

Therefore it is nearly impossible for outside observers to judge accurately what went wrong based only on the final moment of life. In some cases we can make sound judgments based on personal knowledge and intuition, but in many cases we cannot. Only God can know the processes that were at work within a person's soul throughout his or her life. If these processes were intimately and delicately connected to the end, or connected to what weakened the person prior to the end, then it is likely God's perfect judgment takes more into consideration than just the final moment of life. This is why we may rightly discern the quality of an action or its outcome, but only God can judge the person who committed the action.

Human death has been altered by sin just as life has been altered by sin. Here we refer to both death as a process working constantly over time and death as the final moment of life. Death in all its various forms must be redeemed and transformed, not just death that comes by suicide. This means, among other things, that we cannot put all the weight on the last moment of life as the determining factor in a person's eternal destiny. The last moment cannot always reflect the essence of a person's soul or identity as a child of God. This is particularly true of many elderly who have lost their memories, or of young people who die in a sudden accident. There is more to the pattern of a tapestry than the inweaving or unravelling of the final thread.

Dietrich Bonhoeffer thought that the danger in the sin of suicide was in disregarding the reality of God. Yet every willful disobedience or "sin with a high hand" disregards the reality of God. In cases when there is no time for repentance, does this sin then trump God's grace and become unforgiveable? If so, are we meant to think that only our complete repentance leads to the possibility of forgiveness? Those who would take such a position are in danger of putting all the emphasis on the human side of the equation and not enough on God's objective provision of salvation. In transcendence and purity God provided the gift of Christ once for all. In utter holiness God has the freedom to honor the self-offering of Jesus and apply forgiveness to the life most in need of it. Grace is nothing less than an undeserved gift. As God's people we do not fall into the safety net of grace only when we are good, but also when we are bad, when we are failures, else grace is something other than grace.

Salvation as a gift is highlighted in the New Testament as a reminder that we do not free ourselves from slavery to sin.[6] We cannot rescue ourselves. No repentance of our own, however long-lasting or seemingly complete, is perfect enough to set us free. We will only be given a place in the eternal kingdom by God's mercy. Therefore any discussion of personal repentance is unfinished if we do not primarily highlight our mediator, who was the complete and perfect gift which God provided for our salvation. The active and passive obedience of Jesus Christ must

---

6. "Paul sees the human problem as larger than that of repentance and forgiveness of the individual. This is clear from the slavery language in Romans 6: slaves cannot repent their way out of slavery; neither can they be forgiven. They can only be delivered, which is the terminology Paul uses." Gaventa, *When In Romans*, 43.

take precedence over every other inadequate form of human repentance. Christ honored and obeyed the will of God throughout his life and also embraced our death on the cross, in the supreme act of vicarious self-offering, providing atonement.[7] This means Christ reconciled all sinful humans to God.[8] We are ultimately saved by his obedience and self-offering, not our own, and are called to place our faith in him.[9] The Holy Spirit revealed to the early church that the person and ministry of Jesus is connected to the very being of God, which is why God will never turn away from what Jesus accomplished for the world.

So while Bonhoeffer recognizes that suicide is willful sin, despair or hubris that disregards God's reality, the discussion does not end there. Bonhoeffer says that the argument that suicide rules out the possibility of repentance and, therefore, also of forgiveness, is insufficient: "Many Christians have died sudden deaths without having repented of all their sins. This is setting too much store by the last moment of life."[10] The decisive reason why suicide is wrong is not that it precludes forgiveness or removes forgiveness, but because only God the creator and lord of life exercises the right over human life. We are not meant to usurp God's lordship but to submit our very lives to it.

Bonhoeffer's admonition about not weighting down the last moment of life with a greater burden than it can bear, particularly in regard to God's forgiveness and gift of eternal life, is of vital importance. In this regard Bonhoeffer is supported by Karl Barth, who faced the same question about the end of life. In response Barth asked, "What right have we to isolate the last moment of human existence from that which precedes, and to judge a man by this moment alone?"[11] Barth does not excuse or

---

7. For Christian proclamation, the doctrine of atonement cannot be divorced from the doctrine of the incarnation without becoming distorted. For more on incarnation and atonement, see Torrance, *Incarnation*, and Torrance, *Atonement*. Because Christ lived and died and rose in a substitutionary role, salvation by grace alone is applied to our whole being. Also consider the sermons in Rutledge, *Crucifixion*.

8. We are speaking of the ultimate basis for human salvation which God established, while also acknowledging that only the Holy Spirit can make this salvation experientially ours.

9. We do not live from our own faith but from the faithfulness of God who provides the substitutionary faith of Christ, the faithful one who "lays hold of us to bring us into a living relationship with himself." Torrance, *Preaching Christ Today*, 30–32.

10. Bonhoeffer, *Ethics* (2005), 199.

11. Barth, *Church Dogmatics* (hereafter *CD*) 3/4:403–4.

justify suicide, but says we cannot conclude it is an unforgivable sin, not even if we come to think of it as self-murder:

> [Even] suicide in this sense is not as such unforgivable sin. For there are many other ways of "taking" one's own life which may be more foolish and wicked than suicide. We have also to remember the parallel case of criminal murder in relation to others. If there is forgiveness of sins at all, even for the latter sin, there is surely forgiveness for suicide. The opinion that it alone is unforgivable rests on the false view that the last will and act of man in time, because they are the last and take place as it were on the very threshold of eternity, are authoritatively and conclusively decisive for his eternal destiny and God's verdict on him. But this cannot be said of any isolated will or act of man, and therefore not even of the last. God sees and weighs the whole of human life. He judges the heart. And He judges it according to His own righteousness which is that of mercy.
>
> He thus judges the content of the last hour in the context of the whole. Even a righteous man may be in the wrong at the last. Even the most sincere believer may be hurled on his death-bed into the most profound confusion and uncertainty, even though there is no suggestion of suicide. What would become of him if there were no forgiveness at this point? Yet if there is forgiveness for him, why not for the suicide?[12]

For these reasons we should not think the suicidal person's choice in the last moment of life is all-determinative. If there is forgiveness for other confusions and terrible sins, why not for the suicide? God's forgiveness, Barth goes on to say, does not in any sense make the act of suicide legitimate or justify sin. This is true for all other sins we may commit. The fact that Bonhoeffer and Barth hold out the hope of forgiveness does not mean they approve of suicide as a possible choice. They think suicide is wrong, a sin against the God who forgives sin, but they do not think this form of confusion and rebellion has the power to overcome the atonement for all sin which is given in the life, death, resurrection and ascension of Jesus.

God can see more than the final moment of life. God can see all the germinating and contributing factors that influenced or induced the suicide choice. God can also see the other moments of a person's life that are more significant and unerring indicators of one's relationship with God. God can even know whether the person would have repented had he or

---

12. Barth, *CD* 3/4:405.

she survived the suicide attempt.[13] While we may think that the choice of suicide is sin in a particular case, only God can rightly judge the person who makes that choice.

Therefore I do not think Heb 9:27, which says it is appointed for all humans to die once and after this face God's judgment, settles any question about suicide. Some teachers and preachers quote this verse as a definitive reason why suicide cannot be forgiven, arguing that there is no time left for repentance. This move involves both a theological emphasis that may place more weight on human repentance than it can bear—though I do not say this to minimize the significance of repentance in daily fellowship with God—as well as a rationalization about what forensic and eschatological judgment involves.

In prophetic biblical content, judgment may be a historical moment in time or eschatologically a forensic meting out of just deserts at the end of time, but it is also a time when what is unjust and out of balance is put right, where healing takes place, followed by harmony and peace. What we are not told is whether there is an accounting for each and every moment, for each and every decision, or primarily for our essential character—character that is revealed in significant responses to God and others. Christian theology has long made judgment a relational matter, touching on one's response to God's offer of salvation in Christ. Is this "response" only defined by or established in the final moment of life?

Insofar as God's judgment may condemn an individual rather than exonerate or rescue, and insofar as God's decision may bring resurrection life and joy to some while others are cast out of the kingdom, we still have no grounds for declaring we know which way God will decide on any particular person, including suicides. From our perspective, the judgment has not taken place yet, and we should not pretend that we know more than we do. What Heb 9:27 declares are two simple statements. First, we will all die. Second, we will all face a judgment. But more than that, it does not say. It does not declare the basis for God's judgment, negative or positive, nor does it declare that none can be saved by the mercy of God. The one who gave his own righteous life to reconcile us to God is the only one permitted to judge us on that day.

Heb 9:27 comes in the context of a discussion of the earthly and ascended heavenly mediation of Christ, and the very next verse says, "So

---

13. This point is made by Montgomery in chapter 19 below. On the logical compatibility of God's foreknowledge and human freedom, see Craig, *Only Wise God*; cf. Geach, *Providence and Evil*.

Christ also, having been offered once to bear the sins of many, shall appear a second time for salvation without reference to sin, to those who eagerly await Him."[14] While written in Greek, the idiom is Aramaic. In short, the Aramaic term "many" stands opposite the idea of a "limited few," and is an inclusive thought rather than an exclusive one, and sometimes can mean the totality of the whole. But even if it is not the totality of the whole in every context, it is more expansive than constrictive. What does this mean for our discussion? The affirmation that we die once and face the judgment is immediately followed by the promise that the Christ who already bore the sins of many will appear a second time for salvation. We cannot derive from this that Christ did not bear the sins of suicide victims, nor that he will not appear again for their salvation. Just as we have not yet seen the judgment, we have not yet seen the fullness of this salvation.

(4) Does the Bible Directly Address Suicide Or the Eternal Destiny of the Person Involved?

No part of the Bible directly addresses the topic of suicide. C. S. Lewis says this is the case. Karl Barth says this is the case. These are world-class scholars trained in reading ancient literature, whose study of the biblical books was also part of their comprehensive personal worship.

Furthermore, no part of the Bible discusses the eternal destiny of those who die by suicide. Since the topic of suicide is not addressed specifically, there is no specific word of condemnation about it. Simultaneously, there is no affirmation of heavenly reward for such an action. Judgment is appropriately left to the decision of God regarding every suicide mentioned in the Bible, just as with every person who dies by other means, including old age.

In connection with this question is whether the Roman Catholic position is more negative than Protestant teaching on this matter. It seems there are persistent misunderstandings about this. Roman Catholics are duly warned not to commit suicide, and it is categorized as a serious sin against both nature and God's calling to live by faith. But the official Roman Catholic position, as given in the recent Catechism, does not state that suicide is an unforgiveable sin. Any previous statements to the contrary, whether by bishops, priests, nuns, or lay writers throughout

---

14. Heb 9:28.

the world, are overruled or enlightened by this official teaching. Rome's former rules about burial in consecrated ground have also been changed.

And for the other half of the question, Protestant evangelical teaching is not unified regarding suicide, but surprisingly the grace-oriented responses of modern theologians do not exactly break new ground. They were anticipated by earlier theologians going all the way back to Martin Luther. There have been many (but not all) who recognize the wide reach of God's forgiveness of sins, including mercy for persons who despaired of hope and took their own life.

(5) Do Major Theologians Say that Suicide Is an Unpardonable Sin?

So far I can say, no, they do not. Here we are talking about five or six theologians whose names loom the largest in two thousand years of church history, because they were theologically penetrating and highly influential: Athanasius, Augustine, Thomas Aquinas, Martin Luther, John Calvin, and Karl Barth. A couple may have feared God's condemnation in some specific cases, but not likely in all cases. Augustine thought motivation mattered. Barth refused to presume about God's sovereign (free) decision. None encouraged suicide or took it lightly, but none of these made it out to be unforgiveable in all cases or the most reprehensible of all possible sins.

(6) How Can We Affirm the Possibility of God's Forgiveness Without Appearing to Say Suicide Is Permissible?

Martin Luther believed that God's grace was for the suicidal person as well as any other sinner in need of redeeming. Why did he not emphasize this more in his public sermons? Because he was afraid that when conditions became too harsh for some people, they would misconstrue his message and consider death by suicide. Luther's primary reason was his concern for world-weary or unbalanced persons who might take it as permission to destroy themselves. He did not want that for them or their families, nor did he want to promote anything so destructive as popular approval of suicide. How do we think about sin and grace? This touches the heart of the Christian hope for salvation, the very concern of the Reformation.

Luther's theology and biblical interpretation emphasized God's grace, but as a public preacher, one of his great pastoral concerns was to steer people away from suicide by not talking about it too freely. Yet at table with pastors whom he trusted, he did not speak harshly of those who committed suicide. Rather he spoke some of the most gracious and perceptive words about their despondent condition which are found in this anthology.

Even if we believe in God's mercy, should we tell people there is no forgiveness for suicide? Should we scare them away from making such a bad choice?

Samuel Johnson was asked this question by Boswell, and he said we are not free to tell a lie, not even to prevent suicide. His moral clarity was evident, but there was also a measure of wisdom in his response. For scaring people with talk about hell is generally not effective with very despondent people, not even if they already believe in heaven or hell. It does not generally get the attention of those who do not believe either. Karl Barth answered the question by saying that people do not need a prohibition. Rather they need permission to live. We have something better than a prohibition in the Bible, for we have God's gracious permission to live.

(7) How Much Attention Should be Given to Discussing Suicide at a Funeral Service?

Should we instruct from the Bible on why to choose life, or on why suicide is not the right choice? Perhaps that is a discussion for a Sunday sermon or Bible class. Those who attend a funeral do not want to be a captive audience hearing an extended admonition.

At a memorial service it will not be helpful to dwell on the suicide or mention it in a high state of emotion. It is possible that too much attention can do harm both to the family and the guests attending to pay respect. Giving undue attention to the problem of suicide can thrill some persons who are already unbalanced, especially with a funeral for a teen suicide. Someone unstable may be entranced by the emotional drama and then entertain thoughts about a copycat suicide. This does not always happen, but it has been known to happen when there is excessive emotional display at school events among distressed peers.

(8) Should Preachers Discuss Suicide from the Pulpit?

It is natural to shy away from bringing up difficult topics in a public context, but this question is important in light of rising suicide rates. There are many related topics that are triggered in people's minds whenever someone speaks about suicide. These require time for exploration and digestion, conversation with others, and sometimes a follow up sermon is needed. This cannot all be done at a funeral. Perhaps some basic statements at a memorial service can be followed up in a Sunday service where there is more time for development.

My encouragement is to discuss this topic at a weekly congregational service. Questions about suicide in reference to sin and grace, judgment and hope are important topics to vast numbers of Christians. An overarching topic is also the breakdown of a sense of community in our society, which has been accelerated in the last several decades for a variety of reasons.

(9) How Appropriate Is It to Disclose Publicly when Someone Has Died by Suicide?

If done gently and respectfully, the death by suicide may be acknowledged. It seems wise for a pastor to prepare the family in advance, insofar as you can overcome their fear of disgrace by showing implicitly that you do not despise them or the loved one who committed suicide, and pray for them to receive the Holy Spirit's strength and comfort. Within that discussion a pastor may advise a brief acknowledgement, one that does not dwell on the event but which touches on it. Why is this important?

Some of the family may feel shame because they think they are held responsible, or that their caring for their lost family member was inadequate, fearing they will be blamed for not being watchful or helpful. Some family members will be laid low by intense grief. Their loved ones may also be angry at the person who committed suicide because of the intense grief a mother, father, or spouse is going through. These can be volatile emotions, hard to control, and generally they remove strength from the people who are grieving.

The problem with shame is that it tends to isolate, and with this type of wound, isolation is not good. Intruding upon private grief is not good either, but at some point, the spiritually wounded need the support of others. Part of this support can only be given initially at a public service, especially by those who care but do not feel close enough to visit the home. So many are afraid to go because they know the grief is overwhelming. Yet many of these same people will attend a memorial service if given notice and opportunity.

When the speaker even briefly acknowledges that the person who died is a victim of suicide, it frees everyone else in the room from the sense of holding a secret.[15] Any pretense of accidental death is over, for most attending likely know already. They now have permission to shake hands or give a hug without seeming to hold something back. Should a family member choose to say anything about it to a friend at a reception following the service, the way is prepared. Or the way is smoothed for tacit support that does not need to mention right then what has already been said. For this reason it can be a simple grace to touch on the fact and move on.

There is no correct way for every occasion, but I have tried this approach: "We are here to remember and honor the life of [name]. We do not honor the final decision to take his/her own life, [pause] but we do find much in his/her life that was good, and that is what we want to recall and honor today." That may sound too blunt and direct, but when you do it in a soft tone, people sense respect and many have told me afterwards that it changed the atmosphere at the outset of the service. It was almost as if there was a collective sigh of relief. The statement is behind us and we can move on. To date no one has taken it as a judgmental statement, simply a statement of fact, one we cannot change or ignore. Our attention moves to the survivors who need our support. Their loved one is treated with respect. Usually there are good memories that can be included, special personality traits recognized by those in the audience, vignettes, which helps to personalize the service.

(10) Why Didn't They Ask for Help?

Looking for reasons behind a suicide has more to do with our desire for an explanation than with our ability to discern what was in the person's mind leading up to this tragedy.

There are a variety of reasons why people commit suicide instead of asking for help, and the same reason does not apply to every case.

---

15. See Buechner, *Telling Secrets*. Also Hsu, *Grieving a Suicide*, 42–57, for his discussion on lament.

In looking for explanations we should not minimize the complexity of a human life, for the process of abstracting out one motive often causes us to lose sight of other contributing factors. Nonetheless in our personal attempts to understand a tragic death, some motivations or problems appear as dominating features and guide our understanding.

The various reasons why people contemplate or commit suicide are numerous. In books on counseling, entire chapters are written on any one of these aspects. One person cannot continue living in the pain of chronic depression. Another feels slowly crushed by the burdens and disasters of life. People take their own lives out of fear of what they think is coming based on a medical diagnosis or some other form of threat. People kill themselves out of sheer loneliness. Many victims of self-destruction cannot endure feelings of shame. Shame is often a more potent factor than guilt, for it often motivates people to withdraw from friendships or family and become isolated. Shame keeps people from believing in God's forgiveness, and influences people to think life can never be good or "normal" again.[16] Where a sense of guilt and shame is mixed with significant moral failure at odds with one's own ideals, there are those who commit suicide based on a sense of self-loathing.

Yet people can feel no sense of guilt or shame and still be suicidal. Noted psychiatrist Karl Menninger worked with successful and extremely wealthy people who were suicidal though they had no practical problems causing tension and no perceived family conflicts. They felt that their lives were meaningless. Yet they resisted Menninger's advice about giving gifts to make other people happy or establishing foundations that would contribute good works beyond their lifetime, advice that would have connected them to community and immediately provided a more meaningful purpose to their lives.[17]

Surprisingly, a few destroy themselves with the intent to inflict wounds on other people as a form of extreme punishment. Some suicidal people feel they will exact a revenge by taking their own life, and their target of revenge are the survivors whose lives they wish to ruin. This is twisted thinking, to be sure, but seems to fit some actual cases.

These type of examples are all root problems that have to be studied in the literature on counseling. There are select factors regarding teen

---

16. Shame is a powerful force in removing individuals from spiritual fellowship and community. See Patton, *Is Human Forgiveness Possible?*

17. Menninger, *Whatever Became of Sin?*, 152–54.

suicides that require attention, problems which gain strength when they come in combinations.[18]

Our survey in this anthology does not include the counseling room, with its focus on personal factors, but rather is an exploration of the theological questions that commonly follow suicidal deaths. We do understand there is not just one universal reason or contributing factor for all deaths by suicide. Not every person who commits suicide is mentally ill, and not every person had a long struggle with depression. While some who attempt suicide have battled mental illness, numerous people struggle with depression and disorders without attempting suicide.

This word of caution means there is no room for a one-size-fits-all approach. Each person's life can be considered only on its own ground. It is nearly impossible to make sense out of some of these actions and underlying reasons, apart from someone's self-revelations. This is why the therapist has to get to know each individual. People have unique histories even when they seem to fit a pattern. For this reason, the counselor cannot make hasty assumptions about motivation or contributing factors, but asks each person to make self-disclosures about the nature of his or her problem. Without essential disclosures, it is so difficult after a suicide to put oneself mentally into the shoes of the person who died. We cannot have assurance that we have the right understanding. Even the content of a suicide note may not betray or reveal the full truth, or if it seems to, may not make sense to those of us who would have responded differently to the same situation.

Making Use of Resources for Christian Reflection

There are good resources available for counseling and prevention. Our purpose here is to fill in some gaps where preachers and bereaved family are looking for theological reflection, placing suicide within the larger realm of the story of God with us, God for us.

In the end nothing is wrapped up in a nice, neat package. Each one of us must grapple with hard questions as we think theologically not only

---

18. These cannot be detailed here without appropriate explanations and illustrations. However, valuable short books include Gerali, *What Do I Do*, and Leder, *Dead Serious*. Gibson and Mason, *Preaching Hope in Darkness*, offers help on talking to youth groups and Bible studies designed to prevent teen suicide. Important wider discussions include Clinton et al., *Quick-Reference Guide*, especially 274–80; Clark, *Hurt 2.0*; Parrott, *Helping the Struggling Adolescent*; Berman et al., *Adolescent Suicide*.

about suicide but about all aspects of the human condition, along with the great biblical themes of sin and grace, hope and rescue. At the outset I do affirm that God's grace offered in the atoning life and death of Christ is supreme and answers for all human sin and error, including suicide. It is also my fervent hope that nothing presented in this book will encourage anyone to end life too soon or in despair. The same God who made all things can make all things new. The Holy Spirit can add sustaining gifts that enhance life, even in the face of grave problems that do not go away.

Section Two

Historical Survey of Christian Reflection

4

The Bible: Key Narratives

THERE IS NO SPECIFIC command in the Bible about suicide. Does the Bible explicitly forbid what it does not address in a clear and direct fashion? C. S. Lewis said the Bible does not forbid suicide in any passage. He is not alone in that assessment. Yet some want to see suicide as forbidden by the Ten Commandments in Exod 20. This possibility is reviewed in the next chapter. There may be an indirect, tacit disapproval in some passages, but not an explicit command.

The biblical writers never present suicide as praiseworthy or promote suicide as a course of action. King Saul is not blamed for his decision to kill himself, considering the alternative, but telling the story is not the same as promoting Saul's final decision. At that point it may have been the lesser of two evils, but what brought him to that point? While there are realistic references to suicide there is no holding it forth as a model behavior, an option that is evidently better than all endurance of shame, affliction, or personal suffering. Yet suffering is nowhere made light of, for it is always presented as a reason to cry out to God for help.

This chapter offers a short review of places where suicide is mentioned in the Bible, with the exceptions of Abimelech and Zimri.[1] These are not very choice passages for use in funeral sermons, but grieving people sometimes look them up in their Bibles. The examples of Saul or Judas simply tell the tragic end of people who struggled or failed to follow God's way. The negativity in each story is understated but present.

---

1. Judg 9:54; 1 Kgs 16:18–19. For an overview with a focus on Jewish interpretive and ethical evaluations, see Shemesh, "Suicide in the Bible."

However, empathy can be aroused by stories of people who could not overcome guilt, shame, confusion, and loss.

The biblical narratives about suicide are not positive, but the negative aspects include all that led up to the suicides. In one or two cases the suicide might be seen as the lesser of two evils, given the context and the options, yet might never have been considered if previous errors and sins had not been committed. But some misfortunes and circumstances are beyond our control and place us just as much in jeopardy, regardless of what we deserve, as when villagers were captured by slavers or seafaring people captured by pirates. Ancient Jewish moral education likely discussed some of these narratives, probing cause and effect, searching for appropriate responses in both similar and dissimilar situations. They may have served as discussion starters about personal behavior and life choices, something more subtle and indirect than rules for human conduct.

Saul was favored by God when he was called to be Israel's first king. Judas was favored by God when he was called to be Jesus's disciple. Even people especially favored by God have made wrong choices, falling into traps and nightmares. Biblical writers deal with hard realities and human weaknesses. What is significant is that these stories are presented without moralizing commentary. No biblical writer bothers to add that these suicides follow after bad choices and sinful conduct. In fact, it is difficult to find words of condemnation at all concerning these self-inflicted deaths. There may be implied or explicit condemnation for previous actions, but no additional comments discuss their mode of death by self-removal. The plain narrative is sufficient to leave a negative impression of horror and sadness in the mind of the reader.

From a theological perspective, three important points must be recognized. Firstly, no narrative of suicide in the Bible specifically approves of suicide as a human action. This means no account of suicide ever serves as an ethical example for others to follow. Secondly, there is no attempt to declare what is the eternal destiny of the people who committed suicide. God alone determines their destiny beyond death (as with each one of us) and no biblical writer presumes to know more than this or state anything about that divine decision. As some would debate this point regarding Judas, we will discuss this below. Suffice it to say that any judgment declared on Judas may refer more to his betrayal of Christ than to the way he ended his life. Thirdly, no verse in the Bible says suicide is an unforgivable sin. In each case where there is a narrative of suicide it is never used to teach that suicide is an unforgiveable sin, neither by the writer of the narrative nor by any other biblical writer who refers back to one of these characters.

Job's Agony

Perhaps the most agonizing story of human abasement found in the Bible, second only to the suffering and humiliation of Christ, is found in the book of Job. Whether the book was a historical narrative or an inspired story with a theological purpose can be debated in the commentaries. Either way, the story is meant to communicate that bad things do happen to good people, and when things go right or wrong it is not an obvious indication of reward or punishment, of God's pleasure or displeasure.

In this story, I do not see Job as an example of suicide, but as one who was probably tempted to end his own life while enduring great suffering. That very temptation is a form of suffering. Early in his experience of overwhelming calamity, Job's wife tormented him with abusive words that encouraged suicide (Job 2:9). He refused that temptation and continued to endure both spiritual and physical agony. He maintained faith in the God whose ways he could never understand. At one point Job's words express a welcome of death (Job 6:8–13), but he refused to take his own life. Yet he argued with God, defended himself against pestering critics, and cried out to be vindicated. As the days came and went, his friends rebuked him for trying to defend himself. Their words were comfortless as they tried to defend the ways of God. Importantly, they were rebuked by God in the end. Their form of theodicy was unhelpful and incompetent. God asked Job questions which Job could not answer, pressing home the almighty greatness and unsearchable wisdom of the creator, but God did not condemn Job for his vigorous complaints. This is highly significant. The highest affirmation came when God declared that Job had been righteous throughout his life, and that he had done no wrong. In the end what Job really wanted was for God to show up, and in God's presence, his questioning and searching was over.

In the finale, Job was vindicated by God. Therefore the end of the book tells us how to look at the entire story, showing why it was revolutionary in ancient times and why it remains important today. The entire story was a theological corrective to a misunderstanding that is still with us. In ancient times some people believed that if your wealth increased and you enjoyed good health, if your barns were full and you had lots of children, especially sons, then you were marked as someone specially favored by God. In other words, if good things came your way then you were blessed and protected by God. Happiness was a sign that you were a good person and God smiled on you. (There are plenty of examples today of the health and wealth theology which says prosperity is a sign of God's approval.)[2] The book of Job says a resounding "No" to this way of thinking, and may address a misuse of the promises in Deut 28, which were corporate promises. They involved blessings and curses regarding the future of the whole people, not necessarily assurances that every individual who did right would prosper at all times.

Bad things come even to good people. God may love us, be pleased with us, and still allow bad things to happen. This was a revolutionary message in ancient Israel, strange and hard to accept. We need to listen to this message today. On visits to hospitals or nursing homes we hear some people complain in earnest, "I don't know what I did wrong for God to do this to me." It may be they did nothing wrong except live in a dangerous world or have a physical body that finally wore out. You may be a good person and still have to endure hardship, loss, temptation, or other forms of suffering.[3] However hard it may be to bear, this does not mean that God hates you or has abandoned you. Neither does it mean that God turns away from you when you lament and ask, "Why?!" Furthermore, we do not have to call suffering good. Margaret Shuster says, "Let us engage in no sophistry: suffering is evil. . . . Any purpose of God lies beyond suffering, not in it."[4]

In a funeral context we can point out that Job was allowed to grieve as well as complain to God. God did not condemn Job for his anger or for voicing complaint, but Job also found that in the awe-filling, glorious presence of God there was nothing more to say. May the day come for each one of us when the wonder of God's presence removes the terrors

---

2. A good corrective is Fee, *Health and Wealth Gospels*.

3. See the comments on Job by C. S. Lewis in chapter 16 below. Also of interest are the ways the biblical stories of personal hardship and endurance can be used in counseling depressed and suicidal people, including the story of Job. Although space limitations do not permit a focus on counseling here, two relevant studies are Schwartz and Kaplan, *Biblical Stories*, and Kaplan and Cantz, *Biblical Psychotherapy*.

4. Shuster, *Power, Pathology, Paradox*, 220, cf. 163 note 12. "Suffering may be an *occasion* but not a *cause* of growth; it produces criminals and madmen as well as saints. To confuse occasions and causes breeds continual mislabeling of evil as good." Nor need we call suffering a hidden good, though we ask God to bring good into it. In the end, God must deliver us from suffering as well as from sin.

of life on earth, taking us beyond the reach of anything that can harm or sever our bonds of love and fellowship. In the end, God alone can vindicate God's ways to those who have suffered. God alone can resurrect the dead or rescue a damaged human life. God alone can make all things new.

When friends and neighbors are weighed down with pain and grief, we can listen to their complaints and not feel threatened, not offer answers. We are not called to repeat the mistakes of Job's friends. There is no need to prattle on about the ways of God or attempt to justify pain and suffering. Those made uncomfortable by their own fears often talk too much in the presence of people who experience great tragedy and loss. At such times it is best to say nothing at all, or very little (as in "I have no words"). A silent presence and caring touch may do more to encourage the wounded heart than a flow of words.

Samson's Intentional Sacrifice

Samson was a wild man living on the edge of society, someone whose prior great achievements were empowered by God's Spirit.[5] By his indifference and disobedience, he fell from a high place to a very low one. The story is told in Judg 13–16. The Holy Spirit suddenly withdrew all but normal human strength from Samson, which left him completely vulnerable. When overcome by the Philistines he was blinded and made a slave, taunted and abused for the rest of his life. Whenever Samson was put on display at banquets Israel's God was also mocked as a weakling. For a long time he endured shame and misery before he imagined there could be an alternative. Samson finally prayed for God to restore his strength, which implies this was a prayer of personal repentance. He did not request the restoration of his sight or freedom to return to Israel. When supernatural strength was restored he destroyed many Philistines as well as himself, but first he gave his young guide time to get to safety. There is no comment of reproof in Judges pertaining to his form of death, but the moral reproof of Samson's life is embedded in the entire story of his earlier disobedience. Insofar as there is approval of his final action, it comes by way of God's answer to his last prayer: "Let me die with the Philistines!" In response to that prayer, God restored amazing strength to this man. Then Samson died with his victims.

5. Niditch, "Samson as Culture Hero," 608–24.

It is important to remember that Samson was more than a hero in the strong man category. As judge and champion of Israel, Samson represented Israel and her faith in God. His struggle with the Philistines, on one level, was personal. On another level, his conflict was like the later struggle on Mount Carmel between Elijah and the prophets of Baal. To the Philistines his final battle probably looked like it was fought to avenge his gouged eyes and long captivity. But to the Israelite storyteller this was his final opportunity to represent Israel and demonstrate the power of Israel's God to rescue.

The self-sacrificial death of Samson did not serve as a role model in the Bible for others to follow, nor in most later Jewish or Christian interpretation, because teachers could not affirm the disobedience that originally put him in his slavish, blinded condition. Yet the story of his wild life fascinated many generations and made him one of the great characters in literature and faith. Samson's place as a hero in a long line of heroes (Heb 11:32) was secure not because of his disobedience with Delilah, but because of what God did in and through him prior to his fall and disgrace. Even so, the story has often been presented to children and adults as a moral lesson, where they are reminded that Samson became a slave to the Philistines because he was first a slave to his own passions. He paid a tragic price for moral weakness and lack of self-control. Yet there is something fascinating and edgy in this story, something that cannot be reduced to a lesson in morality. God can work in and through "wild men" (male or female) who live on the edge of society, inspiring them to do good, using them to bring rescue to others.

More can be said about his death, however, that touches on our subject. Prior to pushing the support pillars in his final moment, he recognized that both his life and the timing of his death belonged to God. So he sought God's permission and did not attempt suicide apart from receiving God's empowerment. This was no suicide for suicide's sake, no mere succumbing to despair. And so it was a unique case. Donald Bloesch commented on Samson's motivation:

> Just as not all acts of taking the life of another human being are murder, so not all acts of self-destruction are suicide in the theological sense. There is a marked difference between killing oneself to end it all and laying down one's life for one's neighbor out of obedience to God's commandment. The first is born out of desperation and rooted ultimately in disbelief in God's goodness and mercy. The second has its roots in fidelity to God's promises.

> The deaths of Saul and Judas are examples in the Bible of suicide in the sense of self-murder. The death of Samson, on the other hand, is an example of self-sacrifice out of fidelity to God.[6]

In the end Samson's death was not mere self-destruction, but was an act of service on Israel's behalf and a sign of a repentant heart. Somewhere in his unending darkness Samson regained contact with his previous fidelity to God. Perhaps Saul's death was also an act of service on Israel's behalf, as we will see below, and not just an expedient act of self-destruction.

Saul's Defeat

In the long story of Israel's first king, we are told of initial goodness, growing fear, error in judgment, attempted murder, pursuing the innocent, and murder of a priestly family, all within the unfolding tragedy of sensing God's disapproval and rejection. Finally, after a losing battle against the Philistines, Saul committed suicide. He did this in order to prevent his enemies from tormenting him and disgracing Israel by putting him on display as they had once done with Samson. His death is chronicled by the writer of 1 Sam but no word of reproof is spoken there about his suicide, although he was reproved directly for consulting a medium.

When David heard of Saul's death, he composed a lament. Whether it was heartfelt or done for political reasons, the lament was for Saul's entire life, much of which was valuable to Israel. This is a reminder that even when we cannot celebrate the final choice and mode of death, the person who committed suicide may have done much that can be celebrated and remembered with respect. Where this can be brought forward at a funeral service it brings some balance to very disturbed emotions without removing the sense of tragedy, primarily by reminding everyone that this person can be remembered for more positive reasons.

Saul had done much to unify and protect Israel before he took several turns for the worse.[7] He certainly used a sound military strategy that was designed to bring a long-lasting protection to all the tribes of Israel, not just his own.[8] In this way Saul worked for the benefit of the entire

---

6. Bloesch, *Freedom for Obedience*, 221n30.

7. See the extensive discussion of Saul's election as the first king of Israel in Barth, *CD* 2/2:336–93. For other informative studies in narrative interpretation see Bar, *God's First King*, and Gunn, *Fate of King Saul*. While I do not agree with Gunn at every point, there is plenty of sympathy for Saul's predicament in his account.

8. Hauer, "Shape of Saulide Strategy," 153–67. The effort to protect all the twelve

nation. Yet he had also done much to tear apart that unity and earn the disrespect of many. Especially reprehensible was his attack on the priests of Nob for the "crime" of feeding David, a murderous action which many of his loyal soldiers refused to commit (1 Sam 22:17–19). His was a once-good life sadly gone bad. Thus David's lament was magnanimous.

A review of Saul's downfall must look not only at isolated narratives but at the unifying theme running through them. Donal P. O'Mathuna reviews the whole biblical account of Saul's kingship and says, "Saul's root problem is his desire for control over his life and his unwillingness to give that control to God. One of the general themes of the Bible is that Saul's problem is humanity's problem."[9] We all like to control our surroundings and activities, our fortunes and resources, our use of time and the way people perceive our importance. Desire for control is hard to surrender to God. If Saul stands condemned on this point, for not being able to surrender his idea of kingship to God's revision and correction, he certainly does not stand alone.

Saul's downfall began with an act of disobedience. Instead of decapitating Agag, who deserved death because he brutalized and murdered many innocent victims, Saul chose to keep him alive as a prisoner. He probably did this intending to continually humiliate Agag and put him on display, reminding everyone of his defeat as the Philistine's had done with Samson. This was not the swift justice which God demanded, nor the obedience to God's command which the king should have shown before the nation. This act of disobedience did not stand alone, but it was a turning point for Saul, setting him on the wrong path. And it "grieved" the Spirit of God. Afterwards Saul could never regain his inner balance. Elie Wiesel points out many of the strange and tragic conflicts surrounding Saul.

> Misunderstood himself, Saul was incapable of understanding others. He understood no one. He should have been more aware of Samuel's suffering at having to transmit God's word and God's will without being able to change them. He should have tried to understand the conflict of David, who was compelled to replace him though he loved him. Nor did he empathize with his own children, who, out of love for him, tried to stop him from committing the irrevocable. Saul was alone and never managed to go beyond his solitude.[10]

---

tribes together was central to their unity, part of a well-reasoned and prolonged strategy.

9. O'Mathuna, "But the Bible," 349–66, especially 360.

10. Wiesel, *Five Biblical Portraits*, 94.

Wiesel reads the account of Saul as a heartbreaking story of personal decline and moral break down, a narrative filled with anguish and confusion. In the end, utterly defeated in battle and standing near the bodies of his dead sons, Saul asked his servant to kill him, saying, "Otherwise these uncircumcised will come and thrust me through, and make sport of me" (1 Sam 31:4). But the armor-bearer refused. At that point Saul killed himself with his own sword. Then his armor-bearer followed suit. Thus two men controlled their own end as their enemies swept in for the kill.

Many readers empathize with Saul all the way through the account of his tragic life, in spite of his sins and errors in judgment, as David rises to replace him. Saul was given a special role that was eventually taken from him, and we can recognize his pain in experiencing God's rejection even as we see justice in God's decision to do this.

In the New Testament, Saul was never chosen as a negative example in moral education, and in the history of Christian biblical interpretation some patristic writers spoke of Saul more positively than negatively. He was finally rejected by God as king over Israel, but his kingship was not removed immediately, only his right to pass the kingship on to his heirs. God did not instruct Samuel and David to lead a revolt against him and depose him, so there was a season of mercy granted to Saul and his family, though Jonathan seems to be the only one who realized this. Perhaps the extended time offered Saul meant there were still good qualities in him, although mixed with lesser ones that increasingly frustrated his attempts to succeed. Perhaps opportunity was given for personal repentance.

The taking of his own life served a specific purpose. Saul prevented the Philistines from disgracing the living king of Israel.[11] The tragic death of Israel's first king, then, became like an honorable death in battle. Years before he may have lost honor when he refused to face Goliath, but he regained some honor at Gilboa. In the perspective of time Saul's suicidal death was not much reviled in Jewish tradition, nor in early Christian tradition either. As Joyce Baldwin says, "There was some consolation for Israel, therefore, in the circumstances of Saul's death. Though the Philistines became the victors, they were deprived of the satisfaction of torturing and deriding Israel's king. He died an honorable death."[12]

---

11. In more recent times a similar concern was felt by General Matthew Ridgeway in the Korean War when he visited troops on the front lines and place himself at risk. Fearing capture and its consequent propaganda use by the enemy, he carried a live grenade for the purpose of ending his own life rather than surrender.

12. Baldwin, *1 and 2 Samuel*, 172. For a helpful discussion on God's interaction with

A final grace was given to Saul: the loyalty of his retainer to the end. He refused to kill Saul when Saul requested, but soon followed Saul's end by his own suicidal death. This response was not expected of a servant in ancient Israelite society.[13]

Ahithophel's Betrayal

Ahithophel held a high position at the court of King David, but for some reason he joined Absalom's rebellion (1 Sam 16 and 17). When David realized that he lost Ahithophel's support he became afraid, knowing how capable the great man was in analysis and strategic thinking. So David sent Hushai back to Jerusalem to pretend allegiance to Absalom and undermine Ahithophel. The smartest man in Jerusalem advised an immediate pursuit because David was on the run and his supporters were in disarray. Overtake and kill David to secure the kingdom. It was the right strategy but the great opportunity was missed.

In countering this sage advice, Hushai exploited fear. He said Ahithophel's recommended course of action would work in a different context, but was not advisable then. David had so much knowledge of warfare that he was a deadly adversary at all times, particularly in quick engagements involving smaller forces. At that very moment he was like a wounded bear, ready to destroy any who came within reach. If Absalom's troops suffered an initial setback then uncommitted people would not want to join him. Better to wait, gather more troops, and choose a better moment. This counsel was cunning in its mixture of truth and dishonesty, because at that moment David was at a great disadvantage and there would never be a better moment to attack.

Absalom heeded Hushai's advice and delayed to gather additional reinforcements, losing his one chance to deliver a crushing blow. Meanwhile David had time to escape and gather more forces for the upcoming battle.

Ahithophel anticipated defeat the moment his advice was discounted. He went home and put his business and personal affairs in order, then hung himself. Rabbi David Wolpe points out two possible fears. It may be that Ahithophel knew that if David won he would suffer for his betrayal. Or that if Absalom won he would not be allowed to retain his

---

Saul, which seems strange to many modern readers, see 172–75.

13. Shemesh, *Bible*, 163–64.

high position, because Absalom lacked respect for his counsel. Either Ahithophel feared for his life or he could not face loss of prestige and influence in power politics. Wolpe says, "Either way, the Tanach reports the suicide dispassionately. There is not a word of approval or, as might be expected, condemnation. The end of Ahithophel is rendered with austere dignity."[14]

There is another possibility regarding motive. Ahithophel may have feared David's wrath descending upon his family if he went into hiding, and hoped by suicide to shift David's focus elsewhere. He may have been motivated by thoughts of protecting his loved ones.

The ancient Israelite historian told about Ahithophel's suicide matter-of-factly, without adding any moral commentary. The story is simply told and the reader can see Ahithophel's actions in the light they deserve. Furthermore, Ahithophel's hanging foreshadows Absalom's as the narrative tension builds in the story.[15]

In the imprecatory Psalms, David probably had people like Ahithophel in mind just as much as Doeg, the man who induced Saul to declare David an outlaw and murdered the priests at Nob. Saul did not design all his murderous plans on his own, but was fed lies and goaded into distrusting David by schemers like Doeg. Similarly it is not likely that Absalom concocted the rebellion all on his own, though his hatred towards his father had been brewing since the rape and humiliation of his sister, Tamar, by Amnon, which David failed to punish (2 Sam 13). People as cunning and strategic as Ahithophel could prepare for the upheaval long before the event. Even if Ahithophel did not act alone he was a type of all those who betrayed David during the rebellion. He had received David's kindness and favor, served as counselor in his inner circle, and eaten at his table (Ps 41:9), yet Ahithophel was ungrateful and unfaithful. His death is reported dispassionately by the biblical historian, but we can all understand if David's personal reaction was embittered by every memory of previous friendship (Ps 55).

---

14. Wolpe, *David: The Divided Heart*, 112. The reference to the Tanach is a reference to the Hebrew Bible.

15. Battenhouse, "Tragedy of Absalom," 53–57.

Jonah's Resignation

The story of Jonah reads like a parable, full of extreme situations that heighten tension. Jonah was called by God to go to Nineveh and preach to the Assyrians, but he rejected this divine assignment. Jonah was not the only prophet to protest against his mission, and not the only Israelite who would have refused to go to Assyria. When first called to return to Egypt in God's service, Moses argued with God and asked that someone else be chosen. When first called to become a prophet, Jeremiah protested that he was too young for the job. Yet both Moses and Jeremiah served in the end. Only Jonah completely rejected his mission. He put his No into action and travelled in the opposite direction. God sent such a severe storm that experienced sailors became afraid for their lives. When the frightened men interrogated Jonah, he confessed that God controls the wind and waves. Jonah told them that his own presence on the ship was the cause of the storm, and that they should throw him overboard. The idea was his, not theirs.

The sailors feared incurring guilt for his death, but after their attempt to land the ship failed, they did as he suggested. While the biblical writer does not tell us what Jonah thought at this point, Jonah had every expectation of death and no expectation of being swallowed by any "great fish" that would help him survive and spit him out near shore. There is no indication he thought God would deliver him from drowning, so we may safely assume he expected death. When he advised the sailors to toss him overboard, he seemed willing to sacrifice himself for the good of others. Yet maybe his suggestion stemmed from despair more than a death wish.

As the wind raged, Jonah did not just think that circumstances were against him. He experienced God as being against him because God told him to go to Nineveh, a city of Assyrians known for their cruelty. What would the Assyrians do to him? The people who lived near the Assyrian Empire feared and hated them, and so the call of God must have seemed beyond strange. Why would God warn the enemies of Israel or treat them well?

Because he perceived that God threatened his ship, Jonah could have no thought of death bringing relief or reward, for in God's presence, he would face judgment. Jonah would face the very One who was against him, hostile, opposed to his welfare. This was despair indeed for a prophet of God. A woman struggling with cancer, who was estranged from her adult children, said to a pastor, "I think God hates me." That was likely how Jonah felt. While many take the story of Jonah to be historical, others take it to be an ancient parable. There are so many vivid and unusual extremes in the telling which normally belong in parables. However, either way you interpret it, the narrative contains these very difficult elements in the portrayal of Jonah's experience of God.

Martin Luther recognized Jonah's desire to die is indicated in the narrative. He also said that the magnitude of Jonah's despair is not often felt by the reader who already knows that in the end God rescues Jonah from drowning, then releases him from the "great fish." Luther hit the nail on the head when he said, "But you must visualize Jonah's frame of mind in this dilemma. He does not see a spark of life left in him, nor any hope of rescue; nothing but death, yes, death, death confronts him, and he must despair of life and surrender to death."[16] Through eyes clouded by despair, Jonah could not see any rescue in his future. Luther continues,

> And so, since the Lord was not subduing the storm, Jonah wanted to provide a cure for this misfortune by his own death. Surely this was a great sin on the part of the prophet. In addition, it was far greater and more serious because, now that he was about to die, he knew for sure that he had an angry and hostile God. . . . It was a very bitter trial to look at the death that lay before him in this way, to really wish to die, and still to know that God was angry with him.[17]

As only a person in misery can think, Jonah conceived in his own heart that God was hostile to him. Was he right or wrong to think this? The crux of any problem is not what we actually know about God's plan so much as what we think and fear about God's purpose. Or what we think and feel without understanding God's purpose. Our feelings are not a good guide when it comes to our fellowship with God, yet we often base so much on them that we can easily lose our way.

Luther saw Jonah as "a figure of Christ," because Jesus felt this type of despair in the hour of death and because he endured the wrath of God against sin. Luther had in mind the despair Jesus felt on the cross, echoed in the opening verse of Ps 22, and the fact that previously Jesus himself spoke of the "sign of the prophet Jonah."[18] Because the central significance of this sign involved Jonah's being swallowed in darkness and

---

16. Luther, *Luther's Works, Volume 19*, 66.
17. Luther, *Luther's Works, Volume 19*, 13.
18. Matt 12:38–41; Luke 11:29–30.

coming forth alive, pointing ahead in time to Jesus's death and resurrection, Luther said that Jesus recapitulated some of Jonah's experience of despair on the cross. Even after Jesus's life-long trust and obedience in God, unlike Jonah's distrust and disobedience.

Christian theologians say that Jesus recapitulated the historic experience of ancient Israel in the course of his life. What do they mean by this? Jesus, as the Messiah of Israel, summed up in his own singular life major aspects of the history of Israel, including the rejection of God's prophets by some of the very people they were sent to help. Jesus also summed up the misery God's servants experienced in the course of their faithful lives, from Joseph to Jonah. In other words, as the redeemer, Jesus had to suffer as righteous people often suffered in the past, and as they still do in far too many places. This was part of his God-given mission, so that he fully identified with God's people throughout time. Hurting people today, like the woman who felt that God hated her, need to know that Jesus experienced the despair of abandonment as he suffered on the cross (Matt 27:46). Whether mixed with other more positive thoughts from Ps 22 or not, we find the sense of abandonment there, heartfelt and real in its most frightful aspect. By turning his head Jesus pushed away the sour wine from his lips, but he drank the full cup of that despair.

The Hopelessness of Judas

Richard France thinks that Matthew's reference to Judas's suicidal death by hanging is an allusion to the death of Ahithophel, who hung himself after betraying King David.[19] A literary comparison between the first and second betrayer is implied in the mode of death. The abhorrence due a betrayer like Ahithophel was given to Judas in the New Testament writings, with an implied condemnation of the sin of deceit and treachery.

In early Christian literature from the patristic period there is never approval for Judas's suicide, but not much mention or condemnation of it either. His mode of death seems to get dwarfed by the sin of conspiring with Jesus's enemies. Many questions come to mind regarding Judas. For example, was he ever a true believer? If so, why did he turn away? If not, given Jesus's deep perception about personal character, why did he invite Judas to belong to the Twelve?

---

19. France, *Gospel According to Matthew*, 386.

In time, a general idea developed among Christians that Judas died unrepentant at the time of his suicide. This was based on an assumption, not on any known apostolic teaching in the early church. It was generally thought that the outcome should have been different if he had repented, that with God's help he would have regained self-control and not committed suicide. However the New Testament is silent regarding the final thoughts or personal prayers of Judas, and this silence cannot count as evidence one way or the other. Furthermore, his motive for suicide can have more than one plausible explanation. Did he commit suicide as one who lost his mind or as one who tried to expiate guilt?

We wonder about forgiveness. In human terms it appears that Peter was far closer to Jesus than Judas. If so, then Peter's refusal to speak a word in Jesus's defense, together with his outright denials that any personal friendship existed between them, must have been far more wounding to the heart of Jesus than what Judas did. Like Judas, Peter also could have hanged himself in remorse afterwards, but his safety net included the nearness of other disciples.

As Alexander MacLaren stated in a sermon on Matt 27:4, "Be sure of this, that if Judas Iscariot, when his 'soul flared forth in the dark,' died without hope and without pardon, it was not because his crime was too great for forgiveness, but because the forgiveness had never been asked. There is no unpardonable sin except that of refusing the pardon that avails for all sin."[20] He is careful to say *if* Judas died without pardon, because this is really unknown by us. Judas may have prayed for and received God's forgiveness. If so, it could only mean that his suicide did not define the complete truth of his life, however much it showed the anguish and despair he felt at the end.

Ray Anderson on Judas

Unlike many who hold out no hope for Judas, Ray Anderson wrote a book on grace in which he affirmed the wide reach of God's forgiveness. He used Judas as a hypothetical model in order to address people who cannot hear a word about God's grace because of long-felt guilt, shame, and fear. The book's title is *The Gospel According to Judas: Is There a Limit*

---

20. MacLaren, "'See Thou to That!'" 304.

to God's Forgiveness?[21] Anderson thoughtfully reviews all references to Jesus's interaction with Judas.

He starts with Jesus's prayer for guidance in selecting the makeup of the Twelve, a symbol for the reconstitution of Israel. Jesus could choose only twelve young men out of a much larger group of initial disciples. At that time Judas was God's gift to Jesus, someone given in answer to prayer, a special situation which Anderson explores because of the possible insight it brings to Jesus's relationship with Judas. He sees in the Jesus and Judas relationship the development of the theme "love risks failure in order to redeem."[22] His focus is truly on Judas, and he does not use this discussion as a springboard to argue for universalism carte blanche or belittle the significance of Judas's betrayal, a sin that he considers dreadful. There is a full review of what it means for Judas to have betrayed the love of Christ.

Anderson asks many questions that fit the context of each biblical story. For example, he asks us to reflect on the inclusiveness of Jesus's prayer from the cross. "I like to think that Jesus spoke a word even on behalf of Judas when from the cross he said, 'Father, forgive them, for they know not what they do.'"[23] Was not Judas one of "them" at that point? If Jesus could pray for Caiaphas and Annas, for Pilate and his Roman soldiers, and for all of his own people who rejected him, did not his prayer also include Judas? Indeed the prayer must include Judas.

Anderson's study opens up questions about wounded love, the nature of betrayal, the response of shame, as well as the meaning of forgiveness. The element of speculation is intentional because Anderson is trying to examine the range of forgiveness for the reader who is actually thinking about his or her own sins, not those of Judas. Interpretations of Judas that take the opposite tack also involve elements of speculation. It is not the duty of any theologian to assign Judas his rightful place (Acts 1:25), for that assignment belongs to God alone.

---

21. Anderson, *Gospel According to Judas*. This title is not to be confused with the gnostic gospel that purported to bear the testimony of Judas Iscariot and was without historic merit. See Bock, *Missing Gospels*, and Wright, *Judas*.

22. Anderson, *Judas*, 52.

23. Anderson, *Judas*, 23.

God's Foreknowledge of Judas's Role

Matt 26:24 (or the parallel passage in Mark 14:21) says, "The Son of Man is to go, just as it is written of him; but woe to that man by whom the Son of Man is betrayed! It would have been good for him if that man had not been born."[24] Here Jesus indicates a foreordained plan, which took into consideration the traitor's role in this drama. At the same time Jesus warned Judas not to go through with his scheme, offering him a real way out. God can work with multiple options and contingencies in unfolding the divine plan, so Judas was not trapped in the role of betrayer.

If taken by itself this verse implies a preordained role, so the question naturally arises whether Judas had any choice. But the preordained role was for Jesus, not Judas, and Jesus also had real human choice about participating. He was not compelled against his will, though it became a struggle to do the will of God. Was Judas somehow compelled against his will? We have every reason to think that Judas also had a real personal choice. As the creator of time, God's relationship to time is different than ours. This means God's foreknowledge and our human free will can be held together without logical contradiction. God's advance knowledge does not restrict the exercise of human freedom.[25] If Judas had turned away from his betrayal at the pleading of Jesus, the arrest of Jesus would have been accomplished by other means.[26]

When Jesus said it would be better if this man had not been born, the natural way to hear this is that the tipping point came once Judas finalized his betrayal. This statement does not necessarily require an absence of freedom on the betrayer's part, as if Judas had no real choice in handing Jesus over to his enemies. Biblical warnings about God's judgment imply moral responsibility. Personal responsibility implies a degree of freedom of action. Therefore, I think Jesus's warning was a true warning meant to dissuade Judas and implies that he was not a puppet with no mind of his own. A way out was provided which Judas rejected. Yet the words of Jesus imply something more. Whatever this action meant

---

24. This literal reading is provided in a footnote by the New American Standard Bible.

25. Craig, *Only Wise God*; cf. Geach's chapter on omniscience and free will in his *Providence and Evil*.

26. Alexander MacLaren crafted an entire sermon on Judas's opportunity to repent called "The Last Pleading of Love."

to Judas personally it also filled a role in a much greater drama. In this betrayal, God's purpose for the suffering of the Messiah would be served.

As Charles Cranfield observed, even if his act serves a larger purpose, it remains Judas's act and he remains morally responsible for it.[27] Therefore Judas is without excuse. He made his choice and God used it in a greater drama, but it was not a righteous choice.

The Wrong Kind of Sonship
(John 17:12 and the "Son of Perdition")

Jesus speaks of one disciple as lost, "the son of perdition" [or "the one doomed to destruction"]. F. F. Bruce advises against pressing the predestinarian flavor of the Aramaic phrase too far. We are not meant to think Judas was lost against his will.[28]

What does it mean to be a child of hell or a son of perdition? Bruce points to one aspect, that of willingly cooperating with evil in some form. There is such a thing as succumbing to demonic influence and temptation, in which one may be guided or "ruled" by evil without being literally possessed by a demonic spirit, without having one's will and imagination overpowered. There are other routes by which a person can become a fitful servant or a temporary pawn of evil, even if not an enduring one. This happens when human intentions align with a greater evil purpose at work, even when that purpose cannot be clearly perceived or totally affirmed.

The phrase "son of perdition" indicates one who is under the sway of demonic influence or ungodly human influence. Such a condition is personally deplorable for any human being but does not mean, without exception, someone who is predetermined to go to hell and perish eternally. Sometimes our thoughts jump to the possibility of damnation too quickly with regard to specific people, as though there could never be an intervention of the Holy Spirit bearing upon their human spirit in a transformational work of rescue and redemption. The description that applies to a wayward human in one situation cannot be applied constantly at all times, not even to that same person's history. This is seen by looking at two particular examples, Peter and Paul.

---

27. Cranfield, *Gospel*, 424.

28. Bruce, *Gospel of John*, 332. Foreknowledge does not require predestination in a deterministic sense. God can foreknow each possibility without mandating that each possibility is predestined to happen.

At one point Simon Peter was a "son of perdition" in a different way than Judas, when he was the unwitting tool used by Satan to tempt Jesus away from the cross (Matt 16:21–23). Without realizing it, Peter encouraged Jesus to disobey the will of God the Father. Yet Jesus did not end his relationship with Peter or revoke his discipleship after that moment. Nor did he do so after Peter's triple denial on the night of his arrest. The fact that Peter served the will of Satan in a different way than Judas does not mean that Peter was destined to go to hell. Furthermore, as Ray Anderson reminds us, the "son of perdition" language is not isolated to the case of Judas in Jesus's usage in John's Gospel. "We forget that Jesus used such language with others—for instance, when he said of certain Pharisees, 'You are of your father the devil' (John 8:44)."[29] Jesus's opponents also called him a son of the devil, saying Jesus led Israel astray. Anderson adds, "Jesus' use of this language was consistent with the way in which people in that culture accounted for actions in others that they deplored."[30]

Earlier in his career, the Pharisee Saul of Tarsus could have been called a son of perdition, because he attacked the truth and harmed people loyal to Jesus, but by God's grace he was brought to a life-transforming encounter with the risen Christ. And there were believers in churches founded by Paul who were converts from deplorable spiritual and moral conditions. "You were formerly children of wrath " (Eph 2:3, KJV, RSV; compare Eph 2:1–7 with Col 1:13, 21–22). If children of wrath were the equivalent of children of perdition, and the phrases are virtually synonymous in meaning, God seeks to rescue these very people.

Therefore we should hesitate to say we know anything about Judas's eternal destiny simply because he was called a son of perdition. This caution does not disregard the truth about Judas's conduct. Judas served the will of Satan at the great crisis point in Jesus's life. He became devilish in his ingratitude and hostility to Jesus, withdrawing from God's election

29. Anderson, *Judas*, 66.

30. Anderson, *Judas*, 66. Speaking sharply against one's opponents fits the Jewish milieu of the first century according to a variety of biblical scholars, including William Manson, William F. Albright, F. F. Bruce, Cullen I. K. Story, Craig Evans, Craig Blomberg, and Richard Bauckham. Attempts to portray the author of the Gospel of John as being anti-Jewish, claiming the phrase "your father the devil" is inauthentic, fail to take into account Second Temple Period social divisions and rhetorical expressions prior to the destruction of the temple. Consider wording in relevant portions of the Qumran (DSS) documents, particularly the community's references to priests in Jerusalem who did not honor their Teacher of Righteousness: "The Man of the Lie," "The Wicked Priest" and "a congregation of falsehood."

to be the Messiah's close friend and disciple. That was a rejection that entailed the most serious of consequences. Judas rejected the way of discipleship as Jesus embraced the way of the cross. Then what followed? The New Testament does not focus on Judas during Jesus's trials before Caiaphas or Pilate. We cannot track his thoughts. Was Judas unmoved by the sentence of crucifixion? How should we interpret his throwing down the silver and declaring his own guilt (Matt 27:3–5)? Was the self-hanging a manifestation of inner repentance and a cry for forgiveness, whatever else was mixed with it?

Barth said the New Testament does not tell us that Judas converted at the end or give any hopeful word, but neither does it make him a hopeless example of assured rejection.[31] Why not assured rejection? We do not know everything, but there was an open confession of sin and an attempt to make amends.[32] Barth asked preachers neither to preach universalism nor a message of powerless grace. The wickedness of humans is a reality, but a weaker one than the almighty power of the grace of God in Jesus Christ. In the end we are left with a tension which Barth does not attempt to resolve.[33] The New Testament picture of Judas includes remorse, but remorse is not necessarily the same as repentance or conversion. However, remorse can precede and accompany repentance. In the end, what can we say? With an incomplete picture the personal repentance of Judas remains a possibility, though it seems like an outside one to many students of the Bible. It is not my intention to argue one way or the other, only to caution against presuming more than we know. As Peter said, God knows the proper place for Judas, the place where he belongs (Acts 1:25).

Was Judas Condemned Because of His Suicide?

In our review of John 17:12, I have said nothing to exonerate Judas or minimize his betrayal, nor do I forget that Jesus declared he would be

---

31. On the inability to condemn or exonerate Judas on the basis of sparse NT references, see Barth, *CD* 2/2: 476. In this passage Barth also said that there is no promise Judas will be saved as a matter of universal salvation (*apokatastasis*). On this topic see Koonz, "Old Question," 33–46; cf. Burton, "Universalism," 217–18. Also see Colwell, "Contemporaneity," 139–60, and Torrance, *Karl Barth*, 213–40.

32. Barth, *CD* 3/4:408. He is partially supported by van Unnik's interpretation of Judas's final actions. For Barth's extensive discussion on Judas, see *CD* 2/2, 458–506. For an interpretation that saw Judas's action as serving a theological purpose, see van Unnik, "Death of Judas," 3–16.

33. Barth, *CD* 2/2:476–77.

judged for the role he played in the arrest. What is maintained is caution about thinking we know God's ultimate judgment on Judas based on one or two passages where Jesus offers brief comments, in each case almost as an aside, while discussing a more important point. The more important point was that Jesus would be vindicated following his suffering and death. With that assurance he celebrated his last meal with the disciples and instituted it as a continuing meal which would both memorialize his death and point ahead to his return.

However, for those who think John 17:12 is clearly a pronouncement of God's ultimate condemnation of Judas, there is still something more to consider. If you interpret the words of Jesus to mean that Judas was condemned in eternity, then there is a necessary follow-up question. What was the reason for Judas's condemnation?

If Jesus did intend to reveal the ultimate fate of Judas, making a preliminary announcement of God's final judgment on this one specific person, the condemnatory emphasis is on the sin of not believing which led to rejecting and "handing Jesus over" to his enemies. The emphasis is not on the personal despair and suicide which followed after Jesus's arrest. Suicide is not lifted up in the New Testament as Judas's great sin. The weightier matter of betraying the Lord is mentioned. Suicide may be implicitly condemned in the very negative narrative of Judas's death, just as in the case of Ahithophel, but it is never explicitly condemned. Suicide is not declared to be the reason why it would have been better for Judas not to have been born.

Karl Barth on the narratives versus specific commands

Karl Barth affirmed that nowhere in the Bible is suicide explicitly forbidden.[34] Rather than being given a command we are given specific stories about men who did commit suicide. While many good things could be said about parts of their lives, the truth of wrongful deeds is also told. God had gifted the kingship to Saul, but not for the purpose of making kingly decisions apart from God's will and blessing. God had to be acknowledged as the sovereign ruler over the king, which Saul found impossible to do. In all his cleverness, Ahithophel could not see that it was not merely by David's own prowess that he had achieved the kingship, but

---

34. Barth, *CD* 3/4:408.

by God's election. To dispose of David in a rebellion was to act unwisely and wickedly.

Judas was given by God to live in close relation to Jesus and was given special privileges, including gracious and profound personal instruction, and eyewitness proximity to miracles of healing and other significant messianic signs. Yet even with these advantages as a close follower of Jesus, Judas wanted to retain control over some areas of his life.[35] As a result of this error there came a day when horrific choices seemed possible, even necessary. Thus the biblical stories of autonomous living, expressions of self-will, betrayal, and suicide contribute to the one story that communicates the grace of God. In our effort to be sovereign, we resist the mercy of God. Yet in Jesus the mercy of God defeats this sin.[36]

For this reason Barth urged "the Church," which includes every person who represents Jesus Christ (friends in conversation, parents, neighbors, preachers), to communicate the good news of the free salvation of God.[37] The Reformation's evangelical affirmation of the unconditional grace of God is very much needed in our time. Preaching Christ and preaching grace go together. However, the hardest thing to do is to embody this message and live by grace in our personal relations.[38]

With God, the gift and giver are one and the same. To come to Jesus Christ, crucified, risen, and ascended is to come to the one who established reconciliation and renewed fellowship with God. In relationality with him, new life is made possible today, because salvation is not just something given beyond death in a heavenly dimension. In his presence today, by the Holy Spirit, we can receive more than permission to live, even freedom and strength to live. The Spirit of Christ sets us free from bondage to our past sins and mistakes. The Spirit of Christ sets us free from human distortions based on cruel things done to us in the past. In God's unconditional grace we are renewed and our hope does not die.

Recommended Reading for Reflection and for Using Bible Narratives in Counseling:

Karl Barth, *Church Dogmatics*, 3/4, 402–413 (Barth works with both testaments).

---

35. Barth, *CD* 3/4:409.
36. Barth, *CD* 3/4:409.
37. Barth, *CD* 3/4:409.
38. Hordern, *Living by Grace*; this theme is also found in Torrance, *Preaching*.

Kalman J. Kaplan and Paul Cantz, *Biblical Psychotherapy* (a use of Old Testament stories compared with Greek tragic stories).
Margaret Krych, *Teaching the Gospel Today* (a use of New Testament stories).
Mathew B. Schwartz and Kalman J. Kaplan, *Biblical Stories for Psychotherapy and Counseling* (a use of Old Testament stories compared with Greek tragic stories).

5

The Bible: Key Passages

ALTHOUGH THE BIBLE DOES not directly address suicide, in addition to the brief narratives of specific suicides, there are key passages that may say something relevant. In this chapter, we will explore compelling moral teachings of the Bible on questions of life and death.

Genesis 1 and 2: God is our Creator and Life is a Gift

One main theme from Genesis to the Prophets is that God is the creator of the world and the giver of life. We are meant to recognize this truth in gratitude, seeing our lives and those of others as sacred gifts. Life is to be valued so highly that we give thanks every day.

We are created to be bearers of God's image, which means above all that we are made for spiritual fellowship with God. In this gift we are raised above basic animal life and made "just a little lower than the angels."[1] Sadly, gratitude diminishes when life is lived constantly under a great strain or, in the other extreme, when financial success and comfort brings too much ease and distraction. Stewardship of the gift of life is the main reason why we are not to commit suicide. We owe our lives to our Creator.

Of course one may point to other biblical passages that indicate God does not always protect human life in specific circumstances, and then claim these counter the central affirmation of the giftedness of life. For example, the destruction of Pharaoh's soldiers (Exod 14), or the lawless

---

1. Ps 8:4–8, King James Version; Heb 2:6–7.

youth who taunted Elisha (2 Kgs 2:23–25). These stories can be interpreted as incidents where God took away life in an act of judgment on those who threatened harm to the Israelite community. Ultimately God will take away every individual by some form of death, but these seem to be cases where human life was cut short as a punishment.

Yet there are countless examples where there is no hint of God's punishment. Queen Esther put her own life on the line when she came unbidden into the king's presence, and was willing to perish on behalf of her people if he would not receive her. This is a story bordering on reckless disregard for life, but it was a calculated risk which Esther took for the sake of others, not for her own self-advancement. Still, it is a story that tells us there are some things more important than preserving one's own life. As we come to various biblical texts with our modern sensibilities we will usually find something that confuses or appalls us in these type of stories. We read of Elijah's prayer that it might not rain in Israel (1 Kgs 17:1) and realize that drought destroys crops and animal life, in the end bringing starvation and financial distress to many people. Why should a prophet pray for the destruction of life?[2] What did the prophet value above all? Any one of these passages demands difficult thought, requiring a full explanation of historical context, various details and theological considerations. Do they undermine the sense that life is a gift from our creator? Do they counter the command against murder? These are common responses, especially when considering the conquest of Canaan.[3]

Donald Bloesch says, "All these stories remind us that God's commandment against killing protects life, but it does not enthrone life. It was given to preserve life, but not to idolize life. Life is something good, but it is not unconditionally sacred in the biblical perspective. Human life proceeds from God and is designed to give glory to God. Since it is

---

2. The biblical view that God in wrath punishes sin and covenant apostasy seems alien to the modern person who thinks that God should primarily serve human needs and make everyone nice and comfortable. It seems hard for theologians to find the right balance when talking of God's love for all humans or God's anger (opposition to sin and evil), committing errors in both directions. See Lane, "Wrath of God," 138–67.

3. The ancient cultural background of the Israelite conquest account is given in Walton and Walton, *Lost World*. Diverse opinions include Copan, *Moral Monster*, and Jones, "Killing the Canaanites." A review of literary histories from the late Bronze Age (time of Joshua) demonstrates the prevalent use of hyperbole regarding devastation. See Younger, *Ancient Conquest Accounts*. There are several reasons why we should reject an interpretation of genocide; however, this does not mean there were no localized slaughters. William Lane Craig works with questions about the morality of the conquest at www.reasonablefaith.org.

a gift from God, life must be respected and may be taken only for the sake of life."[4] That which leads individuals and community away from communion with God will be opposed by God, in some cases even to the point of death (Acts 5:1–11). In the mindset of the biblical writers, the ultimate tragedy is not physical death but spiritual separation from God.

The gift of life is not ultimate in itself, but given in order that individuals may know and worship God, not only in private but also in community, as a preparation for a greater fellowship with God in the life to come. That which, by our inclination and choosing, counters and opposes the purpose for human life must be opposed by God. God's wrath is always an expression of God's holiness and love, because it is not primarily set against the individual person but against that which turns the individual away from the goal for which he or she was created. Life is a gift, both life on earth and life beyond death. As our primary purpose is to honor God, giving thanks for the gift of life is essential to doing so. But ending life by suicide rarely comes close to honoring God. However, giving one's life in order to save others may honor God. The meaning of the action depends so much on the context and personal intent.

Yet if I may speak pastorally for a moment, statements about the gift of life can sound really glib and superficial to those who undergo trauma, live in social isolation, or live with wounded memories and intense soul sorrow. Suffering can steal the joy of living away, and we cannot pretend to be more pious and accepting than we actually are when this happens. For some people the feeling of gratitude is a far country, an impossibility, when staying alive requires all the energy they can muster. What the Bible presents is the ideal of seeing life as a gift, but the grim reality is that life gets damaged in many ways by confusion, sickness, deprivation, or other aspects of mortality, weakness, sin and evil. Sometimes all we can think about is the distortion of life. In the end, however, the underlying truth is that every human life is a gift from God. Insofar as we can say this, we have a lot of affinity with historic Jewish interpretation. Based on different biblical passages, many rabbis affirmed the sanctity of life and opposed suicide for the reasons that life is a great good, life belongs to God, and life is to be preserved if at all possible.

---

4. Bloesch, *Freedom for Obedience*, 207.

First Thoughts on the Commandment "Thou Shall Not Murder"

In past generations, especially the eighteenth and nineteenth centuries, many funeral sermons for suicidal deaths were notorious for offering very little comfort. They highlighted the command "thou shalt not kill." (Exod 20:13). The preacher often defined suicide as "self-murder," following the ancient example of Augustine. Was this a slight of hand trick or an accurate comparison? Are all suicidal deeds the moral equivalent of murder? To me, in using the word "murder" to describe the act of suicide a transference of meaning takes place that stretches the intent of Mosaic law.

A common understanding developed in the popular Christian mindset, crossing denominational lines, which made suicide ethically equivalent to murder. While many preachers surely meant to discourage future suicides, there is no verse in the Bible that declares suicide the moral equivalent of murder.

Exodus 20:13 was originally intended to forbid murder, especially the widely accepted practice of blood vengeance and clan feuding. That problem was entrenched in ancient cultures long before the birth of Moses. Exodus 20:13 does not refer to the killing of domestic animals for food or killing wild animals for protection of one's sheep. In the remainder of Exodus (or anywhere in Leviticus, Numbers, and Deuteronomy) the prohibition against murder was never seen as a command opposed to individual self-defense or national defense. Nor was it opposed to the need for local justice, which required the life of a murderer to be forfeit. A murderer was someone who plotted another person's death. Someone who killed accidentally, yet without negligence, was not considered a murderer.

Given the full biblical context of the prohibition against murder, but not against all other forms of killing, it is special pleading to argue this verse has suicide in mind or refers to it indirectly. In the larger canonical context this verse is not seen as a controlling referent to all forms of homicide. While over the centuries much Christian interpretation has defined suicide as self-murder, it is never explicitly defined this way anywhere in the Bible. It is a form of manslaughter, and may involve a form of self-hatred, sin, or fear. And insofar as suicide is an intentional act, it is not accidental like other forms of manslaughter. Yet mention of suicide is left out of biblical passages that discuss the distinction between murder and manslaughter, most likely because there can be no further legal punishment for the person who died. However, it is also the case that no biblical laws took away an inheritance based on a parent's suicide (which was later the case in other historic contexts).[5]

The books of the Law make important moral distinctions between manslaughter and murder because the intentionality is different. In ancient Israel, intention was a highly important factor that needed to be determined before appropriate judgment could be reached. The judges had to search and discover whether there was evidence of a previous enmity. Did the killer lie in wait to kill his victim? Or did the conflict arise suddenly in the heat of the moment? Was the action accidental? Num 35:16–25 raises questions which required careful consideration before sentence was passed. The testimony of eyewitnesses was important in order to bring clarification. Circumstances and signs of intentionality or lack of intentionality had to be considered. The point here is that the outcome alone did not determine guilt. Therefore the problem of making a simple moral equation between suicide and self-murder is one of judging from the act alone, without seeing any difference in context or motivation. God alone knows human intentions and the circumstances in which they develop. Even though suicide is intentional and not accidental, because human motives vary it is hard for us to place the right moral valuation on the deed.

Yet there are Christians who do see Exod 20 as forbidding suicide, and God can use their witness too. In his younger days a pastor in a large American city knew a woman whose life seemed troubled. He did not know her well, but she worshipped and attended a class which he taught. Once she asked him a serious question but in a casual way. Did he think the Bible forbids suicide? At that time he answered, "I think the Ten Commandments forbid it. 'Thou shalt not kill' applies." It was a short conversation. After that nothing in her routine changed, nor did her problems seem to lift from her shoulders in any immediate sense. Yet about six months later, she came and told him that she had been suicidal when she asked her question, and the only thing that stayed in her mind afterwards and kept her from killing herself was his answer, "The Ten Commandments forbid it." Maybe today he would answer her differently, but at that time his answer helped her.[6]

---

5. The later medieval European practice of desecrating the corpses of suicides and confiscating property had roots in pagan antiquity, not in early Christian traditions derived from Judaism.

6. I owe this account to Alan Beasley.

Second Thoughts on the Commandment "Thou Shalt Not Murder"

Even if suicide was considered as something less reprehensible than murder, it is unlikely that the prophets of Israel ever thought suicide an acceptable ethical choice in most circumstances. Although suicide was not the primary reference in Exod 20:13, there is nothing said positively to support it. While King Saul's suicide is a possible exception, it came within a context that was negative for other reasons, and was not a moral example for people in distress.

Sometimes people loathe their own existence, finding life too lonely or painful to go on. What should we recall when thinking about taking our own lives? We do not need one specific verse that has a technical reference to this type of death. The totality of God's revelation can form a pattern which shows us what is important. The overarching theme from Genesis onwards is that God our Creator is the author and giver of life. We do not have God's authority over the lives of others, and likewise we must not supplant God's authority over our own lives in a mistaken sense of autonomy. We owe God our lives in worship and service, and it is for God to determine the number of our days.

Consider the question of ultimate forgiveness for those who take other people's lives. Moses instructed the Israelites to place all convicted murderers under the sentence of death and carry out their executions (as would have been done in Egypt), but this instruction did not presume to know anything about God's eternal judgment on that person. There is no discussion of whether the person who commits murder can or cannot be forgiven by God after death. What about Moses and David, both guilty of this crime and eventually repentant? Both later received affirmations of God's grace in various biblical passages. In fact, the question of forgiveness in reference to an afterlife is hardly touched on in the books of Moses or the prophets. Therefore those who use the Ten Commandments to say suicide is self-murder have no grounds for going further and arguing that suicide is an unforgivable sin. Nothing in Scripture states that it is. What the command does affirm is that life is a gift from God and belongs to God. We honor the commandment when we acknowledge God's authority over life.

References to Self-Destructive Behavior

Jewish prohibitions against suicide generally depend on three biblical passages. Exodus 20:13 and Deut 5:17 speak against murder, while the early Noahide law says, "For your lifeblood too, I will require a reckoning," quoting Gen 9:5. As Kalman Kaplan and Matthew Schwartz point out, Rabbinic Judaism has seen this "as a prohibition not only against suicide but against any form of self-mutilation (Babylonian Talmud, Baba Kamma, 91b). The Hebrew Scriptures contain several additional prohibitions regarding self-mutilation, for example: 'Ye are the children of the Lord your God: Ye shall not cut yourselves, nor make any baldness between your eyes for the dead' (Deut. 14:1)."[7]

In context, Gen 9:5 did not refer to suicide *per se*, nor did it refer to all killing. In verse 4 permission was given for humans to eat animals in the time after the flood, but eating or drinking their blood was forbidden. This restriction honors the principle of life as the ancients understood it. Respecting blood as the basis of animal life reminds us that the principle of biological life in humans must also be respected. Verses 5–6 say God requires a reckoning for those who take human life. Verse 6 imposes the penalty of death for those who shed innocent blood.[8] The ultimate punishment emphasizes the seriousness of the crime. Human life is meant to be treasured because it is the gift which God has bestowed upon us. Therefore I am to treasure your life as well as my own, at least to the point of doing you no harm. The context in Gen 9 referenced the problem of someone murdering another person, not ending his or her own life in suicide. However, many Jewish interpreters infer that if we have to honor the principle of life in every other human being, then we also have to honor it in our own being as well. We have to take care of body and soul in our individual lives, which rules out suicide.[9]

---

7. Kaplan and Schwartz, *Psychology of Hope*, 35.

8. For a Jewish interpretation see Cassuto, *Commentary*, 127.

9. Within Judaism personal suicide is generally frowned upon, but the question of legitimacy concerning the so-called mass suicide at Masada has not been approached uniformly in modern times. The evidence was only discovered in 1963, but it seems clear that the majority (or far too many) of those involved had no choice about participating. Yet the alternative prospect of death by Roman crucifixion could not appear less horrific by comparison. See Leventhal, "Masada Suicides," 269–83. Even so, ancient rabbis made efforts to limit times when martyrdom was justifiable. See Abelson, "Suicide," 3–5.

Deut 14:1 is often connected in commentaries with Lev 21:5, another prohibition against shaving and bodily mutilation. The clear implication is that if it is wrong to intentionally dishonor and injure our body (think of the modern problem of juvenile slashing) then it is wrong to destroy ourselves entirely in an act of suicide.

The Open-Ended Sermon on the Mount (The Beatitudes of Matthew 5:1–12)

When a devastated student came to a seminary professor with the news that his father-in-law had just committed suicide, to which Bible passage did his comforter draw attention? To the words of Jesus in the Beatitudes. He said, "'Blessed are the poor in spirit.' And who is more 'poor in spirit' than he who is so scared, depressed, and removed that he takes his own life?"[10] This was a perceptive application of Jesus's words in Matt 5:3 about a wounded human spirit. We use this to introduce the Beatitudes, the be-happy words Jesus spoke to people who lived under a lot of unhappy conditions. Although I will present one interpretation here, there are multiple other ways in which this passage has been used in the history of Christian thought.

I think the Beatitudes, as presented in the context of the Sermon on the Mount, are not commands or lists of ethical instructions. Rather they are amazing spiritual possibilities for the present day within eschatological promises, surprising possibilities that can invade our lives when we turn to God for the power of the Holy Spirit to hope, forgive, find peace, love others, and rejoice in our daily lives in spite of circumstances that tear us down. Jesus gave these words to bring hope to people who faced very difficult lives. When there is so much trouble that people easily wonder whether God has abandoned them, we ask what it means to live in the kingdom of God. Is it really something we can experience? It seems hard to relate to Jesus's words. Where are these anticipations of the world to come actualized now?

For example, what is good about feeling empty and weak in spirit? This is a negative quality of life. If the Beatitudes are about being blessed by God, what did Jesus mean? It seems that he is contrasting extremes in order to raise a new possibility. His blessing statements were given as contrasts to what one would normally expect to find. This was meant to

---

10. I owe this account to Scott Keith.

shock and arrest attention, which was one reason he could hold the attention of a crowd. Here Jesus highlighted the contrast between the daily condition of life most people experience and the condition of life which God wants to bring to us. Coming reversals of sad and difficult human situations are needed, and only when these reversals take place will all wrongs be set right, in the final judgment and resurrection. But the future time of great blessing, when everything that is out of balance will be put right, has not yet arrived. It is in the future. Yet in these blessing statements Jesus promises that the future can break into the present. He also promises that there will be reversals of spiritual fortune in the age to come.

God alone can make the future break into the present, which means that these Beatitudes are not primarily commands or instructions on ethical living, nor a battle plan for self-accomplishment. That would be like adding rocks to the backpacks of weary hikers. Yet by God's gifting we can sometimes enter into this future in special ways, even here and now. To find our hearts free of anger, to discover a calming patience in distress, these are remarkable changes—reversals of what we usually experience and expect. Whenever we are blessed in situations that are not good it is like a sneak preview of the world to come, when God shall renew all things and give the fullness of peace.

Yet for multitudes of Christians these words of promise add tension to their daily experience, for there is a "now, but not yet" character to Christian hope. Positive responses to problematic people are not yet humanly possible apart from God's assistance. Anyone can be kind when he or she is happy, but it is difficult when we are unhappy. Jesus never envisioned a disciple who lives in the kingdom by his or her own strength, wisdom, or righteousness. Thus the Sermon on the Mount can never be reduced to a list of rules or an ethical standard of human conduct. All depends on a provision of assistance that comes through spiritual relationality with God. Christian experience down through time and across cultures testifies that such gifts have been given.

Jesus's words tell of God's nearness to those who suffer and do right, to those who work and are not rewarded, to those who are misunderstood. With divine assistance all things may become new in their lives, even when their outward circumstances do not improve. For example, a young KGB thug worked in Kamchatka in the 1970s. He was astonished and dismayed by Christian people who responded to beatings with a refusal to hate. He sensed a calm inner power that arrested the steady growth of his own ferocity and diminished its hold on his life.[11] Whenever Christians respond gracefully to hard circumstances or persecutions, they are responding according to the truth of the coming reality rather than to their present conditions.

Surprising reversals of expected behavior were witnessed in the early centuries of Christianity. Reversals of social expectations were seen when slaves were treated with respect in Christian meetings, or when orphans were gathered into homes rather than left to starve. Financial assistance from gatherings of Christians helped the families who took in destitute children, and sometimes congregations paid to purchase the freedom of slaves. Reversals of expected behavior were seen when Christians tended the sick during outbreaks of contagious diseases, ministering to total strangers, placing themselves at risk in order to provide nursing care. Such startling conduct brought glimpses of hope into the harshness of the ancient world.

For past graces we rejoice, but every generation of Christians must face battles with self-centeredness and greed, battles with fears about financial security, loss of status, the very type of problems addressed in the Beatitudes. All is not yet transformed. We live out our days in this tension between current experience and future expectation, and this is why Jesus's words remain sharp and penetrating.

What about suicide? God knows there are people who are poor in spirit, weighed down and nearly crushed. God will not forget Jesus's promise to the poor in spirit, but sadly, the poor in spirit cannot always feel any sense of hope. To some people it seems as though God's love is hidden from them. At this time they are looking for blessings they have not yet received, and some of the poor in spirit grow weary in waiting. They are not impatient so much as they feel empty. In despair some even take their own life. These are the very ones who need the reversals and blessings which Jesus spoke about. The poor in spirit include the discouraged, the despairing, the suicidal. Jesus's emphasis is not on what they can do for God, even on their ability to trust in God, but he encourages them to know God does not forget them. They too have a place in God's kingdom.

---

11. Kourdakov, *Persecutor*. Not all Christians survived the beatings with their minds intact. But those unusual responses that gripped his attention were not made possible because people used the Sermon on the Mount as a list of ethical rules to follow. Evidently, the Holy Spirit was working within and through them, bringing to reality things that were humanly impossible apart from the gift of God.

The Unforgiveable Sin—What Is It?

Matthew 12:31–32, Mark 3:28–29, and Luke 12:10 each reference the same saying of Jesus about a sin that is unforgiveable. He says it is the sin against the Holy Spirit. This has led to some confusion, and a lot of people wonder what this means. Some ask, "Have I committed this sin?" Both Matthew and Mark provide the context for the original saying, which guides us to understand the meaning. Jesus healed all kinds of diseases and worked exorcisms by the power of the Holy Spirit. Both healings and exorcisms were messianic signs to all the people. In and through these moments, gifts of healing were given to select individuals, and simultaneously they became signs to the entire Jewish nation.[12] The character of these miracles was totally positive as damaged personalities and broken bodies were healed. Each person engaged by Jesus was given a new harmony and balance. How were these events signs that signified something to the whole nation? They were indications that God's forgiveness and grace was being poured out and ushering in the messianic age. The messianic age was not completely consummated, but it had been initiated and was beginning to bless many people. Each individual's blessing was a sign to the people as a whole that all were to be included in a great deliverance.

Jesus himself understood that these healing signs were made possible by the presence and power of the Holy Spirit, in whom there is no shadow of evil. It was a sign of Satan's ultimate defeat, a sign that God was restoring and rescuing broken lives from a variety of curses and afflictions. The restoration of all Jewish people would be followed by a blessing for the entire human race (in fulfillment to God's promise to Abraham, and the promise to bring rejoicing gentiles to Zion). Even though these healing events were loaded with meaning, they were not recognized or acknowledged by all. Significant leaders rejected their meaning, though a few were more open and welcoming.

While I do not know much about demons, they were part of the narrative landscape in ancient Jewish thought, and there were rabbis who practiced exorcisms when confronted with certain forms of human distress. Demons were considered to be some kind of created spirits in rebellion against God. And Jesus became known as an exorcist who demonstrated supreme authority over demonic manifestations. But his achievements did not protect his reputation from suspicion. Powerful men were hostile to Jesus and told people that he only cast out demonic spirits by the power

---

12. Bolt, "With a View," 53–69.

of the prince of demons. That he was an evil sorcerer, a deceiver who did not represent God and meant to do evil to the Jewish nation.

Jesus responded, "Any kingdom divided against itself cannot stand" (Matt 12:25–29 KJV). In that context, and only in that context, did he say that there is no forgiveness for the sin against the Holy Spirit. The quality of fruit shows the soundness of the tree (Matt 12:31–33). He was the good tree and they should have recognized that he produced good fruit in abundance. He provided exorcisms that set individuals free from evil, also blessing that person's family and community. In each and every case there was cause for rejoicing. Therefore all who observed the ministry of Jesus should have recognized that the things he did were inspired and directed by God, not the demonic realm, always serving a holy purpose and never an evil one. To accuse Jesus of doing good works by the power of evil, was to sin against the source of each miracle, God's Spirit.

Such willfully chosen blindness cuts oneself off from forgiveness. Yet as Michael Green says, this distortion of the truth "is unforgivable not because God will not forgive, but because a man who practices such deliberate self-deception cannot bring himself to the requisite repentance."[13] Marianne Meye Thompson does not think this sin is a single event that can never be undone, nor is it making an insulting remark about Jesus or the Holy Spirit. "Rather, it is a sustained stance toward Jesus that denies the power of the Spirit of God at work in Jesus."[14]

Given these insights, can we find evidence that someone in that dire spiritual condition can turn around and come to faith in Christ? It is likely that Saul of Tarsus once reasoned that the power of Satan was behind the healings of Jesus and the rise of the church, prior to his encounter with the risen Christ on the road to Damascus. He may have cursed the name of Jesus many times. Yet God provided a miracle of grace to open his eyes so that he could recognize the true identity of Jesus and the reality of God's Spirit working among his followers. Even some priests who formerly opposed the ministry of Jesus became his followers. This happened after the resurrection and the fresh gospel proclamation that arose in Jerusalem (Acts 6:7).

This original refusal to recognize the ministry of the Holy Spirit operating in and through Jesus had societal consequences as well, as Clark Pinnock says, for they negated "God's work of salvation, not only for

---

13. Green, *Matthew for Today*, 128.
14. Thompson, "Committing the Unforgivable Sin," 82.

themselves but for everyone."[15] Jesus's statement about the unforgivable sin, then, had a very specific reference to the eyewitnesses of his healing and exorcist ministry, and the primary reference was to the leaders of the Jewish people in that specific generation. This warning about self-chosen blindness and unforgiven guilt was spoken in that historic context and no other, and is not transferable to people of following generations. Other sins have been bad enough in their own right, but they are not this specific sin. You and I have never been face to face with Jesus and called him evil.

Are There Approximate Sinful Attitudes and Actions to the Unforgiveable Sin?

In spite of general agreement in Bible commentaries on the original context and meaning of Jesus's words about the sin against the Holy Spirit, confusion still persists today over pinpointing the unforgiveable sin. It is a perennial question that keeps popping up. Young people ask youth pastors about this sin, some fearing they have committed it. Or family members fear a loved one committed it in the act of suicide. Anytime the question arises pastoral care is needed, so that the question is answered but not too quickly, because the fear is usually real and deeply felt. Sometimes there should be a holy pause before we offer an answer, for we need to honor the question and the concern behind it.

To start with, there is no reference to suicide in the context of the biblical passages where Jesus warns against this unforgiveable sin. Jesus was not talking about suicide, and the content of this specific warning is not transferrable to other subjects (problematic sins) without doing damage to his original meaning. He spoke this stern warning to the leaders of his own generation. Nor is it transferrable to other Jewish people or those who were not alive at that time.

There may be ways in which we approximate the sin of Jesus's generation in our own lives, but approximation is not the same as exact repetition, which is ruled out because the original context cannot be duplicated. We cannot come face to face with Jesus today in the way that was possible back then. There is nothing comparable to being an eyewitness to the healing ministry and vital presence of Jesus. The unforgiven sin against the Holy Spirit was attributing the power in Jesus's ministry to the power of Satan. This rejection was so destructive because it led to a

---

15. Pinnock, *Flame of Love*, 89.

general societal rejection of what God was doing in and through Jesus, which ultimately meant the rejection of both God's Messiah and the gift of peace. Before that generation passed away they lived to see their children and grandchildren engage in the disastrous rebellion against Rome, which led to horrific slaughter, slavery, and further dispersal to distant lands. That was the very opposite of lasting peace for their people.

Given the difference in historic contexts, can we engage today in a sin that is similar in nature and carries a grave consequence? Perhaps by a refusal of the grace that God offers us as we push away the gift of salvation. God alone knows when any person has pushed the gift of eternal life away to the point of no return, like an airplane crossing the ocean without enough fuel to reach land. We cannot say we know. When rejecting grace, perhaps such indifference or hostility to God's gift contains its own judgment. If your hand is closed in a fist you cannot receive any gift that is offered until you open your hand. The problem here it not that God will not forgive, but that we may refuse to receive the gift of forgiveness. To reject the gift is to reject the giver of the gift. To open your hand is to receive the gift in gratitude.

But what counts as rejection? All Christian witness is flawed or incomplete in some way, and may place obstacles in someone's path. Responding to flawed Christian messages and messengers is not the equivalent of responding to Jesus in the days of his flesh. Yet at times there may be some accountability required. God can hold us responsible for our responses to any encounter with truth, according to the light that is given us.

What then about suicide? Jesus did not call suicide the unforgiveable sin. While it is possible that the suicide of an individual betrays a rejection of God's grace, it is also possible that such a death is not motivated by a rejection of God or salvation. Motivations for suicide include more than one possibility, which means that our limited interpretation of a particular death does not necessarily match God's omniscient judgment. Therefore we are in no position to judge the precise meaning of each death, though we are right to count every suicide a tragedy.

Applying the Parable of the Good Samaritan

In Luke 10:25-37 Jesus linked Deut 6:5, on the complete love humans owe God, with Lev 19:18, about the love we owe our neighbor.[16] When the question "who is my neighbor?" was asked, Jesus told the parable of the Good Samaritan. The hero was a member of a despised group, and surprisingly, this Samaritan's actions represented the heart of God. Then Jesus posed the question, "Who was a neighbor to the man wounded by robbers?" The answer came back, "The one who showed mercy." Jesus told him, "Go and do the same."

Can we find ourselves located somewhere in this parable? What response do we give to those in need? Three different travelers came near the wounded man and each one had to make a hard choice: "will I give assistance or not?" A couple passed by the injured man to avoid becoming inconvenienced or endangered by bandits. I might resonate with them. That is a real possibility unless the impulse to serve and protect myself can be overcome.

Suicidal persons may instantly see themselves as the injured man. But I invite them to use their imaginations creatively and see members of their family as the wounded man, though their wounds are yet to come. When they do, what opportunity does a suicidal person have to bring assistance to these persons in need? The opportunity is to refrain from committing suicide. And if necessary speak instead of suffering in silence, speak clearly instead of hinting. Ask God for help to inform your family and friends of your suicidal ideation. This is true even where your circle of trust includes only one or two people, and when doing so requires energy and courage. After asking for their prayers and understanding, even though your troubles do not go away, your love continues to be shown to them by refraining from suicide.

While intense loneliness can seem overwhelming, and mitigate against the personal knowledge that others will experience deep pain in the aftermath of suicide, vast pastoral experience shows that family or friends will be wounded by that choice. If you take your life or I take mine, others will be hurt. Your gift in refraining from committing suicide

---

16. Bailey, *Through Peasant Eyes*, 37: "It is through a love of *God* that the believer is to approach people. This then has profound implications for the how, why, and who of the love for the neighbor." This is the rationale for Jesus quoting Deuteronomy, the great command to love God, first before Leviticus, the great command to love one's neighbor, even though Leviticus comes in canonical order *before* Deuteronomy. It is only through love of God that we can approach love of neighbor/family appropriately and constantly.

may take greater courage and moral strength than ordinary people can muster in other contexts. These are the secrets of each human life that only God knows, and that is why only God can rightly judge the valiant ones who struggle with this problem in comparison with the more fortunate people who never face it.

And can we enter into the meaning of this parable if we are not suicidal? Those of us who know suicidal people need to see them as the wounded person by the roadside, the one who requires mercy. We need to receive strength from God's resources to be inconvenienced. I do not mean "inconvenienced" on an around the clock schedule, unless specially gifted, but available at some point to people in crisis. Sadly, there are also situations where suicidal people cannot be helped in a lasting way but require ongoing medical or psychiatric care. We all have limits as friends or pastors, but we can extend some form of encouragement and support in friendship and prayer. Yet in offering help, we cannot be superheroes. Ultimately the one we love must make the choice to live. No one else is responsible for that choice.

6

Augustine of Hippo (354–430), Thomas Aquinas (1225–1274)

Whence Came the Negative Attitude Towards Suicide?

WHILE AUGUSTINE HAD A great impact on theological development in the Christian West, he alone was not responsible for the widespread negative attitude towards suicide that became entrenched for centuries. Some ancient cultures showed a horror of suicide by harsh reactions to it (such as desecrating a corpse), demonstrating a deeply embedded human revulsion against taking one's life. Not all the same, however, for mythologies, tragedies, stories like Homer's Ajax, all demonstrate that it was not rare. And so the people who became Christian in the early centuries had more influencing them than just a reading of biblical literature. Jewish and Christian teaching emphasized that life was a gift, that we owe our lives to our Creator. However, for many people, harsh daily realities could hide the luster of the gift.

Historian Charles Wrong recalled a conversation with C. S. Lewis which briefly touched on suicide and serves as our discussion starter. Lewis said, "You know, there's nothing to condemn it in the Bible, in the Old or New Testament. I think it [the negative assessment] must be a pagan idea; comes from Plato. I accept it purely on authority."[1]

---

1. Wrong, "Chance Meeting," 111.

Later, Lewis wrote to Vanauken that suicide was disobedience to God. Had Lewis changed his thinking over the years? There is no reason to question Wrong's recollection, but he only gave highlights. What Lewis said to Vanauken was about a proposed course of action, not a discussion of the history of ideas or a question on how to properly interpret the Bible.

In discussing the nature of biblical references, Lewis knew the distinction between direct and indirect, explicit and implicit statements. He understood the use of narratives to communicate truth as well as didactic statements. Narratives were used to affirm or reject a form of behavior, or show that trusting in God may involve a faithful person enduring hardship, as in the cases of Joseph or Job. Narratives often required discussion and commentary. The use of irony was one way the Israelite historians exposed faulty behavior, even without any direct comment on the tragic results that followed.

Lewis's "there's nothing to condemn it in the Bible" raises the right question. Is there a direct condemnation of suicide in the Bible? Norman Geisler said that suicide is "specifically condemned in Scripture" and asserts that "the few cases of suicide recorded in the Bible are condemned by God."[2] It is telling that many of the ancient Jewish and Christian commentators did not reach the same conclusion. For example, a number of them thought that Saul died a heroic and honorable death. We cannot find a condemnatory word in the passage relating the details of his suicide (1 Sam 31:1–13), though the storyteller made clear that his end came after spiritual and moral failures.

Across denominational lines, many contemporary theologians do not agree with Geisler either. This does not automatically mean he is wrong, but it is grounds for caution. Indeed, he could not point to one verse that explicitly mentioned suicide and condemned it, but Geisler made his statement in a forceful way as if there could be no disagreement with his conclusions. There is far more disagreement than he acknowledged, because there is no direct attack on suicide in the Scripture. To say this, of course, is not to say that suicide is ever honored or promoted. The few biblical stories offer negative lessons about the course of sinful conduct, in no way promoting a positive attitude about the preceding sins or the final choice, yet without specific words of condemnation. Dietrich Bonhoeffer argued that suicide is wrong because our lives belong to God, but also said there are no direct prohibitions against suicide in the Bible:

---

2. Geisler, *Christian Ethics*, 165.

> It is a remarkable fact that the Bible nowhere explicitly forbids self-murder, but that again and again it appears only as the consequence of the deepest sin, such as in the cases of the traitors Ahithophel and Judas. The reason for this is not that the Bible approves of self-murder, but that instead of prohibiting it the Bible wants to call the despairing to repentance and grace. Those who stand on the verge of self-murder no longer hear a prohibition or command; they can hear only the gracious call of God to faith, to salvation, and to turning back. The despairing cannot be saved by any law appealing to their own strength; this only drives them into more hopeless despair. Those who despair of life are helped only by the saving act of another; the offer of a new life that is lived not by their own strength but by the grace of God. Those who can no longer live cannot be helped by the command that they must live, but only by a new spirit.[3]

Similarly Karl Barth found it remarkable "that in the Bible suicide is nowhere explicitly forbidden."[4] But that is not the end of the discussion, for he thought the biblical writers gave us something better than a direct commandment. The stories of suicide in the Bible are presented in a negative light, insofar as they are all types of tragedy which happen when God's right to govern and guide is refused, when there is no trust in God's faithfulness and mercy. Such stories show the human disintegration that results when God's grace is flouted. In this way there is an indirect indictment against suicide together with the choices that precede suicide. This must be weighed together with the recognition that there is no direct and explicit prohibition of suicide in the Bible. Bonhoeffer and Barth are in agreement with Lewis regarding the absence of direct statements against suicide in the Bible, but leave open the need for the narrative passages to be considered. Lewis's reference to Plato's position is also precisely correct, and serves as an example of the influence Greek thought had on the early church, especially through the influence of Neoplatonic thought. Not all attitudes in early Christianity were shaped by the biblical tradition alone or by the normative moral teaching inherited from Judaism.

---

3. Bonhoeffer, *Ethics* (2005), 199–200.
4. Barth, CD 3/4:408.

Some Important Greek Philosophers Rejected Suicide

One of the ancient Greek philosophers who rejected the possibility of suicide was the brilliant mathematician Pythagoras. He thought the soul was immortal but moved in and out of various embodiments. However difficult life was on earth, Pythagoras thought each soul placed in a particular body should remain there for a natural lifespan, even when one felt that life on earth was unendurable, nothing more than a prison for the soul. The imprisonment had to be endured and not escaped ahead of time through suicide."[5]

Plato condemned suicide and his influence was extensive. He thought there was a supreme power that should determine how long a soul stayed in a human body. We should not usurp the divine decision regarding our life on earth. Furthermore, every human life should belong to the state. By the state, Plato had in mind a small territory governed by a powerful city. In his theory, the citizen's life belonged to those who were in charge of governing, in the sense that every citizen has a duty to work for the common good. If you are strong and healthy, you must consider the common good and contribute to it, rather than deprive the community of your labor. Plato made an exception for the weak and infirm who can no longer support themselves by their own labor or help feed other people. He did not condemn Socrates for committing suicide, because he did so under necessity. Plato held there were three conditions that made suicide acceptable: (1) if the state orders one to commit suicide; (2) if one suffers unavoidable misfortune that has dire consequences; (3) if one suffers overwhelming shame. In other words, suicide was not always ruled out of court but there should be a good reason for it.

Neoplatonism, a school of thought that built on Plato's philosophy, took a stronger stance against suicide. Only God is allowed to free a soul from the shackles of the body. Neoplatonism was influential at the time of Augustine. All in all, there was a mixed bag of ideas in the ancient Greco-Roman world. On the one hand, some like Plato discouraged thoughts of suicide. On the other hand, other writers, popular ideas, and philosophies like stoicism eroded the value of human life and commended suicide.

According to Wrong, Lewis did not see explicit biblical statements as the primary influence behind the negative Christian attitude towards suicide. This negative attitude developed early in patristic times and continued into the Middle Ages. Even if no biblical passages affirm suicide or

---

5. Russell, *History of Western Philosophy*, 33.

any narratives show it in a very positive light, the greater emphasis may have been the desire to do God's will.[6] There were Neoplatonic influences within society and some areas of early Christian thought, but these influences cannot completely account for the negative attitude towards suicide which developed and became dominant.

The Bible's Influence Apart from Specific Condemnations of Suicide

As Jewish communities did with their Scripture, so early Christian communities used the Bible (with the addition of the New Testament) to emphasize the need to trust in God through all harsh experiences and changing seasons of life. Jewish people could generally see the emphasis on God's faithfulness as a pattern across the stories of ancient Israel. The same was true for Christians reading the stories of the early church in Acts and contemplating historic experiences in the later Roman Empire. Negative memories of harsh persecutions or current experiences of them were held together with the promise of ultimate victory at the end of the age, as given in 2 Thessalonians and Revelation. In the many biblical passages which recount persecutions, there is no promotion of suicide. The living are not encouraged to seek escape in sudden death but rather seek God's grace to stay alive. God's people live with hardship as faithfully as possible in order to honor God, giving assistance and comfort to other suffering people.

No doubt the use of the Bible in Christian fellowship had an impact on attitudes and practices, but it is hard to pinpoint every contributing factor to the development of the very negative attitude against suicide,

---

6. In Droge and Taber, *Noble Death*, 119–26, the authors argue that Paul was speaking of suicide as an allowable option in Phil 1:21–26, allowable only if the individual becomes aware of God's permission to depart. They argue that Paul could conceive of killing himself and simultaneously honoring God. However, Fowl argues there is a persistent theme of joy running through Paul's rhetoric in Philippians that cannot be accounted for by Droge and Taber's interpretation. "Paul sees his current situation as an occasion for joy. He expects to rejoice when he sees the Philippians (or hears about them). Although he is in prison and often mentions his chains, he could at the same time speak of the joy he has in the midst of prison. To the extent that Paul sees death as an advantage, it is not because it releases him from the misery of prison. Rather, it unites him with Christ. In this respect Paul's suicide would undermine his rhetoric in 1:12–26." Fowl, *Philippians*, 55–56. While death is an enemy, it is not the ultimate enemy for Paul, and it remains important how one faces death in order to glorify God. Paul wanted both his life and his death to glorify God.

which became widespread and endured for well over a thousand years. Instead of just one reason, there were probably a cluster or reasons working in tandem, including the natural horror of taking one's own life. In time, laws were established forbidding burial in churchyards for those who took their own lives. This harsh attitude was maintained for many centuries.

Why the Death of Jesus Was Not Seen as an Example of Suicide

Discussions of suicide in the history of biblical interpretation do not usually include the death of Jesus, who anticipated and positioned himself for arrest and death, given traditions of godly prophets and his interpretation of the messianic pattern. In his unique understanding, the purpose and end of the messiah's work must culminate in rejection and death. Jesus thought of himself as the Messiah but with a unique frame of reference. He combined the figure called the "son of man" in Dan 7, and "the servant" in Isa 52–53, as well as with other messianic promises (Ps 2 or 110, plus more). Thus he perceived his life's purpose must include rejection in order to be achieved, with suffering and death coming prior to his vindication by God. Hence, his death would be followed by resurrection. Altogether, Jesus's understanding of the messiah's role did not fit any current Second Temple expectations for what the messiah would do. We may be shocked at Jesus's dedication to this goal, given his understanding of what he would endure and his real human fear of pain. With these guiding factors and the significance Jesus applied to them, the context and content of his ministry meant that he engaged in a God-assigned, purposefully atoning role, not a suicidal one.

Jesus's disciples are also excluded from examples of suicide in Christian understanding. These did not fear death after Jesus's resurrection as they had beforehand, but neither did they court arrest or mistreatment. They went about risking their lives to spread the gospel and suffered many harsh punishments, but that was a measure of zeal and not suicidal ideation. The disciples were willing to suffer and die only if necessary, but in anticipation of resurrection and the fulfillment of God's kingdom. Martyrdom for preaching the gospel was not considered suicide. Their deaths were examples of refusing to resist their persecutors while bearing witness to the truth. These deaths were not used to promote suicide in early Christian communities. Yet in the first few centuries there developed a veneration of the martyr. Some Christian leaders came to see this veneration as a problematic influence, but others honored it.

Augustine Was Not a Lone Voice Raised Against Suicide in the Early Church

Lewis's reference to Plato may also have had Augustine (354–430) in mind. Neoplantonic ideas and influences were advanced through Augustine's use and endorsement, though from other teachers as well. In the theological West there is no one with greater stature than Augustine, whose influence lasted over a thousand years and still continues. Thomas Aquinas, Martin Luther, and John Calvin were all greatly influenced by him and looked to his writings for guidance. Because his prestige was widely acclaimed and his writings copied and distributed for centuries, what he said on the subject of suicide was important to later generations.

Augustine took the command against murder, "You shall not kill," as a blanket condemnation that applied to death by suicide. Many other preachers followed suit down through the centuries. Martyrdom had long been venerated before Augustine's conversion, so it became important to distinguish appropriate forms of martyrdom from suicide. He condemned as unwholesome the desire for martyrdom during times of persecution, which if promoted led to unnecessary deaths among Christians. There were also unnecessary apostasies on the part of those who renounced their faith in order to save themselves from torture and death. So while Augustine condemned suicide as an unacceptable choice, he also discouraged seeking martyrdom. If forced on one, then martyrdom was unavoidable, but it was not to be sought out.

There were others in the early church who opposed suicide, including Clement of Alexandria (d. 213), Eusebius, Bishop of Caesarea (d. 339), and Gregory of Nazianzus, Bishop of Constantinople (d. 374). These theologians were also important and influential. The Synod of Elvira, Spain (ca. 305/306), condemned both abortion and suicide as illegitimate destruction of human life; the condemnation of suicide was designed to prevent Christians from seeking martyrdom when it was not forced on them. (This Council was called shortly after a time of persecution, but unfortunately fell under the sway of extreme people who promoted reprimands of lifelong excommunication without hope of reconciliation, thus moving away from Christ's own example of restoring Peter after his denials (John 21). Here is a reminder of why the early church is not the final arbiter on all questions. The Council of Arles (452) saw temptation to suicide as the work of demonic forces. While these councils are mentioned as historical markers, none of these were ecumenical councils that involved bishops from all the ancient centers of Christianity. They are not the equivalent of the Council of Nicea.

This is not an exhaustive historical survey, but shows that when Augustine wrote there were already other important voices raised against suicide in the early church. Later, in the sixth century, prohibitions against suicide became part of Canon Law. By no means was Augustine the only influence in that development.

Baptismal Confusions and the Question of Guilt

In the early church there were significant numbers of people who thought that water baptism brought remission for all previous sins, but that confession and penitence was required to eradicate the guilt of any specific sin committed after water baptism. This is why many adult converts to Christianity, who had not been baptized as infants, tried to save their baptism until later in life rather than when they first converted. (Acts 2:38 and 16:33 leave little room for thinking this was the apostolic example.) There is evidence that Bishop Ambrose of Milan, a noted preacher, opposed the practice of delaying baptism, but he was unable to influence the common Christian mindset away from this trend.[7] Many people even tried to delay baptism until the moment before death. This practice was a prevalent problem in the early church by the time of Augustine. The underlying assumptions of this practice operate with a serious theological confusion, particularly the belief in the necessity of Christian perfection after baptism or at the time of death.

In the popular understanding of many people, then, unconfessed or unrepented sins at the time of death became problematic regarding forgiveness, for there was not adequate time to show true repentance. The concern involved was not just to feel sorrow and remorse for sins, but to actually demonstrate that very contrition and live a new way, which of course required extra time. Hence, in popular thinking, suicide did not

---

7. Brown, *Augustine of Hippo*, 99.

offer time for demonstrating repentance and thus became something too awful to mention. This mindset is still widespread today.

Augustine of Hippo (354–430)

Aurelius Augustine counts as one of the most influential theologians of all time, and his intellectual impact on philosophy was also great, extending across centuries. As Benjamin B. Warfield said, "It was through his voluminous writings, by which his wider influence was exerted, that he entered both the Church and the world as a revolutionary force, and not merely created an epoch in the history of the church, but has determined the course of its history in the West up to the present day."[8] Augustine had a key role in the history of ideas, the most widely read Patristic writer in western Europe during the Middle Ages. While he primarily concerned himself with other topics, we can find a couple of places where he addressed suicide.

In *The City of God*, Augustine said it is wicked to kill oneself. Persons who commit suicide are guilty of a death—his or her own—and die with this sin on their hands (for this reason Judas was guilty of two deaths, Christ's and his own).[9] But never in this massive work does he say it is an unforgivable sin. From what church historians record of his conflict with the Donatists, we know that Augustine opposed Christians committing mass suicide as a way to escape either a sinful world or persecution.

Is Suicide Permitted to Prevent Moral and Spiritual Contamination?

There were examples in Roman history of women committing suicide after suffering conquest and rape. Should Christian women follow their example? Augustine explained that spiritual purity is not lost when one is raped. "And therefore a woman who has been violated by the sin of another, and without any consent of her own, has no cause to put herself to death; much less has she cause to commit suicide in order to avoid such violation, for in that case she commits certain homicide to prevent a crime which is uncertain as yet, and not her own."[10] Thus a violated

---

8. Warfield, *Studies in Tertullian*, 114.
9. Augustine, *City of God*, 22.
10. Augustine, *City of God*, 23.

woman is not guilty of sin, is not worthy of shame, and should not contemplate suicide. The same problem was faced by male slaves or military captives who did not have complete control over their bodies. People unjustly mistreated or raped by their masters were not to be despised in the church, nor were they to despise themselves. He also used examples from Roman history to say it was better to suffer slavery than commit suicide. Even under humiliating conditions Christians will not be deserted by God. Augustine consistently spoke against suicide for any reason whatsoever, and said it was not to be done to avoid abuse by others, nor as a means to avoid one's own future sins.

> It is not without significance, that in no passage of the holy canonical books there can be found either divine precept or permission to take away our own life, whether for the sake of entering on the enjoyment of immortality, or of shunning, or ridding ourselves of anything whatever. Nay, the law, rightly interpreted, even prohibits suicide, where it says, "Thou shalt not kill." This is proved specially by the omission of the words "thy neighbor," which are inserted when false witness is forbidden.[11]

For Augustine the command in Exod 20 is unconditional and not given with any exceptions, therefore it pertains to every human being, including oneself. "The commandment is, 'Thou shalt not kill man;' therefore neither another nor yourself, for he who kills himself still kills nothing else than man."[12] This passage shows the heart of his opposition to suicide. He called suicide a sin that violates the commandment against murder. As a corollary, he also implies we fail to love our neighbor properly if we fail to love ourselves. Love for others is emphasized. We can follow his thinking, for the act of suicide does not generally encourage, bless, or help the victim's family. The entire Ten Commandments enjoin love of neighbor as a vital part of honoring God.

Did Augustine See Any Acceptable Exceptions to the Prohibition?

In *City of God* 1.21, Augustine acknowledges that there are two times when it is justified to kill another person without incurring guilt. Firstly, public justice does require that wicked people be put to death. Secondly,

---

11. Augustine, *City of God*, 26.
12. Augustine, *City of God*, 26.

an individual might in select cases be commanded by God to kill another (though certainty of God's call to do so would be as rare as a handful of biblical cases). Then he reiterates that, apart from these two possible exceptions, "Whoever kills a man, either himself or another, is implicated in the guilt of murder."[13] In Augustine's eyes, to kill oneself is as wrong as to kill another person.

In *City of God* 1.22, he argues that suicide is not to be encouraged in order to obtain a better afterlife. He cites Jesus's warning to his disciples that they will be persecuted, with the forewarning to flee from city to city when necessary, but he never advised them to escape by any form of violence to themselves. Therefore, suicide is not acceptable merely to escape trouble.

Would the Holy Spirit Ever Guide Someone to Commit Suicide?

During one of the Roman persecutions against Christians, some who were raped committed suicide afterwards by self-drowning. Augustine acknowledged the possibility that these early Christian suicides were obeying a divine prompting or order to take their lives. "It may be that they were not deceived by human judgment, but prompted by divine wisdom, to their act of self-destruction. We know that this was the case with Samson. And when God enjoins any act, and intimates by plain evidence that He has enjoined it, who will call obedience criminal? Who will accuse so religious a submission?"[14] But for him it was only a mere possibility that God called the faithful women out of life in this way, and it seems he used this possibility as an excuse not to judge them too harshly. Yet he had no confidence that they responded to the prompting of the Holy Spirit. Therefore there was nothing he could point to, with any measure of confidence, to endorse the possibility that God might call someone to an act of suicide. Neither could he find anything in the biblical record to support the idea, save the possible example of Samson.

However, in the case of Samson he did not follow a divine command to take his own life. Samson rather asked for God's permission and blessing at the end, with no sign of being constrained by a divine command. Yet even if there was an example of a command to commit suicide in

---

13. Augustine *City of God*, 27.
14. Augustine, *City of God*, 31.

biblical history, which there is not, it would not serve as an excuse for repetition. We cannot sacrifice our children because once long ago Abraham's willingness to do was commended. Only his willingness was commended. The biblical account indicates that God intervened and stopped the killing of Isaac. That episode was a teaching moment in Abraham's life and used to prohibit child sacrifice in historical Jewish theology.

And so Augustine counseled Christians against presuming they were ever guided by a divine command to do anything drastic. For if anyone is not commanded to take the life of a neighbor, then that person who kills another human is guilty of murder. Likewise, he thought, if anyone is not commanded to take his or her own life in a suicidal act, then that person incurs the guilt of murder. Just as your neighbor's life belongs to God, so does your own.

Another question was raised. Would suicide show proper repentance for past sins? Would it propitiate a past wrong or put anything right? He answered, "No man ought to do so on account of his own past sins, for he has all the more need of this life that these sins may be healed by repentance."[15] In other words, use the time remaining to seek God's grace and personal renewal. Live for God's glory each day.

Can We Use Suicide to Send Ourselves to Heaven? Augustine's Severest Condemnation

What then about people who want to die so they can go to heaven immediately? The very desire may seem understandable but it is presumptuous. Augustine gives the sternest warning against this, saying, "No man should put an end to this life to obtain that better life we look for after death, for those who die by their own hand have no better life after death."[16] There are three possible interpretations of this sentence. (1) He means that in general we cannot presume on God's judgment or mercy as an assurance that heaven is our reward, and so must not be presumptuous in this specific way; or (2) he means that incurring guilt by suicide will require a painful purgatorial experience (but one which comes before the final judgment); or (3) he means that there can be no forgiveness after the sin of suicide. "Those who die by their own hand have no better life after death" is a negative warning, but one that is not spelled out to a sufficient

15. Augustine, *City of God*, 31.
16. Augustine, *City of God*, 31–32.

degree for us to adjudicate between options 1, 2 and 3. We cannot turn it into a declaration that suicides are automatically damned. In fact, no such statement has yet been found, to my knowledge, in Augustine's large body of literature. Furthermore, because he did endorse the idea of purgatorial suffering in order to purify and ready the soul for the joys of heaven, we cannot rule this out when we consider his intended meaning in this warning. While it may seem like a borderline case, Augustine still qualifies as a major theologian who refused to say the sin of suicide is unforgiveable in every case.

We also have to remember the early church's struggle to arrive at a sound theology of water baptism and its role in the Christian's life. Augustine was caught up in the mode of thinking which was so prevalent in the first few centuries, namely that after baptism people had an opportunity to "pass to their Lord" pure and undefiled, with all past sins blotted out.[17] Many seem to have feared committing a willful sin after water baptism, because they were not sure a willful sin would be forgiven, or they feared any minor sin would taint them after their baptism. This was a major reason why a lot of converts put off getting baptism until they thought they were near the end of life. It is important to say this whole approach involved a misunderstanding of sin and grace, as well as baptism. Perhaps Augustine missed an opportunity to correct this misunderstanding. No one passes to the Lord pure and undefiled. Every person dies in a condition of sin that requires Christ to be both justifier and sanctifier.[18] The Christian can die in joyful hope, but that joy and hope is not based on any human ability to have sin purified and completely removed prior to the moment of death.

Be that as it may, Augustine, if we understand him correctly on this point, does think the suicide is likely to face God's disapproval or condemnation (though it is not clear whether he thought the punishment would be purgatorial and temporal or of eternal duration). "It is wicked to kill oneself."[19] And if it is a wicked action to kill oneself then suicide must be avoided. Therefore Augustine contributed greatly to the church's abhorrence of suicide because of his pervasive and long-lasting influence as a theologian.

---

17. Augustine, *City of God*, 32.
18. 1 Cor 1:29–31.
19. Augustine, *City of God*, 32.

Augustine's Psychological Understanding: Some Suicidal Deaths are Yearnings for Peace

Augustine often demonstrated a deep understanding of human nature and an ability to analyze human motives, truly deserving credit in the history of ideas for his pioneering work in psychology. In the Greco-Roman world, ideas varied about what happened after death, but there were two prevalent options. Many feared that their spirit would enter into a shadowy realm. They might remain a long time in shadows, in isolation without any communication with loved ones. The other option was to believe that they simply ceased to exist. Augustine considered both of these ideas contrary to Christian teaching.

Regarding those who think they are annihilated at death, what would be their real underlying motive when considering suicide? He answers that the desire for peace, for freedom from trouble, is often their real motive when contemplating suicide. They do not really seek annihilation; rather, they seek to be free of a harsh burden that weighs them down.

> When someone who believes that at his death he will cease to exist is driven by unendurable troubles to yearn for death, he makes his decision and takes his life. He has the false opinion that he will be totally annihilated, but his natural feeling is a longing for peace.... Every willful desire for death is directed toward peace, not toward nonexistence.[20]

Here Augustine's psychological understanding is penetrating. He looked deep into the human condition in order to make sense out of the very desires that prompt unusual behaviors. Many suicides were nothing less than a desire to escape an unendurable life, and that remains just as true today. I sometimes wonder whether Augustine had the right temperament to be a patient counselor of despondent souls, but he certainly had the requisite insight. Centuries later, Martin Luther learned a special lesson in Christian fellowship and pastoral care from reading Augustine on Gal 6. His insight was that when dealing with any fault or sin in another person's life the stress should be placed on redemption rather than reproach, on the other person's welfare rather than on reproof and scolding.[21] Luther valued this insight from Augustine and gave it high praise.

20. Augustine, *On Free Choice*, 105–6.

21. Luther, *Commentary on Galatians*, 359–60: "When Paul addeth: 'Considering thyself lest thou also be tempted,' [Gal 6:1] he gives a very necessary admonition to beat

Was Augustine's Opposition to Suicide Rooted in Neo-Platonic Philosophy or the Bible?

William Clebsch argued that Neoplatonism strongly influenced Augustine, in which worldview self-hatred is not compatible with the dignity of participating in the world-soul.[22] But did it influence him more than biblical theology? As there is no specific prohibition against suicide in either Old or New Testament, did Augustine somehow read the prohibition into rather than out of Exod 20:13, which had a clearer reference to murderous homicide? Possibly he misstated the literal reading of the text, given the original context, but Augustine was always interested in the spiritual interpretation of a biblical passage. He focused on this primarily because the spiritual reading helps us apply God's truth to our own life and context. Augustine might have answered criticism of his biblical interpretation by saying that he had found the spiritual meaning of the passage and correctly applied it to the question of suicide.[23]

Did Augustine Teach That Suicide Was Unforgiveable?

Eventually suicide came to be seen as a pernicious act of murder, called "self-murder." It became one of the three sins that were considered to be unredeemable. The other two were adultery (or any gross sexual misconduct never repented of), and apostasy in the form of repudiating that one was a follower of Christ.[24] Some chose apostasy to avoid torture during a time of Roman persecution, which generally involved a public cursing of Christ and an offering to the emperor. Those who later wanted to rejoin the community were not quickly welcomed back into fellowship. Too many Christians thought such disloyalty was (almost) unforgivable, especially if they had handed over Scripture to be burned or pointed the authorities to a pastor. To emphasize the horror of this sin a long penitence was required before they could return as fully participating communicants.

---

down the sharp dealings of pastors who shew no pity in restoring those that are fallen. Augustine saith, 'there is no sin which any man hath done, but another man may do the same.'"

22. Clebsch, "Editor's Introduction," ix.

23. Froehlich, "Take Up and Read," 5–16. On the importance of a spiritual reading as well as literal, see also Froehlich, *Sensing the Scriptures*.

24. Clebsch, "Editor's Introduction," x.

The early church found it humanly impossible to apply Jesus's admonition to forgive seventy times seven. In addressing this fact of church history, which appears either as a failure to live by grace or a communal horror of what a later generation called "cheap grace," we can ask whether the threats and horrific persecutions of the second and third centuries so traumatized many of the church leaders that they perceived no other way to hold the faithful together. It is hard to understand all the spiritual, psychological, and social dynamics of the era when so many congregations suffered destruction, with their leaders torn by predators in the arena and their manuscripts of the New Testament tossed into bonfires. How does one forgive a traitor? We can further ask whether the New Testament doctrine of grace was properly understood in the patristic era.[25] None of this was particularly Augustine's fault, who taught that we are sinners saved by grace through faith in Christ. However, given his stature, his negative attitude toward suicide encouraged an enduring disapproval in the history of Christian thought.[26] Yet he never said suicide was always unforgiveable.

Thomas Aquinas (1225–1274)

After Augustine, Thomas Aquinas was the most influential theologian in the West in the centuries prior to the Protestant Reformation, and his

---

25. This point is raised in Torrance, *Doctrine of Grace*. Torrance's book was discounted by some scholars because he traced the uses of "charis" (grace) to make his point, but did not study the uses of "agape" (love). Even if this criticism has some bearing on the discussion, the evidence Torrance amassed cannot be totally dismissed. He cited many indications that there was an insufficient grasp of the concept of grace in the early centuries. This problem was sadly prevalent in both east and west. German and French scholars also see evidence the early church neglected Paul prior to Augustine, which did not enhance the patristic concept of grace or help counteract legalism: see Stendahl, *Paul Among Jews*, 85n12. J. C. Beker says Paul's influence on the patristic period was minimal and that the apologists avoided his writings. See Beker, *Paul the Apostle*, 30. On the other hand, there was a vast reaction against Novatian's harsh rejection of compassion towards repentant sinners, so that councils at Carthage, Rome, and Antioch condemned Novatian's anti-grace stance.

26.. Amundsen "Did Early Christians," 285–95, reviews Droge and Tabor's *Noble Death* and says, "'It is a profound irony of Western history,' they maintain, that Christian theologians, beginning with Augustine, 'condemn the act of voluntary death as a sin for which Christ's similar act could not atone.'" Droge and Tabor credit Augustine with giving an added impetus to the negative assessment of suicide, which eventually led to the widespread popular understanding it was beyond the reach of God's grace. However, it must be reiterated, Augustine did not teach that all suicide was beyond the reach of forgiveness.

immense influence within the Roman Catholic Church continues to the present day. His genius status is unquestioned. He was a masterful theologian, a gifted expositor of Scripture, and a brilliant philosopher.

Aquinas accepted Augustine's classification of suicide as a sin of murder and raised self-preservation to the status of a universal natural law. In his discussion of vices in the *Summa Theologica*, "Question 64" deals with aspects of murder. Article 5 deals specifically with suicide.[27] First, he agrees with Augustine that Exod 20 forbids all intentional homicide, including self-destruction, for if you kill yourself you kill a human being. There are three reasons why it is unlawful and wrong to kill your own self. The first is the observation that every living thing in nature keeps itself alive and resists corruption (sickness, weakness, and danger) in so far as it can. "Wherefore suicide is contrary to the inclination of nature, and to charity whereby every man should love himself. Hence suicide is always a mortal sin, as being contrary to the natural law and to charity."

The second reason for rejecting suicide is because every part belongs to a greater whole. "Now every man is part of the community, and so, as such, he belongs to the community."[28] Aquinas says that suicide injures the community and should be avoided for this basic reason. In this, he agrees with Plato and Aristotle.

The third reason is that life is God's gift to us. "Hence whoever takes his own life, sins against God. . . . It belongs to God alone to pronounce the sentence of death and life, according to Deut 32:39."[29]

Aquinas's teaching method involved taking a position and then presenting objections.[30] Consider these objections: (1) It is clear that murder does an injustice to another person, but suicide does no comparable injury to another, so why is it wrong? Aquinas answered that murder is not only a sin because it is contrary to justice but also because it is contrary to charity (love and respect). Suicide is wrong "because it is opposed to charity which a man should have towards himself: in this respect suicide is a sin in relation to oneself."

(2) The second objection was that if a public magistrate has authority to put an evildoer to death, and is himself an evildoer, he should be allowed to execute himself. Against this logic Aquinas answered, "But no

---

27. Aquinas, *Summa Theologica*, 1462–64..
28. Aquinas, *Summa*, 1463.
29. Aquinas, *Summa*, 1463.
30. Aquinas, *Summa*, 1463.

man is judge of himself." It is not lawful for a man in authority to put himself to death, although he may commit himself to the judgment of others.

(3) A man should be able to kill himself because it is lawful to suffer a lesser danger in order to avoid a greater danger. "Thus it is lawful for a man to cut off a decayed limb even from himself, that he may save the whole body. Now sometimes a man, by killing himself, avoids a greater evil, for example an unhappy life, or the shame of sin. Therefore a man may kill himself."[31] Should we kill ourselves to avoid a greater evil?

Concerning this third objection, Aquinas said that God has given man a limited domain in which to exercise his free will, and there are many decisions we can legitimately make within that domain, but the decision to end our own life is not included. Rather, "The passage from this life to another and happier one is subject not to man's free will but to the power of God." Those who seek suicide to escape some evil do not realize that the most fearsome evil we can face in this life is death, so it cannot be a case of committing a lesser evil to escape a greater one. Some people contemplate taking their lives because of sorrow or shame for committing a sin, but Aquinas advises against the attempt, because "by so doing, one does oneself a very great injury, by depriving oneself of the time needful for repentance, and because it is not lawful to slay an evildoer except by the sentence of the public authority."[32]

He then picked up on Augustine's example of women concerned to keep their own purity when threatened with rape. Aquinas saw suicide as a greater sin than anything people would seek to avoid. He said a woman "commits no sin in being violated by force, provided she does not consent, since without consent of the mind there is no stain on the body, as the Blessed Lucy declared."[33] Furthermore, we should never kill ourselves to avoid committing a sin in the future, for it is uncertain what will happen in the future. "God is able to deliver man from sin under any temptation whatever."[34] In other words, wait and see if God won't provide a way of escape from sin and abuse, or provide fortitude to endure suffering. Thus no person should commit suicide in order to "avoid penal sins" or "bear penal evils," for these are lesser evils than suicide.

31. Aquinas, *Summa*, 1463.

32. Aquinas, *Summa*, 1463.

33. Aquinas, *Summa*, 1463. The reference is to Saint Lucy of Syracuse. According to tradition she gave her property to the poor during the Diocletian persecution, was denounced as a Christian by her fiancé, and died a martyr in 303.

34. Aquinas, *Summa Theologica*, 1464.

This brief but clearly stated discussion by Thomas Aquinas had a great impact on subsequent generations. The acceptance of Aquinas's position meant that the person who committed suicide violated both revealed and natural law in the eyes of the church, which led to both societal and religious condemnations of suicide. Philosophical and theological condemnations of suicide combined, which seemingly made it out to be particularly reprehensible by comparison with other crimes. Harsh laws of retaliation against the person who unsuccessfully attempted suicide were enforced, as were economic sanctions against the family of an actual suicide victim. People who died by suicide were not permitted proper rites or burial in churchyards, and sometimes corpses were mistreated and left exposed as a public warning. Some of this involved pagan customs more ancient than Christianity, depending on the location. Not all negative societal developments can be placed at Aquinas's door.

Although he never advocated such harsh measures, his stature as a theologian meant that his name would be used and misused whenever the awful nature of suicide was discussed. This entire consensus of condemnation was not challenged intellectually very much before John Donne did so in the seventeenth century (see chapter 9 below). Many priests and bishops lost sight of the fact that Aquinas never said that suicide was an unforgivable sin. It was a sin to be avoided, he argued, but there is an absence of any statement that God must condemn forever the person who commits suicide. Such a posture would have been presumptuous. Those responsible today for the official position of the Roman Catholic Church on suicide (see chapter 20 below) show they respect the boundary Thomas Aquinas refused to cross.

7

Martin Luther (1483–1546)

As THE LEADING REFORMER and translator of the Bible in Germany, Martin Luther gave guidance to pastors and congregations concerning the care of souls. There is every reason to think he had his own personal struggles with depression and weariness, which may have enhanced his sensitivity about dark thoughts. The earlier reformer Jan Hus had died a violent death after being promised safe conduct. Rome placed Luther under the ban, which meant he could be murdered by anyone without fear of prosecution (outside the jurisdiction of his prince), and so Luther always expected to die a violent death. Many worries weighed on his mind regarding his role as a reformer, including the welfare of his family, church, and the German people, all of which might face harsh consequences because they stood with him. Some days, the weight of these worries must have seemed crushing. It would have been odd if he had not struggled with fearful and negative thoughts.

The record indicates that Luther did struggle with inner tensions as well as real practical problems in the public arena. He had bouts of despondency, but not a total loss of hope. Luther soldiered on without being free of all doubts and inner struggles. Erik Midelfort says, "Luther held that a certain despair was necessary to the spiritual life. Without an experience of one's own total worthlessness, one might well develop the stony heart that could question God's justice."[1] Even so, the experience

---

1. Midelfort, "Religious Melancholy and Suicide," 42.

can be like a descent into hell, and can be quite incapacitating. There were some days when Luther could not get out of bed.

Community, Music, and Laughter Help Ward Off Despondency

From his own personal experience, Luther warned that the devil tempts more easily in solitude. He noted that the devil tempted Christ in solitude, and David yielded to an adulterous impulse when he was alone and idle. Luther said, "I myself have found out that I never fall into sin more frequently than when I am alone." The devil may tempt us to despair as soon as entice us to commit some particular sin. Whether from temptation or from something rising up inside our own condition, Luther thought that solitude could produce self-destructive moods. "Solitude begets sadness. Very pessimistic and sad thoughts come into our mind. We consider more carefully everything that is bad, and if anything has gone wrong in our affairs, we brood over it more intensively; we exaggerate it as though no one were unhappier than we are, and we imagine that all our affairs will have a very bad ending."[2]

Because negative thoughts can fester in solitude, Luther counseled depressed people to seek society, hear the gospel, and sing songs at public worship. "Depressed hearts should flee solitude and engage in any sort of conversation with friends, for conversations contribute to diverting the heart from heavy thoughts."[3] When the wife of a suicidal man wrote for counsel, Luther responded that they were under spiritual attack, for the devil hated them both because they loved Christ. He advised, "Be very careful not to leave your husband alone for a single moment, and leave nothing lying about with which he can harm himself. Solitude is poison to him. For this reason the devil drives him to it."[4] He advised reading news, telling stories, or anything likely to "excite him to laughter and jesting."

2. Plass, *What Luther Says*, 1326.
3. Plass, *Luther*, 1326.
4. Luther, *Letters*, 91; cf. 59: Luther wrote directly to another woman whose husband survived an attempted suicide, returned to his right mind, confessed faith in Christ, but subsequently died, "That your husband inflicted injury upon himself may be explained by the devil's power over our members. He may have directed your husband's hand, even against his will. For if your husband had done what he did of his own free will, he would surely not have come to himself and turned to Christ with such a confession of faith. How often the devil breaks arms, legs, backs, and all members! He can be master of the body and its members against our will."

Once the mood was lightened, she was then to "quickly recite comforting verse from the Scriptures."[5] Luther reiterated that the man should not be left alone and should not be surrounded by too much silence, even if he gets angry about a little noise. "It does not matter if he becomes angry about this. Act as if it were disagreeable to you and scold about it, but let it be done all the more."[6]

While Luther never countenanced suicide as an appropriate escape for depressed people, one cannot read Luther for long without sensing that he could fully empathize with their struggle, not necessarily because he himself had suicidal thoughts but because he knew the frightful power of dark moods. Thomas Oden notes that "Luther urged not judging too harshly those who take their own life in order to avoid a perceived greater evil." A young woman committed suicide to avoid being misused sexually by a nobleman, and he was asked whether she was responsible for her death. "Doctor Luther said: No: she felt that this step formed her only chance of safety, it being not her life she sought to save, but her chastity."[7]

Luther did not want the woman to commit suicide to save her virginity and self-respect, but he did not fault her for taking such a drastic step to avoid giving herself to someone else's evil. Philosophers might have been able to explain how suicide was a greater evil, but fear of violence does not focus the mind on learned distinctions. In her ordinary perception this woman thought that suicide was a lesser evil, and Luther refused to condemn her for it.

On the other hand, Luther can refer negatively to an act of suicide. He said there were presumptuous sins which do not honor God, as when Christians tempt God to help them rather than place their trust in God. An example of this is when a person is sick but refuses medicine, asserting that God will heal and protect without medicine if God wishes it. To this Luther said, "Whoever does not use medicine when he has it and can make use of it without injury to his neighbor neglects his body and runs the risk of being a suicide in God's sight. One might in similar fashion neglect food and drink and clothing and shelter, be foolhardy in one's faith, and say, 'If God wishes to protect me from hunger and cold, he will do so without food and clothing.'"[8] Luther sometimes referred to suicide

---

5. Luther, *Letters*, 91.
6. Luther, *Letters*, 91.
7. Quoted in Oden, *Classical Pastoral Care*, 21–22.
8. Luther, *Letters*, 241.

as sin, and in the case of Jonah said it was a "great sin" to wish to die.[9] However, because he always called the failure to trust God a great sin we cannot limit this warning only to examples of suicide.

Suicidal Ideation Is an Attack Against One's Life

Veit Dietrich lived in Luther's home and ate at his table when he was a university student, serving as Luther's private secretary to help with correspondence. They continued a long association afterwards. Dietrich wrote down many of Luther's comments on various topics. On April 7, 1532, he recorded what Luther said on suicide. Of principal importance is that suicides are not necessarily damned in Luther's estimation.

> I don't share the opinion that suicides are certainly to be damned. My reason is that they do not wish to kill themselves but are overcome by the power of the devil. They are like a man who is murdered in the woods by a robber. However, this ought not to be taught to the common people, lest Satan be given an opportunity to cause slaughter, and I recommend that the popular custom be strictly adhered to according to which it [the suicide's corpse] is not carried over the threshold, etc. . . . Magistrates should treat them quite strictly, although it is not plain that their souls are damned. However, they are examples by which our Lord God wishes to show that the devil is powerful and also that we should be diligent in prayer. But for these examples, we would not fear God. Hence he must teach us in this way.[10]

The old custom of treating a suicide's corpse differently from other corpses has no theological significance, but Luther thought it should be maintained as a possible check against future suicides. Midelfort says that Luther approved of burning the bodies of suicides in order to deter others from contemplating suicide.[11] Without knowing the extent to which cremations were practiced in such cases, it seems in this regard that Luther made a concession to established custom. However much this response was misguided, it likely came from a true pastoral desire to prevent the spread of suicide. Especially feared was a softening of societal attitudes

---

9. See above Luther's discussion on Jonah in chapter 4.

10. Luther, *Table Talk*, 29. Luther's editor Theodore G. Tappert explains, "According to popular belief the corpse of a suicide was not to be carried out of the house "over the threshold."

11. Midelfort, "Religious Melancholy and Suicide," 41–56, especially 42–43.

against it, something that might remove a preventative support for other troubled people. In a later generation John Wesley shared the same concern. While this is historical, it has little theological bearing on the questions we grapple with today.

What is of greater importance is that Luther did not think suicide was an unforgiveable sin. Luther said this clearly with reference to people oppressed within their own minds. As in his day, different people have all types of reactions to suffering, adversity, and strain. Some are strong to begin with and stay strong. They can endure much pain and disappointment, but the longer trouble lasts, their inner resources of strength and hope are diminished, and they become weak. A sense of hopelessness develops, dark moods increase. Ordinary people experience the full spectrum of emotional turbulence, with some moving into danger.

Luther's primary concern was for those who are weak and worn down in their inner life, already under assault from within. An old bridge has pylons becoming weak to the danger point, one day collapsing under the weight of traffic. This is but a picture of inner human breakdown, preceded by a loss of strength and support. The bridge does not collapse under the first impact of duress, but under the final one which it cannot resist. How strong is a person? How weak can he or she become? How can strength be restored?

In Luther's understanding, some people are overwhelmed by interior struggles the way others are overwhelmed by robbers. Their suicides are acts of desperation and weakness rather than indications of moral failure or rejection of Christ. Their examples of weakness serve as warnings to all Christians, who must pray daily for God's support and not presume they can face personal hardships without divine assistance. Yet Luther feared publicizing God's grace for this particular sin, because he feared it would send a confused message to people already troubled with depression or seeking to escape from difficult circumstances. He did not want to say there was no forgiveness, but he also did not want to confuse the weak and misdirect them by talking too freely about forgiveness, out of fear that suicide might be made attractive to troubled people.

Luther saw suicidal ideation as a form of attack against a person. Even though the thoughts seemingly arise from within one's own mind and emotions, belonging to the afflicted person in one sense, these are assaults which threaten one's welfare and have to be fought against in order to survive. The philosopher Ludwig Wittgenstein presents an affinity with Luther's insight. Throughout his life he had been "unsettled by feelings of self-hatred, psychological loneliness, and urges to kill himself," says one biographer, though he never attempted suicide.[12] In a letter dated 1920, Wittgenstein wrote, "Surely one cannot will one's own destruction and anybody who has visualized what is in practice involved knows that suicide is always a rushing of one's own defenses."[13] Separated by a few centuries, both Luther and Wittgenstein spoke of the inner life plagued by suicidal thoughts as a life under attack. Luther almost anticipated the modern psychological concept of a death wish that works against one's own best interest.[14]

A Role for Diabolical Temptation and Interference

Heiko Oberman informs us that Luther did believe in a higher spiritual being who is malevolent towards the human race and in extreme rebellion against God. But that does not mean he accepted all ideas held in his day about the spiritual realm or occult. Oberman says, "Christ and the devil are equally real to him: one was the perpetual intercessor for Christianity, the other a menace to mankind till the end. To argue that Luther never overcame the medieval belief in the devil says far too little; he even intensified it and lent to it additional urgency: Christ and Satan wage a cosmic war for mastery over the Church and the world. No one can evade involvement in this struggle."[15] While Luther felt his main defense against evil was faith in Christ, he could believe this conflict was real and still reject many superstitions. He advised professions of faith, such as, "I am baptized, I belong to Christ, he is my redeemer." He also advised scorn for the devil (and here his language often became coarse). Luther's purpose was to do battle with anything that slanders Christ. Furthermore, he did not encourage the torture and burning of people accused of witchcraft.[16]

Luther saw a role for devilish agents goading people into a state of despondency. Despondency can become a tool used to drive people to despair. In *The Large Catechism*, Luther discussed the last petition of the Lord's Prayer.[17] Here he enlarged on all that the prayer "deliver us from

---

12. Waugh, *House of Wittgenstein*, 49.
13. Waugh, *Wittgenstein*, 35.
14. Menninger, *Man Against Himself*.
15. Oberman, *Luther*, 104.
16. Oberman, *Luther*, 107.
17. Luther was not innovative in seeing Satan as a personal agent who rages against God, which he understood to be a spiritual being that cannot be literally described

evil" means, saying, "this petition includes all the evil that may befall us under the devil's kingdom: poverty, shame, death, and, in short, all the tragic misery and heartache of which there is so incalculably much on earth." Clearly not all of these miseries are due to demonic interference, but any fear of these troubles can be inflated by the demonic to instill a state of hopeless despondency. "Since the devil is not only a liar but also a murderer, he incessantly seeks our life and vents his anger by causing accidents and injury to our bodies. He breaks many a man's neck and drives others to insanity; some he drowns, and many he hounds to suicide or other dreadful catastrophes."[18] Because of these dangers, we must pray every day for God's protection and deliverance. The primary danger in the phrase "he hounds to suicide" is not demonic possession, with the human will nearly obliterated, but demonic interference with a human life through various forms of oppression, deprivation, and subtle mental attack.

The Problem of Confused Human Thoughts

Negative thoughts can arise without any diabolical interference to goad or inflate them. We have our own proclivity to think dark thoughts and edge out good ones. Luther's concept of sin as condition, that which taints every area of human life, led him to see that not all the thoughts in one's head are positive or even neutral. We are capable of thinking thoughts that are not life-enhancing or "friendly to our own interests." These might be negative judgments against ourselves or suspicions directed at other people. Therefore not every thought is worthy of acceptance and some

---

or mentally pictured, even as he habitually used simple and picturesque language in his references for the sake of communication. We often translate Matt 6:13 as "deliver us from evil," but the verse may be properly translated "deliver us from the evil one." The Greek genitive can be translated either of two ways. For reasons why the translation "evil one" (masculine) is to be preferred over "evil" (neuter), see Cullmann, *Prayer*, 66-67. Metzger said this verse "can better be translated 'rescue us from the clutches of the evil one.'" Because various hermeneutical errors (concerning passages in Genesis, Job, Isaiah, and Ezekiel) developed down the centuries, feeding into false statements and exaggerations, corrections are needed today without discarding the reality of a predominating evil. See Allison, *Encountering Mystery*, 42-46; Bloesch, *Holy Spirit*, 209-21; Ramm, *Offense to Reason*, 100-105; and Welker, *God the Spirit*, 195-211, which includes a warning by Ernst Käsemann not to reductively psychologize all encounters with evil in biblical passages.

18. Luther, *Large Catechism*, 79.

have to be fought against and repeatedly rejected. This is part of "drowning the old man," to use Luther's phrase.

In Luther's understanding "no one is righteous" (Rom 3:10) does not mean that all our thoughts are wicked, but that every thought may be tainted by sin, even if the corruption is very slight. There are still many vestiges of good in human beings in our fallen condition (now unable to reach the original ideal), because God originally created us good. That goodness has not all disappeared, and much of life depends on it.

Yet our good qualities may be slightly corrupted, as iron is corrupted by just a little bit of rust, as water is tainted by a tinge of bacteria. One illustration comes from a small town in rural Montana. The town had two wells that provided a water supply. The water tasted wonderful and did not have chlorine in it. But tests showed that it had too many parts per billion of an herbicidal chemical that had been dumped along the railroad many years earlier. The poison seeped into the well water over time. The water tasted great, but was tainted with a trace of poison. Like that water, human thought and imagination does not have to be totally bad to be mixed with impurities. Guided by biblical strictures on the unreliability of the human heart, Luther knew that our innermost thoughts and feelings can be so affected by sin that they cannot be completely trusted. The integrity of life can be enhanced or undermined from within.

James Loder was a theologian, philosopher, and counselor who wrote an interdisciplinary study of human development.[19] One of his insights was that no human being can be equated with his or her thoughts and desires as a matter of self-identity, for attitudes, thoughts and desires are something we *have*, not what we *are*.[20] Because thoughts and desires are something we have, not what we are, they can be examined and weighed in reflection. However, this is not to say that the examination is easy or does not involve assistance.[21] When specific desires are recognized as

---

19. Loder, *Logic*.

20. Our deepest core identity is that we are human beings who are created and redeemed by God in Christ, not that which we think, feel, or desire, however much these aspects of individual experience fill our daily lives. That we are not to be defined or slavishly controlled by all our desires also has therapeutic interest in psychotherapies not tied to any religion. This is but briefly touched on in Koonz, "Matters of the Heart," 209–12.

21. As traditional psychoanalysis is extremely difficult work for both counselee and counselor, so are other forms of therapeutic counseling. The counselor works with the counselee's self-disclosures in the mutual search for understanding, and in spiritual care this may involve vulnerability on both sides of the conversation. Loder did not think a logico-causal chain had to be established from early onset to the contemporary

influential, we can choose for them or against them, hold them tightly or try to let them go. Sometimes we must even fight against wayward desires and reject their right to define, guide or control us. Many desires are good and do not require a hostile response, but not all desires are worthy of affirmation. Our inner life is so important that we must make it a matter of daily prayer. This is not to become overly introspective and narcissistic, but to invite the Spirit of God into all aspects of life. What happens in our inner life affects our human spirit and relationality with others.

Furthermore, not all negative thoughts tell the suicidal person the truth. Not all desires lead to good outcomes. To dwell on some thoughts is to entertain a distorting confusion or destructive temptation, to let a provocateur whisper untruths in your ear. Sometimes a deadly contest can occur in the inner life, and matches what Luther (and later Wittgenstein) said about a person's life being attacked from within. While the New Testament writers speak of temptation from outside, as from a devilish tempter, they also speak of temptation from within, from an individual's own human nature (called "the flesh") in response to personal or worldly desires. Regardless of how the thought originated, the temptation has to be recognized for what it is in order to be resisted. Where and when we sense we are under attack internally, we need to seek God's help and assistance. We do so in private prayer or in fellowship with other people. Luther welcomed the prayers of others on his behalf as a matter of necessity.

Why We Should Be Slow to Blame the Victim When There Is Death by Suicide

This moves us into the question of moral responsibility. Although Luther did not use our modern psychological terminology, it is fair to say that he had an insight of psychological and spiritual depth. Whatever is going on internally, the failure to win against dark thoughts in an inner struggle may be the moral equivalent of a person succumbing to robbers on a

---

moment in order to understand the nature of a problem and find its personal resolution. The pastoral counselor may pray with the person that God's Spirit will guide one into a deeper self-understanding, and also provide the renewing balm for the soul that is needed. Sometimes the Holy Spirit allows the conflict to be intensified before the answer is found that brings deep healing and inner harmony. Congruence comes when insights fit the terms of a conflict which hinders coherent "interaction between the self and the world" and brings resolution "with maximum sufficiency and without excess." Loder, *Transforming Moment*, 222.

forest trail. (Three on one is not a fair fight, as martial arts expert Bruce Lee said.) Facts of human weakness are real factors in both contexts, and do not necessarily put the one in danger of a harsher judgment from God than the other. While morality is involved in human choices, and I do not wish to argue otherwise, we are left with an important question. Is emotional or mental weakness more of a moral problem than physical weakness? Luther seems to say "No" by using the analogy from physical weakness. This is not to argue that there is no personal responsibility when someone chooses to leave safety behind, but that the circumference of that responsibility may be drawn smaller than previously thought.

If we do not blame a man for being weaker than those who attack him on the road, why do we blame our neighbor for being weaker than the thoughts that attack internally? Only God knows the origin and content of those assaults. Only God can judge righteously with complete understanding of what led up to a tragic end, putting our weakness in its proper perspective. God knows when the attack in a person's mood or thought life comes as a temptation from the outside, or from a mental breakdown, or as a flaring expression of one's own self-centered nature. Hence only God can judge the person who succumbs. This is why we cannot speak arrogantly about the suicidal person's final sin as though it were worse than other types of sin.

Pastorally, Luther never advocated giving in to depression. Rather he recommended various remedies to people who struggled with despondency. He advised praying at public worship and praying each day at home, singing songs in church and in solitude, or gathering together with other people as often as possible to assuage loneliness. Thus, he wrote hymns for the churches to sing, primarily to teach theology, but also to bring encouragement and comfort to those who are helped by music. Concerning the question of sin and salvation, Luther did not see suicide as an unforgivable sin. Yet he hesitated to broadcast this out of fear that his comforting and hopeful words would be twisted into words of permission by those tempted to suicide.

8

John Calvin (1509–1564)

JOHN CALVIN WAS THE major Swiss Reformer, a masterful expositor of the Bible whose commentaries still offer valuable insights. He lived in greater personal safety than Luther, and this made possible the full use of his brilliant mind in writing systematic theology.

The topic of suicide was not dealt with in Calvin's *Institutes*. We find his comments only in a couple of sermons, one dealing with Saul and the other with Ahithophel. He saw their despair and deaths as just rewards, because Saul hunted innocent David and Ahithophel conspired against him, but this did not mean they were following God's will when committing suicide.[1] Both Catholic and Protestant people had a horror of suicide, associating it with demonic influence or possession. This was one reason why Calvin did not need to address it very often. When he did preach on the sixth commandment (Exod 20:13) he spoke against violence, but did not mention suicide.

Suicide as a Form of Disobedience

The chief argument Calvin made was that in committing suicide a person is being disobedient to God. The essence of this disobedience is that a person will not submit to the will of God. God has the right to number our days. God has given life to us for a purpose. God alone has the right to take life away. It is not up to us to decide when we are done living.

---

1. Watt, "Calvin on Suicide," 463–47.

"Thus God, having sent us in this world, wishes us to stay in it, and he has placed us in a post which we must not leave until God orders us to do so."[2]

He did not see suffering as something to be escaped if it was God's will for a Christian to endure it. Christians will often live through difficult times and suffer personal setbacks. As Jeffrey Watts says, "Calvin saw no bounds to the degree of patience required of Christians. Simply put, they were to endure all sorts of torture, misfortune, and disgrace."[3] After death they will receive God's grace and mercy extensively and eternally.

In these summaries and bare extracts from sermons, much is left out that Calvin put into them. There is a danger that he is made to sound unsympathetic to human trials and problems, which was not likely the case. There is evidence he had a warm heart.[4] We need to see the direction his mind was going and the hope he was anticipating beyond temporary human suffering. Indeed there are experiences that are hard to endure, suffering that is appalling, and sadness that is overwhelming. Where is God's purpose? In our own trouble we cannot see how we may be used to alleviate someone else's suffering, or demonstrate faith, hope, and love which may encourage someone else to enter into fellowship with God. Trusting in God in hard circumstances means that we believe God sees the whole picture even when we cannot, and that God's promises in Christ are true.

The sin of suicide is that we refuse to trust in God to walk with us for the duration of life. Calvin says, "It is against nature that a man kills himself regardless of the method. We have this natural sense to flee from death; we have a certain horror of death, which God has instilled in us. . . . God engraved in the hearts of all persons this apprehension so that death terrifies and shocks them."[5] This fear and repugnance of death is fitting. Even the animals try to stay alive. Therefore suicide is contrary to nature. Jeffrey Watt says, "In rejecting suicide as contrary to nature, Calvin was reiterating Aquinas's argument that suicide violated natural law in that all things love themselves in the state of nature."[6]

Watt's study also demonstrates that there was a second component of Calvin's rejection of suicide, namely "his belief that self-murder

---

2. Watt, *Choosing Death*, 68.
3. Watt, *Choosing*, 71.
4. Stauffer, *Humanness of John Calvin*.
5. Watt, *Choosing*, 72.
6. Watt, *Choosing*, 72.

is caused by diabolical possession."[7] And in this Calvin was not saying something new but rather something representative of Christian theology in the late Middle Ages. However, "Neither Augustine nor Aquinas said anything about the devil causing suicides."[8] If Calvin spoke of people who committed suicide as possessed by a devil, the terminology he used was inherited and could convey more than one meaning.[9] In numerous places, he spoke of sin leading to a deplorable or diabolical condition. When he spoke of suicide leading to a diabolical rage this phrasing did not necessarily mean that he thought a person was demon possessed, though he might have done so. The phrase diabolical rage usually was an indication of a demonic influence that led to a negative end. This is seen in the example of King Nebuchadnezzar's fury (Dan 3:19): "In considering this fury, we ought to take into account the power of Satan in seizing and occupying the minds of men. For there is no moderation in them, even if they shew some great and remarkable hope of virtues,—for, as we have seen, Nebuchadnezzar was endued with many virtues; but as Satan harassed him, we discern nothing but cruelty and barbarity."[10]

Whenever Luther saw suicidal deaths as victims of a devilish temptation to take their own lives, he did not hold the victims totally accountable. Which one of us can choose our own temptations? Luther did not necessarily think the suicide was damned, though no sinner is safe apart from God's grace. Yet it appears that Calvin thought the suicidal person shared in the blame.[11] This is not easy to sort out or explain, so what is offered here is tentative.

Calvin thought the demonic realm, if given opportunity, could somehow suppress the normal human instinct for self-preservation, which is a gift of God, and thus move a person towards a state of fury or stir up trouble to induce a state of desperate rage. In this condition, men or women jump to their death, hang, stab, or poison themselves. Somewhere along the way, the instinct for life and the knowledge that it is God's gift has been obliterated.

7. Watt, *Choosing*, 73.
8. Watt, "Calvin," 469.
9. This was a common understanding in Medieval Europe because even learned people were not always careful to distinguish between behaviors that were strange due to natural or supernatural causes, or distinguish between types of mental illness or health limitations (whereas the ancient Chinese did make such distinctions).
10.. Calvin, *Commentaries*, 226–27.
11. Watt, *Choosing*, 73n19.

In this process of degradation, a man or woman may share some of the blame, having started down a path they were warned not to follow (by Scripture, family, conscience). As their personal choices degraded their lives, they reached a point where they did not know what they were thinking or doing. Given this analysis, Calvin is not necessarily saying that all suicidal people were demon possessed. Rather, just as spiritual and moral problems do not develop suddenly overnight neither do suicidal thoughts. Many life experiences and choices are woven into the fabric. The victim may have made earlier choices which contributed to this tragedy. (Yet we can ask, what if a previous victimhood of suicide victims resulted in inner weakness?)

Insofar as he thought someone's personal journey did lead to a rage that caused suicide, it may be that he despaired for that person's salvation. Yet this is speculation. Calvin never (to my knowledge) said that damnation was certain. It is possible that he might have interpreted the final rage as a sign of God's punishment or removal of grace, certainly as the absence of the fruit of the Spirit. If so, his concern would not be about the final moment alone but on previous and additional factors, especially poor choices.

The Question of Repentance

Calvin's position was that human repentance is not the cause of salvation, though it is the proper response to God's forgiveness in Jesus Christ. "Both repentance and forgiveness of sins—that is, newness of life and free reconciliation—are conferred on us by Christ, and both are attained by us through faith."[12] Salvation comes first and contains every reason for repentance and honoring God. Repentance is not the condition for God's forgiveness, because nothing we do conditions God into being gracious. God first brings the kingdom of Heaven near so that we may enter into it.[13]

No one can seriously attempt repentance without being persuaded of God's forgiveness. It is necessary for a person to recognize grace in order to know that he or she belongs to God. No true reverence of God becomes possible without knowing that God is generous and ready to

---

12. Calvin, *Institutes*, 3.3.1, 592. Cf. *Institutes*, 3.4.21–23, 751–54.
13. The next couple of paragraphs are a summary of *Institutes*, 3.3.1–21, 592–618.

heal our wounds. Trust, obedience, and repentance are life-long ways we live out that reverence.

Calvin distinguished between "repentance of the law" and "repentance of the gospel." In the first the sinner remains trapped in a disturbed state, like Cain or Judas fearing God's wrath, and in the second he or she lays hold of Christ as medicine for all wounds, as real comfort for all dreads. "Repentance of the gospel" never ceases to hope in God's forgiveness and grace.

Faith and repentance belong together just as faith and hope belong together, but they are not to be confused. It is faith that makes repentance possible. Repentance is the true turning of our life to God, which includes but is not limited to turning away from that which offends God. However, any personal turning to God requires a "new heart" (Ezek 18:31; Jer 4:1–4), and this essential gift must be given by God. The Holy Spirit regenerates and gives new life, adopts us as God's children and begins to sanctify us, but this does not free us from personal warfare in this life. There is a conflict within our desires as something in us contends against God's control. The dominating sway of sin is abolished and victories provided, but sinful proclivity does not cease to dwell in us.

For Calvin this means there is no spiritual and moral perfection in this life for any Christian prior to death. In our inner conflicts and miseries, we are humbled by the consciousness of our own weakness, and yet in Christ we are freed from guilt. We are entangled in vices and wayward ambitions and must daily fight against them. As we move forward, we are both mindful of deserving judgment and of God's amazing mercy, a recognition that does not lead to despair. "Repentance of the law" is used by Satan to encourage one to flee from God and remain in sorrow. In "repentance of the gospel," one flees to God, remembering God's goodness and Christ's benefits. The Holy Spirit helps us turn towards God in a variety of ways, using different starting points with different people and situations. With the Holy Spirit's help, people who have lived counter to God's honor and justice can turn and give glory to God.

Can a volitional sin like suicide be forgiven when there is no time for repentance? Calvin did not deal with this question directly. Yet he did not think Jesus (nor later Paul) excluded forgiveness for volitional sins, save the sin of blasphemy against the Holy Spirit.[14] Faced with a local suicide attempt that did not lead to immediate death, he counseled the

---

14. Calvin, *Institutes*, 3.21–23, 616–19.

stricken person to prayerfully ask forgiveness and renew faith in Christ. While never encouraging suicide, he did not declare it (or the attempt) beyond the reach of Christ's atoning work.

For Calvin, God's election and Christ's atoning work are the objective foundation of our salvation. God's gift provides reconciliation in Christ (2 Cor 5:18–21). In the course of our lives, the Holy Spirit graciously works to connect us to God through Christ in faith. Repentance may affect our spiritual fellowship with God in daily life, but it does not establish the ground of our salvation. The mediation of Jesus Christ, who serves now as our great high priest in the Father's presence, embraces and overcomes the inadequacy of our human repentance.

Some Reformed theologians speak of his "vicarious humanity."[15] This phrase emphasizes Jesus's positive human relationality with God, his complete turning toward God as our human representative. This miracle was ultimately what God provided for us from our side of the divine-human relationality. Jesus's vicarious obedience was both active and passive until the moment he died. His active obedience was the fulfillment of the law, his fulfillment of the work of God's servant-son (Messiah), and all his positive human righteousness. His passive obedience involved his participation in our weakness and suffering unto death, in which he suffered God's judgment on sin. Jesus's active and passive obedience form one whole self-offering and cannot be separated or compartmentalized without skewing our understanding of the incarnation and atonement.

Calvin did emphasize Christ's obedience to God's law, yet he also understood that Christ's vicarious role should be seen in broader contexts than can be conveyed in legal terminology. Christ embodied the original design for communion between God and humanity. Although not a dominant motif in his theology, Calvin did see atoning significance in the entire human life of Jesus. "He has achieved this for us by the whole course of his obedience."[16]

---

15. See Torrance, "Vicarious Humanity of Christ," 127–47. Here there is a connection with themes found in the ancient Eastern theologians, particularly Athanasisus. Cf. Crisp, "On the Vicarious Humanity," 235–50. See also Colyer, *T. F. Torrance*, 97–123. Other theologians who address this theme include Ray Anderson and Christian Kettler.

16. "From the time when he took on the form of a servant, he began to pay the price of liberation in order to redeem us." Acknowledging that the Apostles' Creed jumps from the birth of Jesus to his death and resurrection, Calvin adds, "Yet the remainder of the obedience that he manifested in his life is not excluded." Calvin, *Institutes*, 2.16.5, 507–8.

No other human has embodied perfect faith and walked in complete harmony with God, hence no other human can live (or repent) in such a way that God's mercy and forgiveness is secured by it. This securing of hope was made possible by God's miracle of sustaining grace from Jesus's boyhood to manhood. Thus we say that the life of Jesus was God's gift to us from beginning to end. In salvation history, God came to us in grace from God's side, while simultaneously providing the right human response from our side in the life of Jesus.

Thus we do not look to ourselves for the hope of salvation. "Our life is hid with Christ in God" (Col 3:1–4). Our human repentance in the final hour of life, even if beautiful and holy, never finishes a perfect pattern. There may be a genuine calling out to God for mercy, but we call out as those who need rescue. The priestly life, death, and resurrection of Jesus was vicarious, expiates all sin and guilt, and reconciles us to God. Here is the ground of our salvation, not the adequacy of any other human repentance. We can only give thanks.

The Absence of Spiritual Fruit Demonstrating Righteousness

Calvin affirmed justification by faith in Christ, yet he also saw growth in sanctification as a sign of faith and repentance. The fruit of the Holy Spirit is love, joy, peace, gentleness, patience, kindness, harmony. Genuine spiritual fruit is wonderful and encourages everyone (Gal 5:22–23). We rejoice that the Holy Spirit does produce fruit in the individual lives of God's people and in congregations, according to the will of God. Yet what if this righteous fruitfulness (sanctification) is not evident at the time of suicide? The question is not Calvin's but is our own. It is raised because Calvinist preachers at suicide funerals in the 1700s and 1800s often spoke about the need for sanctification as evidence of faith, stating that its absence around a suicide did not give reason for hope but mourning. They very much thought they were in line with Calvin's thought about this, although Calvin did not address this specific issue directly.

My response is that we are not given the role of determining who demonstrates holy fruit and who does not. While it is not wrong to celebrate the public quality of the "fruit of the Spirit," especially when it openly radiates out of someone's life, we are still limited the moment we try to make comparisons. Ultimately only God can say who bears spiritual fruit and who does not. We should be careful of judging by outward appearances, as when the prophet Samuel made this mistake with the older sons of Jesse. So much inner truth is hidden from us too.

Regarding those who are less joyful or more difficult, we cannot always see the fullness of what God already has done in their lives. God may have sustained faith in more trying circumstances than we can imagine (Rom 8:26–27). While God may do a spiritual work of grace in one person, with openly positive results, God may also do a hidden work in another person's life. No two people present the same starting point in their response to life events or God's inner work of renewal. Therefore, their spiritual progress as individuals cannot be known by our observations or comparisons with others. One person may seem to make less progress than another, and yet have overcome far greater hurdles. As C. S. Lewis says,

> Some of us who seem quite nice people may, in fact, have made so little use of a good heredity and a good upbringing that we are really worse than those whom we regard as fiends. Can we be quite certain how we should have behaved if we had been saddled with the psychological outfit, and then with the bad upbringing, and then with the power, say, of Himmler?
>
> That is why Christians are told not to judge. We see only the results which a man's choices make out of his raw material. But God does not judge him on the raw material at all, but on what he has done with it.[17]

We cannot see what God sees, which is why we are told not to judge. Many spiritual battles are fought and overcome in ordinary human hearts, but not in every case the same. Some people face greater difficulties than others. If none can be saved but by the imputation of Christ's righteousness, we all belong to the needy set who require grace.

What About Demonic Temptation, Oppressive Interference, or Possession?

The idea that suicide involved a form of demonic temptation, oppression, or even possession (involving overpowering influences, dissociation of mind and will) had been around for centuries before Calvin's birth. When we read Luther or Calvin on demonic influence, we must not assume that

---

17. Lewis, *Mere Christianity*, 91.

we all work today with exactly the same understanding they did. Nor is it easy to jump back to the New Testament era and identify exactly what Jesus faced in some of his encounters with the demonic, but that does not mean that no linkages can be made.[18] (This is difficult territory and we all need to continue rethinking our assumptions, even as we attempt to link our thought to theirs and evaluate testimony from different cultural and historic contexts.)[19]

The problem with using "diabolical fury" as the primary description of suicide is that it gives the impression that a person who commits suicide is demon possessed (controlled by evil).[20] What if in particular circumstances Calvin actually thought this to be the case? If so, that is not grounds for us to identify the spiritual cause of those deaths in this way. The problem with seeing diabolical possession as the leading cause of suicide is that other contributing factors are too easily excluded: unendurable human mistreatment, ongoing physical pain, breakdown of health due to malnutrition or degenerative diseases, intense mental fears not due to the demonic realm, or ingesting poison (paint was not lead free). These conditions were around in Calvin's day and any discussion that leaves them out lacks comprehensiveness.

Calvin did not think all temptation was of demonic origin, for he saw much emphasis in the New Testament on both the flesh (the

---

18. See the discussion of 1 Cor 8 and 10 in Fee, *Jesus the Lord*, 126–128, especially 127n2.

19. Of relevance are recent calls for interdisciplinary, cross-cultural discussions: see Acolatse, *Powers, Principalities*; Vaughan, *Phenomenal Phenomena*. Such discussions were also the subject of the Warfield Lectures at Princeton Theological Seminary, delivered by Professor Philip G. Ziegler of University of Aberdeen on March 18–21, 2024. Careful historical studies of the occult may provide significant comparisons, but cannot be detailed here.

20. Modern neurological insights do not necessarily rule out all interferences or communications of trans-subjective reality (spiritual evil or holy angels) with human beings, yet many psychologists operate within a reductionistic framework and see the totality of reality through the lens of a worldview that excludes the supernatural. When speaking reductively about reality (as in "this is nothing but . . .") the problem is not with the psychologist as psychologist but with the psychologist as philosopher. There is the opposite problem with people who see a demon behind every bush, which is problematic for mental health and not representative of the worldview of the biblical writers. "In the Bible, demon possession was an unusual thing. Although people were driven crazy by demons, yet there are cases of lunacy in the Bible which are not attributed to demons. Furthermore, the sticks, stones, trees, etc., were not viewed as under the control of divers spirits. The context in the Bible is that demon possession is seen in the setting of a law-abiding universe, while an animistic society does not view the universe as law-abiding." Bales, "Relevance of Scriptural Interpretation" 123.

proclivity of our self-centered nature) and the world (the attraction of being noticed and seen as important) as sources of temptation as well. For example, the temptation of the flesh may appeal to diverse natural desires, whether for pleasure or for revenge. The temptation of the world may offer proud status. What is twisted in our inner desires does not require a demonic source to excite. Much suffering is caused by people abusing people. Some of the suicides in Calvin's area happened after exposure of criminal behavior.

But the demonic reality as a source of temptation is also affirmed in the New Testament. This subject needs to be rethought without some of the excesses of earlier times. Difficult work remains for us because we need safeguards against extreme fantasies, and no one has all the answers. With this in mind, both Luther's and Calvin's understanding of demonic temptation was formed by historic Christian convictions and experiences, not easily written off as a "limitation of their time," however we think we have advanced beyond their day. Neither Luther nor Calvin gave in to many of the superstitions of their time. Neither blamed everything on the devil or excused human choices, whether influenced by powerful temptation or not.

I acknowledge that I am not philosophically opposed to Calvin's understanding that there are spiritual sources of temptation designed to unhinge the human mind. The attack need not be focused on the individual, as in C. S. Lewis's imaginative model of a junior devil on assignment in *The Screwtape Letters*, though that is also a possibility. Without that concentrated and specific focus, the demonic realm can still impact the individual by unhinging the greater society, damaging family relationships, or undermining economic stability which is necessary for survival. There are various ways calamities come, many through human power plays which cause famine (Stalin's collectivization of farms, for example) or bring war. Additional disasters come through the natural order in the form of earthquakes or drought. Anything that debases, disrupts, or destroys human society is welcome to the powers at work in cosmic evil. Christian tradition affirms that rebellious spirits strive to bring about such ends, and within this overall picture any destruction of a family or individual serves that greater purpose. Because human reasoning and personal choices are always involved in great societal changes, there may be a focused spiritual influence targeting key people. This remains an open possibility, but not one we can know with certainty in any case.

Spiritually speaking, the end goal of the demonic realm is to damage, degrade, or destroy human beings.

Yet there are many possible paths to self-destruction. We have our own capacity to misuse power and freedom, debasing our own souls in the process, whether the process involves envy, lust, theft, murder, or other pursuits. In some cases there can be an unconscious but hidden interrelationship between the role of the human and the forces of Satan. As Marguerite Shuster says, "the corruptible human will, which is inclined to sin, is precisely the will through which—not just upon which—Satan works."[21] Whether knowingly or unknowingly, we can contribute to that which brings greater destruction to other members of society. We can also work against our own personal welfare in multiple ways.

People under great personal strain respond in different ways. Suicide was frightful, tragic, and seen as "demonic fury." Actual demonic agency was potentially involved, but not necessarily so. Perhaps alcoholism and despair were enough to work the mischief (think of Arthur Miller's tragic play, *Death of a Salesman* as a modern example). Even if Calvin ever thought demon possession was a fitting explanation for some particular case, still, the use he made of "diabolical fury" does not require it in every case.

Calvin on the Unforgivable Sin

In his reference to the unforgivable sin (Matt 12:31–32, Mark 3:28–29, Luke 11:14–26 and 12:8–10) in the *Institutes*, Calvin stated that the sin against the Holy Spirit is the only unforgivable sin, defined as the opposition of those who determine, knowingly and maliciously, to extinguish the truth. He saw apostasy as an expression of this sin as well as a sign that a man was possessed by the devil. "From this it follows that pardon is not denied to any individual sins except one, which, arising out of desperate madness, cannot be ascribed to weakness, and clearly demonstrates that a man is possessed by the devil."[22] We know from the history of Christianity, however, that some apostates return to the faith and would not presume to say there is no grace for people in their condition.

In the original context, the sin against the Holy Spirit in Matthew was attacking Jesus by attributing his healing miracles and successful

---

21. Shuster, *Power*, 139.
22. Calvin, *Institutes*, 3.3.21, 617.

exorcisms to the work of the devil. You cannot denounce the work of the Holy Spirit observed in Jesus's ministry and at the same time profit from that work. In Mark's context, the sin against the Holy Spirit was deliberately shutting one's eyes to the light and then, in self-chosen blindness, calling Jesus's exorcisms and healings the evil operations of the devil. People who do this do not even seek forgiveness. The main difference between the enemies of Jesus and Peter in his temporary apostasy was that Peter knew he did wrong, immediately felt shame, and wept bitterly. His nighttime renunciation "I do not know the man" was a temporary expedient to save his own skin rather than a deep hostility. By contrast, hostile eyewitnesses observed the ministry of God's Spirit in Jesus and rejected him. These passages are not about the sin of suicide or the incompleteness of human repentance. Calvin attempted to understand blasphemy against the Holy Spirit as Jesus did. He did not define suicide as blasphemy against the Holy Spirit.

Calvin on the Sin of Judas

Calvin did speak about Judas in his Commentary on the Harmony of the Evangelists, Matthew, Mark, and Luke. In his comments on Matthew 27:5 he points out that Judas threw away the money which was his reward for betraying Christ, as well as his life.

> This is the price for which Satan sells the allurements by which he flatters wicked men for a time. He throws them into a state of fury, so that, voluntarily cutting themselves off from the hope of salvation, they find no consolation but in death. Though others would have permitted Judas to enjoy the thirty pieces of silver, by which he had betrayed Christ and his own salvation, he throws them down. . . . Thus, though God does not put forth his hand, wicked men are disappointed of their desires, so that, when they have obtained their wishes, they not only deprive themselves of the enjoyment of unsatisfying benefits, but even make cords for themselves. But though they are their own executioners by punishing themselves, they do not in any respect alleviate or diminish the severity of the wrath of God.[23]

We learn from this that Calvin thinks Judas will face God's wrath. We ask the question, "Why?" Calvin answers that God is wrathful because Judas

---

23. Calvin, *Commentary*, 271.

betrayed a righteous man to be arrested and murdered. The thirty pieces of silver are mentioned because Calvin thought greed was Judas's chief motivation. The main criticism is not that Judas ended his life by suicide. Judas's inner discomfort which led to that end was God's judgment on his great sin, the sin of rejecting the love of Jesus and betraying him to his enemies. Calvin did not use this verse as an opportunity to speak against the sin of suicide. Nor did he use it as an occasion to say that suicide cannot be forgiven. Judas carried the heavy burdens of dishonesty, greed, and betrayal.

Summary Review of the Patristic to Reformation Period

Among the four great theologians presented above, Augustine and Calvin come the closest to fearing the condemnation of God on some persons who committed suicide. Yet they never declare the sin of suicide is always beyond the reach of God's forgiveness. Augustine thinks it possible for the suicide to face God's negative judgment, which may involve purgatorial punishment, but he did not state in clear language that suicide must lead to eternal condemnation (certainly not in all cases). Augustine had come to think about purgatory as a possibility for people who died. In its historic development, the purpose of purgatory was always to prepare souls for heaven, not hell. While Augustine and Calvin used the sternest language regarding suicide, neither declared it must be thought of as an unforgiveable sin at all times.

Aquinas and Luther discouraged suicide but never removed the hope of forgiveness in their theology and pastoral care. Aquinas and Luther do not consider the act of suicide to be necessarily an unforgiveable sin. Hostility to God that involves the rejection of love and grace was seen as the greatest danger.

These four theologians are of great historic significance. That none of them say suicide is always unforgiveable is highly remarkable. None endorsed suicide as an acceptable alternative to living by trusting in God, even if one's life involves suffering, but they did not encroach upon God's sovereign freedom to redeem sinful and broken people who committed suicide.

We have reason to be less willing than former generations to isolate this sin out of the whole human mess and condemn it more harshly than other sins. While a more hopeful attitude concerning God's forgiveness may seem presumptuous to some, it seems to me that the prevalent attitude about sure damnation works with a clear presumption that is unwarranted. As we all live and sin and die, we must entrust everyone who enters death to God. All sin condemns, not only suicide, and all people can receive salvation and new life only as a gift. Jesus of Nazareth embodied that gift and is risen and ascended to extend the farthest reach of God's mercy. We entrust ourselves to him in faith and hope.

9

John Donne (1572–1631)

THE ENGLISH POET JOHN Donne was a popular Anglican preacher. He wrote a lengthy attempt to change public attitudes toward the problem of suicide. His book was titled *Biathanatos*, which William Clebsch says is slightly garbled Greek that means to die violently. He used the term "self-homicide" for suicide. Donne did not see suicide condemned as harshly in the Bible as the Christian churches taught people to condemn it since the time of Augustine. It was not his purpose to totally excuse suicide or in any way to promote it. Rather Donne wanted to change the harshly judgmental attitude people were taught to adopt against the person who attempted or committed suicide. Not only were victims forbidden proper burials, but the family suffered from social ostracism as well as from legal punishments that impoverished the surviving family members.

On a personal level, Donne did sometime confess that he had considered taking his own life on more than one occasion. Although his poetry betrays a positive attitude toward death–to know we will die helps us live–nonetheless he never counseled others to commit suicide. Rather he counseled people to be more charitable to those who committed suicide and said it was a Christian's duty to look for good motives rather than bad ones. "Nor can there be any suspicion that he himself eventually died that way," said his son.[1] Even so, he wrote the book at a low point in his life, then preserved it for posterity but did not publish it. Publishing it in his

---

1. Clebsch, "Editor's Introduction," xiii.

lifetime might have brought serious legal reprisals, damaging Donne and his family economically.

John Donne (1604–1662) the son of the poet, published *Biathanatos* in 1647, sixteen years after his father's death. The fact that the Puritans were growing strong in England probably protected the book, for their unfavorable attitude toward Thomas Aquinas and Roman Catholic theology initially allowed for criticism of tradition. Needless to say the book would probably have been proscribed elsewhere in Catholic lands had it been more widely available. Even so, prior to its publication, certain theologians in the Church of England gave Donne their private opinion, in sincere friendship, that even though his words were intelligent and winsome it was too problematic to publish. Somehow he had erred. Their proclivity was to disagree with his conclusions though they could not say exactly where he had erred in his reasoning, at least not to their own satisfaction or his.

Three Arguments

What was the nature of Donne's uphill battle? It was not to remove suicide from being thought a sin, but to temper the interpretation of this sin with greater sympathy and less arrogance, so that uncharitable severity towards the surviving family might be eliminated. His goal was to reduce legal and social hardship for the survivors. He began by challenging the way suicide was categorized in Christian teaching as an unpardonable sin. He said that people who damn the suicide victim usually operate from one of three positions.

> Either they misstate that this act always proceeds from desperation [i.e. despair of God's mercy], and so they load it with all the abundant denunciations available from scripture, Fathers, and histories. Or they entertain the dangerous opinion that there is in this life an inability to repent and an impossibility of returning to God, and that this is apparent to us; otherwise, the act could not justify our uncharitable censure. Or else they build upon the foundation that this act, being presumed to be sin, and all sin presumed to be unpardonable without repentance, this is therefore unpardonable because the sin itself precludes all ordinary ways of repenting it.[2]

---

2. Donne, *Suicide*, 7.

Let us separate the three arguments for the sake of clarity. Each statement represented a common reason why people thought a suicidal act could not be forgiven. (1) People "misstate that the act of suicide always proceeds from desperation (despair of God's mercy)." Donne said, "I answer that not all desperation is sinful."[3] Among a variety of examples he pointed to the priest sent to convert infidels, saying it would not be sinful "to despair that God would give him the power of miracles." The priest cannot count on God's miraculous intervention for the purpose of making conversions more appealing, nor for the purpose of saving his own life from deadly enemies. The priest cannot count on God doing that which he so earnestly desires, but he goes into a desperate situation anyway. This is one example of desperation which is not counted against the priest in Christian thinking, and would not prevent him from being venerated after death.

Or to take another case, if a man killed himself in order to extinguish a terrible temptation of the flesh, the result of this desperation would be evil; "yet the root itself is not necessarily so."[4] In other words, the motivation could be seen as an attempt to honor God by assuring the sinful temptation would be avoided. This does not make the act of suicide good, but does not indicate despair of God's mercy. The condition of desperation can be mixed with thoughts of fidelity to God rather than infidelity, with faith rather than its absence (something only God can know). Donne held that the sin of desperation is very bad, but "since it may exist without infidelity, it cannot be a greater sin than that is."[5] Furthermore, in Scripture there are examples of people who killed themselves yet were so far from despairing of God's mercy that they considered it an honor to glorify God's name by their self-sacrifice.

(2) People "entertain the dangerous opinion that there is for some in this life an inability to repent and an impossibility of returning to God, and that this is apparent to us; otherwise, the act of suicide could not justify our uncharitable censure." Concerning this second objection to suicide, Donne rejected the belief that God has made some people unable to repent. This is as wrong as thinking God has made some people unable to sin. Suicide is not an outward sign that returning to God is impossible. Suicide does not indicate an outcome predetermined by God.

---

3. Donne, *Suicide*, 7.
4. Donne, *Suicide*, 8.
5. Donne, *Suicide*, 8.

(3) Suicide is "presumed to be a sin and all sin is presumed to be unpardonable without repentance, therefore suicide is unpardonable because the sin itself precludes all ordinary ways of repenting it." This third way of thinking is still prevalent today, namely that this form of death both requires a subsequent repentance in order to be forgiven and simultaneously denies that opportunity. Donne reminds us that certain things are called sin in the Bible and in church teaching in order to serve as a restraint on our own actions, not in order to condemn someone else by a restriction of God's grace. When we condemn the suicide by declaring we know what God's judgment will be for that individual, we have the wrong spiritual focus. Donne then offers various arguments. One is that we cannot presume there is no repentance even though we could not possibly hear it or see any sign of it. What is true repentance? Donne answers by quoting Clement of Alexandria concerning the Christian life: "To do no more and to speak no more those things whereof you repent; it is not to be always sinning and always asking pardon."[6] This means a suicidal person may not be in the same category as those who wish to repeat offenses and constantly seek pardon. The wish for the sin to never be repeated is a sign of grace, and that wish may predominate at the time of death. It is not possible to say there is no repentance in the suicide's heart concerning matters that trouble his or her soul.

The attitude of repentance involves coming before God as a complete beggar, and Donne thinks a suicidal person may be capable of this: "Of one who died before he had repented the good Paulinus charitably interprets his haste, 'That he chose rather to go to God a debtor than as free,' and so to die in his debt rather than to carry his discharge from it."[7] In other words, the suicide who does not leave time for repentance, like the murderer in the Old Testament, could do nothing but throw himself on the judgment of God in order to obtain mercy. We all must come to God with empty hands, with lack of merit. As theologian Rod Rosenbladt once said, "Following Luther, what do I think I contribute to my own salvation? I answer: my sin, my need." It takes away nothing from the suicide because he or she is a beggar in need of God's mercy, for every person must come before God in the same way. What is eternal life if not a gift beyond anything we deserve?

6. Donne, *Suicide*, 10.

7. Donne, *Suicide*, 10. According to Clebsch the reference is to Paulinus of Nola (353–431), a French Christian who became a bishop in Italy and was known for his asceticism.

Thus Donne does not conclude that every suicide entails repentance, but that some suicides may include repentance. Some people may seek God's mercy in the very last moment of life. This is why we cannot judge the person, for only God knows someone's true spiritual condition and psychological motivation.

Donne acknowledged that suicide goes against the way God designed us to live. As for suicide being a sin against the law of nature Donne says, "Every act that does not agree exactly with our religion will be a sin against nature," but concludes that "self-homicide is no more against the law of nature than any other sin."[8] In other words the act of suicide does not deserve to be singled out as being more heinous than other sins. This discussion touched on Roman Catholic teaching up to Donne's day, which was used to justify public disapproval of suicide and harsh measures directed against the surviving family members, which he sought to undermine.

Discussing the law of reason as regards church tradition, Donne said there are examples in church history that show suicide is acceptable if it is done to protect the seal of Christian confession in the face of torture. Here was a type of example which was not condemned by all early theologians. Thus Donne does not regard all suicide as a violation of the law of nature, which is a disagreement with Thomas Aquinas, nor does he regard all suicide as a violation of the law of God. He does not side with those who think the Bible condemns suicide per se. This was not the same as encouraging the act, only discouraging false human judgments about the act.

Donne deserves to be read not in summary form, as presented here, but in his own words. The entirety of his discussion shows his deep commitment to the Christian faith and his wide reading of the most ancient Christian writers. His interaction with earlier theologians is often instructive and shows the multiple ways he supported his case. Neither wanting to exonerate suicide nor encourage it, he sought to take it from its position as a sin so unredeemable that the suicidal person must be thought immediately cast out of God's presence, and move it into view as something that could be encircled by God's grace. This was not just a treatise on moral theology for Donne, but an attempt to alter societal attitudes so that the families of suicide victims would be punished less and helped more. He saw surviving family members as victims who needed to be supported in Christian community, not shamed unmercifully.

---

8. Donne, *Suicide*, 14.

10

John Wesley (1708–1791), Samuel Johnson (1709–1784)

JOHN WESLEY LABORED TO preach to the poor who could not afford to rent church pews and were largely neglected by the established church in his day. His tireless efforts and the extensive impact of his preaching may have prevented England from experiencing a revolution as bloody as the French Revolution. Historians have given Wesley enormous credit for his positive impact on his generation. In his vast preaching as an evangelist his focus was on the individual's need for Christ. Surprisingly, it is difficult to find a reference to suicide in his published sermons.

Wesley on the Death of Samson

Samson was blinded and worked as a slave, but prayed for a return of divinely-given strength so that he could push over the supports for the roof. Samson prayed audibly, Wesley says, to divert the Philistines' anger away from the Israelite people and place it on himself. He asked for strength to die in this way in order to vindicate God's glory and bring relief to the Israelites, through the destruction of the very lords gathered around him, mocking his weakness at their banquet. Wesley thinks Samson's motivation mattered to God and that God's Spirit prompted him to ask for this opportunity. Regarding the prayer in Judg 16:28, Wesley says, "This prayer was not an act of malice and revenge, but of faith and zeal for God, who was there publicly dishonoured; and justice, in vindicating the whole common-wealth of Israel. . . . [God] would never use his omnipotence to gratify any man's malice."[1]

He says this of suicide in biblical context, "This is no encouragement to those who wickedly murder themselves: for Samson did not desire or procure his own death voluntarily, but by mere necessity [by this confrontation with the oppressors of his people]."[2] God would not have affirmed and answered this prayer if God were displeased by Samson's motive. His death was voluntary in order to bring relief to his own beleaguered people. Some deaths by suicide are a form of self-sacrifice on behalf of others, some are more like the result of a wild animal caught in a trap, and others are a form of self-murder. Wesley does not classify all deaths by suicide as self-murder, which he saw as a wicked sin, for some contexts and motivations move the action into a different moral category.

John and Charles Wesley Hoped for the Redemption of Saul

Charles Wesley (1707–1788) worked together in ministry with his brother John, in a relationship that included mutual support and encouragement, discussing practical wisdom and biblical insight. Charles was gifted in poetry and composing lyrics for hymns. Some of his compositions are still sung and treasured in churches today, including "Love Divine, All Loves Excelling" (1747) and "Christ the Lord Is Ris'n Today" (1739). His Advent song "Come, Thou Long-Expected Jesus" (1744) and Christmas hymn "Hark, the Herald Angels Sing" (1734) are beautiful and joyous, joining many of Charles' other hymns as examples of theology which John Wesley endorsed and proclaimed. With this in mind, we look at a shorter poem by Charles, called a Scripture hymn, which reflects on 2 Sam 1:17 and retells David's lament over the sad end of King Saul (dated 1762):

> For evil may I good return,
>   Kindness for bitter hatred show,
> With pious grief sincerely mourn,
>   The fall of my relentless foe,
> His faults with tenderest love conceal,
>   His shining qualities commend,
> And cordial consolation feel
>   In hope—that hope was in his end.[3]

1. Wesley, *Wesley's Notes*, 968.
2. Wesley, *Wesley's Notes*, 968.
3. Wesley and Wesley, *Poetical Works*, 163–64.

Charles Wesley thought David hoped for the forgiveness of a man guilty of pursuing and harming innocent people. At the very least he affirmed that God could be merciful to such a man. There is no hint that his death by suicide somehow prevented God from showing mercy.

With this in mind we turn to a short poem reflecting on 1 Sam 28:19, on the specially allowed appearance of the Prophet Samuel to Saul before the day of battle. In a word of judgment Saul is told that the Philistines will be victorious and he will not be rescued. Samuel concludes by saying, "therefore tomorrow you and your sons will be with me." John Wesley once considered this verse and pointed to the poem his brother wrote:

> What do these solemn words portend?
> A gleam of hope when life shall end.
> Thou and thy sons, tho' slain shall be
> Tomorrow in repose with me!
> Not in a state of hellish pain
> If Saul with Samuel doth remain,
> Not in a state of damn'd despair,
> If loving Jonathan be there.[4]

These gracious words arise from a generous and benevolent reading of the end of Saul's tragic life. There is a gleam of hope for those trapped by sin and circumstances in a condition of hopelessness. Saul will be with righteous Samuel and Jonathan. Perhaps Samuel's words only meant Saul would die and be in a state of death, but Charles Wesley suggests there is a hint of something more, something better that does not end in frustration, sin, pain, and darkness.

Wesley considered that Saul may have turned to God in the end. First Sam 28:20 says that after hearing the word of doom, Saul fell full length upon the ground and was very afraid. Wesley says, "As if the archers of the Philistines had already hit him, and there was no strength in him, to bear up against these heavy tidings: especially, as we cannot doubt, but all his past sins were now brought to his remembrance and what authority

---

4. Wesley, *Sacred Poetry*, 639. The 1870 edition by George Osborn changed the words "not in a state of hellish pain" to "not in a state of health or pain," which weakens the meaning. John Wesley thought that God's judgment took place at the moment of death, when the departed either goes to heaven or hell. Thus, in his favorable embrace of his brother's verse, Wesley is open to the possibility of forgiveness ("If Saul with Samuel doth remain, Not in a state of damn'd despair.") Here is indirect evidence that he did not consider suicide to be an unforgiveable sin, certainly not one that was the all-determining factor in God's judgment. Charles could imagine Saul with Samuel and Jonathan, and it seems that John accepted this possibility.

has any man to affirm, that he felt no contrition all this time? Altho' it did not seem good to the Holy Ghost to leave it upon record?"[5] Here there is not a hint that Saul's death by suicide undid his repentance. Wesley knew the historical context well enough to understand that had Saul been taken alive, Israel's disgrace would have been far greater.

Wesley on Ahithophel

During Absalom's rebellion, the brilliant political strategist Ahithophel sided with the prince against his father. Second Sam 17:23 recounts that when Ahithophel realized that Absalom would not follow his advice, ensuring David's victory, he went home, "set his house in order, and strangled himself." Wesley says, "See here contempt poured upon the wisdom of man. He that was more renowned for policy than ever any man was, played the fool with himself more than ever any man did. See likewise honour done to the justice of God! The wicked is snared in the work of his own hands."[6] The trap ended in suicide because there was no alternative that would help Ahithophel, but beyond calling this disaster a form of justice, Wesley did not say anything specifically about suicide in terms of God's eternal judgment.

Wesley's References to Suicide Are Without Stigmatization

When we look at what Wesley did with narratives of suicide in the Bible, we often find that he makes no comment specifically pertaining to the act of suicide itself. Commenting on 1 Sam 31:4, which tells of Saul's suicide, Wesley gave censure about Saul's mode of death, yet quoted the earlier insight of Matthew Henry (1662–1714) with reference to verse 8. He said this text "makes no mention of the souls of Saul and his sons, what became of them after they were dead: secret things belong not to us."[7]

In these notes on Bible passages, Wesley does not stigmatize suicide and make it out to be a more reprehensible sin than all other sins. We also consult his journals and letters on the same passages. If we look up the few references to Judas, what do we find? Nothing about Judas is whitewashed, but there is no statement about suicide making his spiritual

---

5. Wesley, *Wesley's Notes*, 1026.
6. Wesley, *Wesley's Notes*, 1053.
7. Wesley, *Wesley's Notes*, 1029.

condition worse than it was while he lived. Wesley thought that Jesus knew there was something spiritually wrong with Judas Iscariot from the beginning. Judas, at times, demonstrated that he had a problem with anger as well as covetousness.

However, when Jesus sent the disciples out in pairs as evangelists, Judas was also sent and his ministry was blessed with results the same as the others. Wesley said this shows us that "our Lord can and doth send salvation to men even by those who will not accept it of themselves."[8]

In Acts 1:25, Peter states that Judas turned aside from his ministry and apostleship "to go to his own place." Wesley says, "To go to his own place—that which his crimes had deserved and which he had chosen for himself, far from the other apostles, in the region of death." It appears that all Wesley can say is that Judas chose to die, but he does not attempt to declare God's judgment. It seems he thought Judas was spiritually lost before the betrayal, even when he first became Jesus's disciple.[9] Whatever Wesley thought of Judas's spiritual condition before or during the betrayal of Christ, Judas's death by suicide is not commented on with any moralizing strictures against the sin of suicide. What are we to conclude by this? Nowhere does Wesley encourage death by suicide. He called it "self-murder" more than once, a wicked sin. But he knows there are many other sins that can rightfully be called "wicked" and does not stigmatize suicide.

An Opinion Shared Privately

However, once in private correspondence, Wesley took a very hard line against suicide. He argued that after the fact of death the laws against suicide should be invoked against the victim. Yet these sentiments were not expressed in a sermon or public address.

In a letter dated April 8, 1790, Wesley bemoaned the fact that the laws against the crime of suicide are rarely applied. "If all self-murderers are mad, what need of any trial concerning them? . . . The question is, Was he mad in other respects? If not, every juror is perjured who does not bring him in *felo de se*. But how can this vile abuse of the law be

---

8. Wesley, *Works Volume VII*, 181.

9. "So one even of them whom God had given him is lost. . . . The son of perdition signifies one that deservedly perishes." Wesley, *Wesley's Notes*, 163.

prevented, and this execrable crime effectually discouraged?" Wesley answers his own question.

> By a very easy method. We read in ancient history, that, at a certain period, many of the women in Sparta murdered themselves. This fury increasing, a law was made, that the body of every woman that killed herself should be exposed naked in the streets. The fury ceased at once. Only let a law be made and rigorously executed, that the body of every self-murderer, Lord or peasant, shall be hanged in chains, and the English fury will cease at once.[10]

The Latin phrase for the verdict Wesley demanded, *felo de se*, meant "felon of himself." This was a reference to suicide in English common law, which meant that an adult who committed suicide was declared to be a felon. As such a male adult's land or property was forfeit to the Crown. The money from the sale of which went to the king's almoner to be given to the poor. This basically put suicide on the same level as treason, the primary legal ground for confiscating property and giving it to the king (without the money going to the poor). It was a sure way to impoverish a family and leave them no means of support. Additionally, the body of the deceased in this legal category was given a shameful burial at night with no mourners or clergy present. The severity of this punishment fell harshly upon the family, particularly as an economic hardship if the suicide was a father or husband who owned property that would be taken away. The demeaning nighttime burial was also a social disgrace. Concern for the welfare of these innocent family members and the need to treat them kindly was probably the chief reason why many juries refused to bring in this verdict.

Therefore, Wesley's judgment seems overly harsh and troubles us. Here we must review the bigger picture of his life's accomplishments before we pass judgment. What more do we know about his personal life that bears on his attitude toward suicide? Was this letter evidence that Wesley was in a melancholic or aggressive mood? According to some studies of his life, Wesley did struggle at times with a state of depression. Many high energy people who accomplish a lot on the public scene, or who endure great hardships in their work while driving themselves beyond physical endurance, have bouts of severe depression. There is some

---

10. Wesley, *Works Volume XIII*, 481.

evidence of this in Wesley's life from time to time, but there are also gaps in relevant information.

The possibility of a personal bout with depression, however, does not mean that Wesley was really not against suicide. Clearly he did not approve of it. He did not see it as an option for God's people to choose. He did not want to give permission for any person to end this way.

Speculatively, it may have been the case that Wesley's vast contacts with despairing prisoners in London might have influenced his pastoral response. In an age when an eight year old child could be hung for stealing money or transported for stealing bread, prisoners without private means lived in filth and went hungry (as graphically shown in episodes of *Garrow's Law*).[11] Contact with such horrid conditions might have made Wesley less patient with those living in better circumstances who complained or contemplated suicide.

James Clemons reminds us that we get a distorted picture of Wesley if we do not keep in mind the complete record of his achievements. Clemons says, "[Wesley] had been at the forefront of many progressive ideas involving prison reform, emancipation from slavery, employment, education, and medical care for the poor."[12] Furthermore, Wesley's harsh comments on suicide were only presented in a private letter, written when he was an elderly man near the end of his life. This was not offered in a sermon or meant for publication. As harsh as his words sounded then and still sound today, the motivation behind them was certainly a pastoral concern to discourage any future deaths by suicide.

In conclusion, there can be no doubt that Wesley saw suicide as a terrible sin. But we also see that, given the firmness of his opposition, he did not say suicide was an unforgivable sin. Any statement like that is absent in his collected writings. In this way, he joins those theologians who leave judgment and mercy in God's hands.

---

11. The television series *Garrow's Law* is based on the life of barrister William Garrow (1760–1840). The point is not that this series is perfectly accurate about the details of Garrow's life in every scene, but that the general conditions of prison life are accurately presented as reprehensible. These were conditions which Wesley and his group had long worked to ameliorate. Wesley did prison ministry in person, encountering many horrid scenes. The English writer and magistrate of the same era, Henry Fielding, was also horrified by legal corruption and prison conditions.

12 Clemons, *Sermons on Suicide*, 36.

Samuel Johnson (1709—1784)

Samuel Johnson was an eminent writer and critic in the eighteenth century, whose remarks were recorded by James Boswell and published in what became the most famous biography in the English language. C. S. Lewis held him in high esteem and continued the tradition of respectfully calling him "Dr Johnson" in his lectures, conversations, or letters.

Does God Play Tricks?

Once, as Boswell and Johnson were preparing to set out on their trip to Scotland, the conversation turned to suicide. Boswell asked about a Christian who dies before properly repenting of his most recent sinful act.

> I stated to him an anxious thought, by which a sincere Christian might be disturbed, even when conscious of having lived a good life, so far as is consistent with human infirmity; he might fear that he should afterwards fall away, and be guilty of such crimes as would render all his former religion vain. Could there be upon this awful subject, such a thing as balancing of accounts? Suppose a man who has led a good life for seven years, commits an act of wickedness, and instantly dies; will his former good life have any effect in his favour?

This question involves whether the good can outweigh the bad, or vice versa, in God's judgment. Boswell's question presupposes that he primarily views sin as actions committed rather than a manifestation of an underlying spiritual condition. In this view, so common to many Christians across the centuries, sins are kept track of by the divine Judge and weighed against good actions. Those who do good deeds will be rewarded and those who do bad deeds will be punished accordingly.[13] Boswell asks whether a final sin can undue God's gift of forgiveness and salvation, a question still asked by many people today. Johnson's reply seems to comply with Boswell's conception of just rewards, but also indicates that God's promise of salvation holds.

> Sir, if a man has led a good life for seven years, and then is hurried by passion to do what is wrong, and is suddenly carried off, depend upon it he will have the reward of his seven years' good life; God will not take a catch of him. Upon this principal

---

13. Jer 17:10.

Richard Baxter believes that a Suicide may be saved. "If, (says he,) it should be objected that what I maintain may encourage suicide, I answer, I am not to tell a lie to prevent it."[14]

What does Johnson mean by "God will not take a catch of him"? The phrase did not mean "to catch ahold of something" as in catch a tossed ball or catch a fish. Rather it meant, as Percy Fitzgerald explained over a century ago, to take an unfair advantage of someone. "'God Almighty will not take a catch of him'— that is, will not take him by surprise; take an unfair advantage of him."[15] To Johnson, if God promises to save a person it is a sure and constant promise, not one subject to change. For example, if God promises to save us by grace through faith in Christ, the promise will not be changed at the end of our life or removed altogether—there will be no surprises unworthy of God's holy character.

Even if one interpreted this phrase in a semi-Pelagian way, so that a good use of free will is made in response to the gospel, or so that human moral living is taken into account as a factor in salvation (or as evidence of faith in Christ), Johnson's reply meant that the rules of the game will not be changed in the final inning. The final moment will not cancel out seven years of righteous living. If not meant in a semi-Pelagian way, the point is the same—God will not cancel out the years of trusting in Christ just because it was hard to trust in the final moment.

What are we to think of this? We should disagree with Boswell's presupposition that human merit affects or secures salvation, but not the principal Johnson espouses: God does not change the way of salvation from one moment to another. God does not offer grace for a long season and suddenly remove it at the end. The offer is lasting.

This is a significant point for us to consider. The promise of grace does not only hold good up to the point of the final moment of life, when suddenly salvation becomes based on something else, such as our ability to have enough faith, hope, and love. That scenario would make God's promise unreliable and place every person in danger. Johnson's unique expression means God's promise of forgiveness may be relied upon. Because God does not change the way of salvation, centered in the atoning work of Christ, "a Suicide may be saved." He referenced English theologian

---

14. Boswell, *Boswell's Life of Johnson*, 498.
15. Fitzgerald, *Examination*, 71–72.

Richard Baxter (1615–1691) for support. Baxter did not consider suicide an unforgivable sin and Johnson was in agreement with him.[16]

As to that which ultimately defines the individual in God's sight, there is an affinity with the insight expressed in the twentieth century by Dietrich Bonhoeffer (see chapter 3 above), that the emphasis should not all be placed on the final moment of life. We need to remember that even when "we are faithless, God remains faithful" (2 Tim 2:13).

Johnson on Scare Tactics to Discourage Suicide—What Should We Do?

Johnson was also aware that saying there is grace for suicide seems too permissive. With due consideration for the concern to protect life, he did not adjust his theology to accommodate the fear of encouraging suicide. "I am not to tell a lie to prevent it." We are either saved by grace through faith or not. If Johnson read Eph 2:8–10 correctly, then it is right to affirm salvation by God's grace regardless of the unfortunate ways this message can be distorted. Additionally, it is questionable whether affirming God's gift of forgiveness actually does encourage suicide. Affirming God's gracious permission to live may be more freeing than forceful prohibitions against suicide, though in some cases providential negatives have saved lives too.

Should We Declare This Sin Unforgiveable in Order to Prevent More Occurrences?

Sometimes those who have suffered from a relative's death will test to see if a minister really thinks there is forgiveness for suicide. It is as though they think, "You said there was hope for forgiveness at the funeral, but maybe you just said so to make us feel better, not because you really believe it." There may be a lurking fear that has not been resolved. Relatives of people who committed suicide may attend other funeral services in

---

16. Although Baxter worked within the Calvinist tradition, he rejected the idea of limited atonement. He worked for moderation in settling the disputes of the English Civil War. Boswell said, "I asked him [Johnson] what works of Richard Baxter's I should read. He said, 'Read any of them; they are all good.'" Boswell, *Johnson*, 499. C. S. Lewis borrowed the phrase "mere Christianity" from Baxter, who said in 1680, "I am a Meer Christian" (See West, "Richard Baxter"). For both Baxter and Lewis, the word "mere" meant essential, not trivial.

order to test one pastor's words by what another says, being highly sensitive to any nuances in tone or wording about whether suicide is forgivable or unforgivable. Is there really solid theological ground for any hope of forgiveness? While some seek assurance of possible forgiveness, other people worry that if we say forgiveness is possible we remove a necessary barrier that prevents suicide.

Shortly after I conducted a funeral for a young man who committed suicide, a man saw me in passing at the local post office. The recent funeral was fresh in his mind. His own son had committed suicide some years earlier. While looking at his mail, he casually said to me, "Pastor Mark, don't you think we should tell young people that suicide is an unforgivable sin? Just to scare them from doing it?" My immediate answer was, "No, because it's not true." This answer came almost mechanically as I sorted my own mail. I meant that God can forgive sin, including this sin, not that I knew God's ultimate judgment concerning any particular person.

But it was about twenty minutes later that I realized I had been tested. The long-grieving father was checking my spontaneous response to gauge my true thoughts: did I really believe there was forgiveness for this sin? That question was his chief concern, hidden under the subterfuge of scaring young people away from taking this unalterable course. It seemed he was testing my answer for consistency or inconsistency. If I spoke about God's grace in a funeral sermon, well that was nice, but did I really believe it? There are some questions that haunt relatives for years to come, and the question of grace is of central importance: did Christ die for this sin too? Yes, Christ also died to atone for this sin.

A dark cloud descends upon family members who have lost a loved one to suicide. Observing their grief, we want to scare someone else away from making the same mistake. We may want to say that suicide is unforgivable in order to save another person's life, sparing another family from wrenching grief. Samuel Johnson was aware of this impulse, but found it insufficient reason to say a suicidal death could not be forgiven. "If it should be objected that what I maintain may encourage suicide, I answer, I am not to tell a lie to prevent it."

11

Søren Kierkegaard (1813–1855)

DANISH PHILOSOPHER SØREN KIERKEGAARD wrote on the borderland of philosophy and theology, writing consistently against the philosophy of Hegel which had so strongly influenced the theologians of his day. We cannot go into all the ways in which he interacted with Christian teaching and practice. He was very provocative in his lifetime and remains a stimulating influence.

Kierkegaard published *The Sickness Unto Death* (1849) under the pseudonym "Anti-Climacus." He said there are people who recognize they are in despair, correct to see themselves as in despair, but wrong to think that other people are not in despair. In a variety of ways, despair is a universal sickness. Many people do not want to acknowledge their spiritual condition and so distract themselves with diversions and busyness. Some know they are doing this while others do not seem to be aware, but "the level of consciousness intensifies the despair."[1] Suicide is an intensive form of despair, which he also referred to as "despair in weakness." Furthermore, "the opposite of being in despair is to have faith." Faith for Kierkegaard came when the human spirit is transparently grounded in God, "in the power that established it," rather than in false groundings which cannot support and sustain the human spirit.[2]

Despair in weakness is not empty, however, for it contains an element of aggression. "No despair is entirely free of defiance; indeed, the

---

1. Kierkegaard, *Sickness Unto Death*, 48.
2. Kierkegaard, *Sickness Unto Death*, 49.

very phrase 'not to will to be' implies defiance. On the other hand, even despair's most extreme defiance is never really free of some weakness. So the distinction is only relative."[3] A despair of defiance becomes bondage when the defiant person confronts the calamity of suffering by refusing the comfort of eternity. The self can be lost in despair, and suicide is an obvious way this happens. Yet the common wish to be someone else, someone other than who we are, should be viewed by shaking one's head (in pity), just as with the wish to die. For both wishes reveal despair, though the first looks more comical than the second. What is important for such a person is to realize and declare why he does not wish to be himself, which may move him into a state of defiance. Sometimes living (and continuing to live) is the greatest form of defiance, which happens when the decision to live springs from within rather than from external pressures. The decision for suicide often presses on a person from external pressures.

Sickness Unto Death is filled with psychological reflections, reminding us that the role of the human spirit cannot be neglected in anthropological understanding. The strength or weakness of the human spirit affects meaning making, which impacts us both mentally and emotionally, contributing either to hopefulness or despair. Kierkegaard had a deep knowledge of what made a human being a human being, and what made life on earth seem like an unbearable burden or an exquisite opportunity. These insights, however, do not provide ready answers to common questions. We also want to explore his journals and mine them for clues. A more thorough examination of Kierkegaard would need to pay attention to the many things he says about suffering, which are more extensive than his comments on suicide.

Does the Bible Prohibit Suicide?

Does Kierkegaard think suicide is forbidden in the Bible? The short answer is no, not by any explicit command. But this specific absence of a prohibition adds something to the mystery which he observed regarding the popular disapproval of suicide. Writing in 1854 he said, "Why is it that although Holy Scripture does not actually contain a definite prohibition against suicide, although significant character-philosophers allow, yes, praise it, although as far as I know no pagan religion forbids it—why,

---

3. Kierkegaard, *Sickness Unto Death*, 49.

then, is it that in common daily exchange in the market and on the street suicide is spoken of again and again as cowardice?"[4]

If we probe we may find that people call suicide cowardice based on personal reactions to their own battles with life's external and internal pressures. Family survivors often feel a great emotion of anger toward the one who left them via suicide. Intense anger can arise from a sense of abandonment and rejection which wounds them, something of a deeper emotion than disgust at the sight of someone else's cowardice. So at every turn of the page there are opportunities for more psychological discussions. As an observer, Kierkegaard was right to note the negative reaction to suicide "on the street." Those who minister today will uncover reactions of anger mixed with grief in the wake of a suicide, as well as responses that are more empathetic.

Elsewhere, he carefully notes how family members suffer in the aftermath of suicide. In *Stages on Life's Way*, he writes about a girl from a distinguished family who committed suicide. He says, "If the girl had just considered the mortal agony she can cause another person, I believe she would have refrained."[5] It is difficult to exaggerate the agony of the survivors, especially those who invested loving care and shared difficult life experiences together. Awareness of the pain inflicted on family and neighbors was a key reason for societal disapproval.

Does Cowardice Play a Role in People Refraining from Suicide?

In a private writing of 1854, Kierkegaard goes on to say that living can be a form of cowardice (the opposite of his defiance remark in *Sickness Unto Death*). These were partial reflections not meant for publication. "There is scarcely any doubt that it is precisely cowardice which restrains a goodly number of men from suicide." It is possible that those who are afraid to die accuse those who commit suicide of cowardice out of envy or out of a desire to find consolation in their own misery. "Perhaps it is also because man snatches after every fragment of compensation—so he consoles himself by thinking that he displays courage by living—for to take one's own life is cowardly." Perhaps Kierkegaard thought there were people living around him who would have chosen suicide but for

4. Kierkegaard, *Journals and Papers*, 443.
5. Kierkegaard, *Stages on Life's Way*, 298.

cowardice (the fear of death); yet even if this were an apt description of some suffering people, it would not be true of all.

Certainly not true of all people whose lives are extremely difficult. Victor Frankl wrote of concentration camp survivors who persevered against great odds. So much that counteracted despair depended on whether the sufferer perceived his or her life to have meaning.[6] Other perceptive observers of the human condition find people who embrace duty in the face of hardship, including responsibility for the welfare of others who need assistance. This is the opposite of cowardice. Bravery and goodness can be demonstrated more often and more quietly by the weak than by the strong. This is a theme that appears in the movie *The Magnificent Seven* (based on the earlier *The Seven Samurai* by Akira Kurosawa). In this western remake the gunslingers defend a vulnerable town from a large group of raiders. One of the village boys meant to express admiration for the character of Bernardo O'Reilly, played by Charles Bronson, but he did so by expressing a negative comparison with his own father. The boy says essentially, "I wish I were like you, not like my father." The actual words are, "We're ashamed to live here. Our fathers are cowards." Immediately O'Reilly spanked the boy for disrespecting his father. Then he gave his own valuation of the men of the village.

O'Reilly (Bronson) said, "Don't ever say that again about your fathers, because they are not cowards. You think I am brave because I carry a gun; well, your fathers are much braver because they carry responsibility for you, your brothers, your sisters, and your mothers. And this responsibility is like a big rock that weighs a ton. It bends and it twists them until finally it buries them under the ground. And there's nobody says they have to do this. They do it because they love you, and because they want to. I have never had this kind of courage."[7] Such impoverished but loyal parents exemplify the opposite of Kierkegaard's example of cowardice, for they refuse to abandon those who need their care, even though each and every day is an abject struggle for survival. There are surely people who reject suicide not because they are afraid to die but because they will not abandon their family responsibilities. This only goes to show that one valid insight into the human condition cannot cover all cases with accuracy.

---

6. Frankl, *Man's Search for Meaning*; cf. Scully, "Victor Frankl at Ninety," 39–43.
7. Sturges, *Magnificent Seven*, 1:50–1:51.

What can we glean from these selections? On the one hand, Kierkegaard did not think the Bible definitely prohibits suicide. This would lead one to think that he did not see suicide as an unforgiveable sin per se. On the other hand, he did not promote it or think it acceptable. In another entry from 1854, he considers suicide as a false alternative, largely based on his understanding of the role of suffering. To even mention the subject of suffering, however, without adequate discussion of all his insightful commentary may do Kierkegaard a disservice. We need to read and explore far beyond what is offered here. His commitment to Christianity was neither superficial nor unaware of the agony of human disappointment and sorrow.

Life Is Not Always Good

"For the very reason that this life, from a Christian point of view, is a suffering of punishment and for the very reason that Christianity promises a blessed, an eternally blessed, existence when the last suffering, that of death, has been endured, it displeases God if someone arbitrarily breaks out of this existence."[8] He goes on to say that the argument that life is always good and that suicide should always be regarded as a form of ingratitude is a lie. Life is not always good and suicide is not always reprehensible due to ingratitude. No distortion of the truth is needed to argue against suicide, because such arguments miss the point. There is suffering, and for most of us, if not all, suffering must be embraced. When we suffer we need to seek God's purpose in it for the present or future, or spiritual assurance that there is a purpose in it, though this will be like walking a path strewn with thorns. "For the simple reason that this life is a suffering and for the simple reason that eternal salvation awaits the one who patiently endures it, Governance is opposed to suicide."[9]

Those who want to pursue more of Kierkegaard's thought in depth can also search out his understanding of God's providence. This discussion cannot be divorced from one's understanding of God's sovereignty, a highly significant doctrine for which there is not agreement among Christian theologians. In my own understanding, sovereignty means that God will move history to its rightful conclusion. This does not mean that

---

8. Kierkegaard, *Journals*, 443.

9. Kierkegaard, *Journals*, 444. For a study showing the greater complexity in his thought on suffering, see Evans, *Kierkegaard's "Fragments" and "Postscript"*, 161–84.

God ordains each negative event that occurs or directs the choices of every intelligent creature, including those in a state of rebellion. For reasons known only to God, there is the possibility of many things temporarily existing which are contrary to God's will, including the vast misuse of human freedom. Praying "Thy will be done on earth" implies that much in this life is still contrary to God's will.

Here is a profound mystery which remains dark and impenetrable at this time. I agree with Hugh Ross Mackintosh, the teacher of James S. Stewart and T. F. Torrance, who said we must never identify God's will "with what just happens." That would lead to a deterministic philosophy or fatalism, which is contrary to the biblical worldview. Mackintosh is worth quoting here.

> Never forget that much in the world is utterly alien to God's nature—cruelty and cancer for instance. His will is opposed, dead opposed to these facts. So to speak of them as phenomena through which He is transparently manifested is absurd. We must never identify His will with what just happens. These evil things—and there are mysteriously many of them, in the world and in ourselves—obscure God, and if we continue to know Him, it is in spite of them, not because of them. You can't rise from cancer to cancer's God, . . . The apostles only just overcame these difficulties; they triumphed over the stark actualities of tragedy and death by a faith which all but broke under their weight. Something wonderful had happened, something connected with Jesus, which actually enabled them to rest in the knowledge of God in spite of these dark things.[10]

God's overarching sovereignty means that the destructive power of death and evil will not have the final say. Yet God's sovereignty does not necessarily mean that God directly sends each measure of suffering. And the doctrine of providence means that God can introduce good into (or after) tragic moments of life which is beyond our ability to anticipate. In providential mercy, God can cause suffering to serve a better end than devastation and destruction, but this cannot be made obvious to us in every instance.[11] This is not said as an explanation of Kierkegaard but

---

10. Mackintosh, *Experience*, 62.

11. Mackintosh says, "Our grasp of the Father certifies to us, indeed, the fact of Providence, but the method or process of providential guidance is as much hidden from the Christian as from others. We cannot look on at God's operations through His eyes; we cannot see the details of His purpose in the world from the inner side, or as He sees them." Mackintosh, *Experience*, 56.

rather as an alternative to thinking that all suffering is preordained or approved by God. Even if there exists a temporary evil that is contrary to God's will, there are ways in which God's grace can enter into the suffering which God allows us to encounter in this life. Without this possibility, it is nearly impossible for many people to face the reality and extent of human suffering.

Suffering is part of the human experience, yet something that cannot be explained or appreciated from this side of the grave. Returning to Kierkegaard, he concludes his reflection by saying, "It is the same here as when the children must wait in a dark room on Christmas Eve—precisely because the parents know how much has been done to increase their happiness and that the time is used for that purpose—for that very reason impatience is frowned upon."[12] Kierkegaard also thought that Christianity does not offer immediate consolation for all forms of suffering. That fact adds to the depth of suffering in daily experience. In saying so he was very realistic about the hard struggles which so many people face, but without robbing them of the Christian basis for hope. Having Christ does not give us an advantage over others in this regard, but rather gives us a pattern for trust and faithfulness through hardship and pain, a pattern that promises to end in death and then move forward into resurrection to new life.

---

12. Kierkegaard, *Journals*, 444.

12

Two Victorians
George MacDonald (1824–1905), Charles Haddon Spurgeon (1834–1892)

GEORGE MACDONALD WAS A Scottish poet and Congregational pastor. It is said that he wrote novels primarily to supplement his meager income, but I also think that telling and writing stories were a great outlet for his imagination, and the world is richer for it. Not that he was a first-rate novelist, for C. S. Lewis assures us that he was not. Yet there is a sensitivity and goodness that enters his stories and hangs on some of his characters like dew on the morning grass. Lewis acknowledged that MacDonald's fantasy adventures, as we would call them, were unsurpassed. "What he does best is fantasy—fantasy that hovers between the allegorical and the mythopoeic. And this, in my opinion, he does better than any man."[1]

He also wrote a few fairy stories which are engaging. If the novels were not all crafted well, it may be because of distressing worries that prompted fast writing, for in the nineteenth century publishing paid based on word count if a story was sold. He had a poor family to clothe and feed, feeling a great strain when some churches refused him employment or reduced his salary because of his theology.

Without high regard for the novels, Lewis delighted in *Phantastes*, *Lilith*, and the *Curdie* books, which he read prior to his becoming a Christian in his adult life, and which he said baptized his imagination

---

1. Lewis, *George MacDonald*, xxix.

more than he understood at the time. He continued to draw spiritual inspiration from MacDonald after he became a Christian. Lewis feasted on his many stories, but also on his prayers in *Diary of an Old Soul*. He read repeatedly the three volume set of *Unspoken Sermons* until the end of his life.[2] Thus, for several reasons, he called George MacDonald his spiritual mentor. Some readers cannot understand *Phantastes*, for example, yet somehow when they are done reading they feel as if their life has been changed.

MacDonald as writer and preacher had a personal quality of holiness, intelligence, and wisdom that was recognized by several of his noted contemporaries. G. K. Chesterton was proud to write the introduction to the biography written by his son Grenville.[3]

Another literary association was with Reverend Charles Dodgson, who wrote under the name Lewis Carroll. MacDonald served as an encouraging mentor to Dodgson, who visited his home many times and one day handed him an early draft of *Alice in Wonderland*, asking for his opinion, as years later J. R. R. Tolkien was to do with Lewis, who in turn encouraged Tolkien to write more until the story was finished.

The love of telling stories was passed on to his son Ronald, and grandson Philip MacDonald, who wrote detective thrillers such as *The List of Adrian Messenger* and *Murder Gone Mad*. Philip seems a more able craftsman and is definitely easier to read today, but the tone is worldly-wise and hard-boiled compared with his grandfather's. Even so, his grandfather could also write about some very mean characters. While some critics said they were too nasty to be true, several kings of old were just as wicked. When the critics said some of his characters were too good to be true, MacDonald thought some saints were just like them. Both extremes were possible and everything in between, because spiritual choices are possible. His fodder for stories were people he had known as well as imagined.

Grenville says that although his father delighted in moments of play and irresponsible fun, "the atmosphere of sadness so prevalent in his youth was still often about him, yet never obscuring the snow-clad alps of his faith." He extracts the following quote from *The Hope of the Gospel* (1892): "More of sorrowful than of joyful men are always standing about

---

2. George Sayer, *Jack*, 106–8; see especially Sayer, "Lewis and George MacDonald," 24–33.

3. MacDonald, *George MacDonald*.

the everlasting doors that open into the presence of the Most High."[4] At the very least he could empathize with those whose necks were bowed by hardship and trouble, filled with weariness of spirit.

With this in mind we come to one brief reference to suicide in a sermon titled "Life," based on John 10:10. To prepare the way MacDonald says,

> What does the infant need but more life? What does the bosom of his mother give him but life in abundance? What does the old man need, whose limbs are weak and whose pulse is low, but more of the life which seems ebbing from him? Weary with feebleness, he calls upon death, but in reality it is life he wants. It is but the encroaching death in him that desires death. He longs for rest, but death cannot rest; death would be as much an end to rest as to weariness: even weakness cannot rest; it takes strength as well as weariness to rest.[5]

A few sentences later he says,

> Lowsunk life imagines itself weary of life, but it is death, not life, it is weary of. Never a cry went out after the opposite of life from any soul that knew what life is. Why does the poor, worn, out-worn suicide seek death? Is it not in reality to escape from death?—from the death of homelessness and hunger and cold; the death of failure, disappointment, and distraction; the death of the exhaustion of passion; the death of madness—of a household he cannot rule; the death of crime and fear of discovery? He seeks the darkness because it seems a refuge from the death which possesses him.[6]

Thus MacDonald acknowledges that the unconscious prayer of all humanity, in all groaning and travail, is "More life!" And he then moves into what he thinks it meant for Jesus to promise more life, abundant life.

This insight, that the suicide is not rejecting life in its fullness, gives us pause for reflection. To George MacDonald, the suicidal person is rejecting death, actually saying no to familiarity with death in some form that is too heavy to bear.

---

4. MacDonald, *MacDonald*, 343–44. The sermon "Hope of the Gospel" is in MacDonald, *Unspoken Sermons*.

5. MacDonald, *Unspoken*, 297.

6. MacDonald, *Unspoken*, 297.

Charles Haddon Spurgeon (1834—1892)

Spurgeon was a noted preacher in London. He was a Baptist with a mix of Calvinist and Arminian leanings which at times tugged him in different directions. He also fought a long battle with depression, which he acknowledged on some occasions.

In a sermon called "Christ the Destroyer of Death" (1876), Spurgeon spoke about death as the enemy of the human race. Only in difficult and strange circumstances can it seem anything but a foe, for "it is not in nature, except in extreme pain or aberration of mind, or of excessive expectation of glory, for us to be in love with death." To desire death, then, is a departure from our normal abhorrence of death. Then he added, "It was wise of our Creator so to constitute us that the soul loves the body and the body loves the soul, and they desire to dwell together as long as they may, else had there been no care for self-preservation, and suicide would have destroyed the race."[7] He continued by saying,

> It is a first law of our nature that skin for skin, yea, all that a man hath will he give for his life, and thus we are nerved to struggle for existence, and to avoid that which would destroy us. This useful instinct renders death an enemy, but it also aids in keeping us from that crime of all crimes the most sure of damnation if a man commit it wilfully and in his sound mind; I mean the crime of self-murder.[8]

Spurgeon's opinion of suicide is given almost as an aside, but nonetheless it stands out. If a suicidal death is committed by someone of sound mind, then it results in God's condemnation and damnation, which I take to mean (in Spurgeon's mind) exclusion from forgiveness and eternal life. In the remainder of his sermon he returned to the theme of death being an enemy but had nothing more to say on our topic. The context, then, does not really help us get underneath his words with greater understanding. What are we to make of this bold declaration that suicide results in the sureness of damnation "if a man commit it wilfully and in his sound mind"?

Here is a popular distinction made between a sound and unsound mind, but Spurgeon does not give a reason why it is important, why suicide must require damnation if committed with one's mental balance

---

7. Spurgeon, *Sermons* 22, 700–701.
8. Spurgeon, *Sermons* 22, 701.

intact. He makes an assertion but offers no reason to back it up. If he gave a reasoned argument then we could examine it, but he leaves us without one.

Was suicide the unforgivable sin mentioned by Jesus? Based on the expositions Spurgeon gave when he preached on the unforgivable sin, we cannot think so. He correctly identified that sin as blasphemy against the Holy Spirit in the context of Jesus's ministry. In each Gospel book, the historical context of that warning is the same. Jesus's learned enemies could not best him in argument nor deny that he cured the sick, so they claimed that he healed and delivered people from evil spirits by the power of Satan. They witnessed the healings and exorcisms of Jesus, knowing these were done by the endorsement and power of God, then called this ministry evil, as if Jesus borrowed power and authority from an evil source. Such an attitude betrayed hearts turned away from God and willingness to turn other hearts away also. They would not be rescued. This was the immediate and only context in which Jesus spoke of the unforgiveable sin. The motives for the vast majority of suicides, where we can learn anything of context and motivation, are a far cry from this particular sin. And the original historical context is not replicable either. Nowhere in the Bible is suicide referred to as the unforgiveable sin. To his credit, Spurgeon exposited these Gospel passages without reference to suicide.

Did Spurgeon consider suicide unforgivable because there was no time left for repentance? If so, this reason was held in common with a great many others. However, he did not actually say so in his remarks. Many people share the same concern about lacking time for repentance. In chapter 3, we present theological responses to this concern by Dietrich Bonhoeffer and Karl Barth. All human repentance is incomplete and requires the mediation of our savior. None of us are saved by the adequacy of our repentance. Why would Spurgeon limit the effectiveness of the mediation of Christ in regard to this sin without limiting it in regard to other sins? If there is an inconsistency here, it should be challenged.

What more can we say? Spurgeon did qualify his judgment as applying only to suicide by someone possessing a sound mind. Here is recognition that not all suicides are committed by people suffering from mental illness. Motivations for suicide are not restricted to just one group of people with medical afflictions in mind or body. Some people are afraid of enduring shame, public ridicule, or hardship in life, and they look with horror on specific problems that confront them. In several of his sermons, Spurgeon acknowledged that life itself can be more frightful than death. For example, "Never fear dying, beloved. Dying is the last, but the least matter that a Christian has to be anxious about. Fear living—that is a hard battle to fight, a stern discipline to endure, a rough voyage to undergo."[9] Some do look at their circumstances with clear eyes, unclouded by mental illness, and still fear living. But why in his mind a self-chosen death is more reprehensible for those lacking than possessing mental illness is not made clear. There is no biblical passage that says the act of suicide is worse for one category of person than another.

There seems to be a human assumption that divides people into false categories, offering a greater empathy for the emotionally and mentally disturbed person than someone of sound mind whose nerves fail in fear or shame. Perhaps Spurgeon thought that it was a question of accountability, that "to whom much is given much is required," where thinking persons with a sound mind have more to account for than those who do not.[10] There is nothing wrong with this concern about bearing responsibility, but it cannot take us to any final conclusion. We should not presume to know how God judges (or redeems) the person of sound mind whose desire to live is overwhelmed by opposing factors.

Is Suicide to be Equated with Murder?

There is one place, however, where Spurgeon comes close to giving a reason for his belief that suicide closes the door on salvation. In his sermon "Fear of Death" given in 1874 (published posthumously in 1908), he speaks of people who are tempted to end their lives.

> And to end his life by his own hand would be a dreadful deed—it would prove that he was not the child of God, for "You know that no murderer has eternal life abiding in him." I mean, of course, if such a deed were done by anyone in possession of his senses—I am not giving any judgment on those who are not in the possession of reason and who are not accountable for what they do. If any man in his sober senses were to commit suicide, we could entertain no hope of eternal life for him.[11]

---

9. Carter, *2200 Quotations*, 52.
10. Luke 12:48.
11. Spurgeon, *Sermons 55*.

By defining suicide as self-murder, he equates such death with murder and an absence of love, quoting 1 John 3:15 as a proof text that no suicide can inherit eternal life. Should we agree with Spurgeon? Nowhere does any verse of the Bible say that suicide cannot be forgiven. Nowhere does any verse explicitly identify suicide as murder or self-murder, though it is an obvious homicide. In context, 1 John 3:11–18 presents the test of love, as stating the underlying reason for Christians to share material goods (food) with their needy brethren. The opposite of love is hate, exemplified by Cain's murder of Abel. We are to follow our Lord's example of self-offering in service to others. In meeting basic human needs, there will be opportunities for us to give and express love. When we give to the needy, we lay down our lives for one another. There are other ways to exemplify love beyond feeding the hungry and clothing the destitute, but this is the basic message of 1 John 3. Love is to be lived out in practical ways.

Suicide is a homicide, but is it of the same nature as murder? The danger of making this equation is that it judges by the result of the act alone, without regard to intention. Yet even the Mosaic Law recognized there were different types of homicide, in which intention played a role in determining guilt or innocence, as well as appropriate punishment, whether death, banishment to a city of refuge, or acquittal.

Concerning intent, most suicides happen because people are under grievous affliction. With some exceptions, it is usually the case that their intention is not to destroy another innocent person. People may feel they cannot tolerate physical, mental, or emotional pain any longer. Some think they might leave the world a better place by removing themselves. These are not the usual intentions of a murderer motivated by lust, hatred, revenge, or desire for personal gain at someone else's expense. While malice is sometimes a motive for suicide, as in the desire to wound someone else's spirit, it is not as typical as the desire to be free from deep inner pain or heartfelt despair. However, self-loathing may be part of that inner pain.

Is There Room for Dialogue with Spurgeon?

Regarding the hope of God's forgiveness, Spurgeon said in another sermon the same year (1876), "I believe that, often as I transgress, God is more ready to forgive me than I am ready to offend, though, alas, I am all too ready to transgress."[12] Is God not "more ready to forgive" the suicide than the victim was ready to transgress? While we do not speak presumptuously and say that God must forgive in each case, is it not also presumptuous to declare that God cannot forgive in any case? Can we really say which type of sin is "the most sure of damnation"?

In a sermon preached in 1893, Spurgeon said, "However great your sin at present is, do not make it more by insinuating that he cannot forgive you. For of all sins this must be the most cruel, to think that he is unable to forgive. This stabs at Christ's Saviorship, which is his very heart."[13] By suicide do we remove ourselves from the saving power of Christ? If so, is not our power to die made greater than Christ's power to save? Once again, the discussion comes back to how much weight we should give the final moment of life.

Do not think that Christ cannot forgive you. This is a good word for the person tempted to give up in despair. Some think their life can never be forgiven. We affirm Christ has the power to save, regardless of your past and present.

Spurgeon's Personal Struggles

Spurgeon suffered with severe bouts of depression in his adult life.[14] At times, he experienced enough despondency to understand its terrible power to rob of joy and strength. He tried to thank God for his bad days, saying they wounded his heart and prepared him for reaching other troubled souls as a preacher. Spurgeon was a public preacher more than a counselor. In this role he chose to rebuke suicidal thoughts. He did this to honor the gift of life and to dissuade people from succumbing to deadly temptation. On both counts we can applaud him, for he was motivated by a deeply empathetic concern for souls. As his preaching had an overwhelmingly positive impact on his own generation, Spurgeon's life and ministry were a gift from God.

---

12. Spurgeon, *Sermons 22*, 573.
13. Carter, *Quotations*, 81.
14. Amundsen, "Anguish and Agonies." See also Spurgeon, *Lectures to My Students*, for his advice concerning despondency, which has the note of authority from personal experience.

13

G. K. Chesterton (1874–1936)

GILBERT KEITH CHESTERTON WAS a writer and critic who impressed many of his non-Christian contemporaries, including George Bernard Shaw. He wrote as a Roman Catholic Christian in the role of public commentator on intellectual fads, writing with discernment and wit, using humor to stir up the imagination. He also wrote novels and the Father Brown detective stories.

Ingratitude for the Gift of Life

Woven into a wide-ranging discussion is his belief that suicide is a great sin because it is "the refusal to take an interest in existence; the refusal to take the oath of loyalty to life." Writing in response to someone who made light of suicide and thought it should be more widespread, Chesterton said,

> The man who kills a man, kills a man. The man who kills himself, kills all men; as far as he is concerned he wipes out the world. His act is worse (symbolically considered) than any rape or dynamite outrage. For it destroys all buildings: it wipes out all women. The thief is satisfied with diamonds; but the suicide is not: that is his crime. He cannot be bribed, even by the blazing stones of the Celestial City. The thief compliments the things he steals, if not the owner of them. But the suicide insults everything on earth by not stealing it. He defiles every flower by refusing to live for its sake. There is not a tiny creature in the cosmos

at whom his death is not a sneer. When a man hangs himself on
a tree, the leaves might fall off in anger and the birds fly away in
fury: for each has received a personal affront. Of course there
may be pathetic emotional excuses for the act. There often are
for rape, and there almost always are for dynamite.[1]

How does the person who commits suicide kill all other people? What exactly does this mean? Chesterton essentially says the person who commits suicide is ungrateful for the gift of life, because there is a refusal to honor any life. Once, a man told his pastor that he could not live with his despondency any longer, and wanted to discuss the reasons why he was thinking of taking his own life. While probing the man's self-revelations, the pastor turned to this passage in *Orthodoxy* and asked him to read it out loud. Seeing himself as in a mirror, the man realized he lacked a sense of gratitude, and this opened the door to re-examining life experiences and discussing them in depth. The challenge in Chesterton's words shook his resolve to commit suicide.[2]

The spiritual problem of ingratitude corrodes and distorts the human spirit, twisting one's proper response to life, and so is something to be aware of in self-reflection and spiritual counseling. In Rom 1, Paul lists ingratitude as the primary sin against God committed by the human race. In pastoral moments, we pray for a freeing power that helps people overcome this condition. The emphasis here is on seeking God's help. Simply being told we are ungrateful does not make us instantly become more grateful. A cognitive change is required, a recognition of something formerly unnoticed which helps us re-evaluate our situation and life history.

Gratitude is an attitude that may be cultivated, but only to an extent, because there is a spiritual dimension to gratitude that needs to be present to enhance its strength and sustain its longevity. Gratitude includes recognition that a gift has been given in the context of a relationship. By virtue of the gift of life we have a relationship with our Creator God, and in acknowledging this relationality we see the fuller extent to which our life is a gift. Every human being has experienced turning away from God. Yet through reconciling grace, given in the life, death, resurrection, and

---

1. Chesterton, *Orthodoxy*, 65.

2. Earl F. Palmer, private conversation with the author, 2007. Every person cannot be helped by the same kind of conversation. Medical or psychiatric intervention may be needed, as well as communal support. It is helpful, however, to see that people can respond to significant insights and reconsider their choices.

ascension of Jesus Christ, the very God we avoid in fear or indifference offers a restoration of divine fellowship to each and every person.[3] There are opportunities in this God-gifted relationality. Holy Spirit-to-human spirit interaction can take place, wherein each created person may discern a new freedom and purpose to live for God's glory.

Sometimes spiritual healing comes in the context of praying for the healing of memories. There is no ready formula, but any answer God provides can touch the past as well as the present. Anything God's Spirit does regarding our past can open up a new future. In James Loder's study of the spiritual pattern of transformation, he discovered that even people who have gone through horrific experiences and mentally deranging traumas can find spiritual healing, even to the extent that the meaning of the original trauma is changed.[4] Not that past events can be altered as if they did not happen, but the meaning we make of it all can be transformed so those events no longer dominate and distort our lives today. The transformation of meaning-making and spiritual and emotional healing often go together. Regardless of a personal history that weakened the human spirit, marred any sense of joy or eroded a sense of gratitude, the presence of God's Spirit can interact with each life in a transforming process that makes all things new. God's love is a power not a sentiment, and is able to bring order into chaos.

Is the Suicide Like the Martyr?

In the Roman Empire persecutions were not always the same in intensity in every region, but for more than two centuries all people were made aware of the government's deadly hostility towards Christianity, noted in both pagan and Christian literature. In those primal years of Christianity, many non-Christians took note of the vast array of people who treasured the gospel above life itself. It must have seemed highly unusual, even eerie, when those who died cruel deaths did not curse their tormentors in return. Victims praying for gladiators made a deep impression and

---

3. Regarding the attempt to limit the scope of salvation, see Torrance, *Atonement*, 181–92. On the ascension of Jesus and his ongoing priestly mediation, see Torrance, *Atonement*, 265–314. A basic introduction that features the ascension is Christina Baxter, *Ready for the Party?*

4. Loder, *Transforming*. Cf. Seamands, *Redeeming the Past*, which is the more readable of the two but presented with less theoretical support.

Christianity increased in numbers and public esteem.[5] Time and again the martyrs embodied the hardest teaching of Jesus, "love your enemies, pray for those who despitefully use you."

The early Christian martyrs were radically different than the anarchists of Chesterton's day or the suicide bombers of today, where people give their lives in order to murder innocent people. Christian witness, after all, did not bring destruction and mayhem to others. Chesterton reacted when someone belittled the martyrs by implying they were wasted acts of suicide.

> I read a solemn flippancy by some freethinker: he said that a suicide was only the same as a martyr. The open fallacy of this helped to clear the question. Obviously a suicide is the opposite of a martyr. A martyr is a man who cares so much for something outside him, that he forgets his own personal life. A suicide is a man who cares so little for anything outside him, that he wants to see the last of everything. One wants something to begin: the other wants something to end. In other words, the martyr is noble, exactly because (however he renounces the world or execrates all humanity) he confesses this ultimate link with life; he sets his heart outside himself: he dies that something may live. The suicide is ignoble because he has not this link with being: he is a mere destroyer; spiritually, he destroys the universe.[6]

Speaking provocatively, Chesterton does not mean that the act of suicide destroys the physical universe, but in a very personal and subjective sense it does the equivalent as far as one human life is concerned. That person's involvement with everything in the world is obliterated by choice. This, I think, is the meaning of "spiritually, he destroys the universe." Suicide may involve elements of hostility and rejection.

Chesterton then probed Christian history to discover why martyrdom was praised but suicide was condemned. More recently, Jennifer Michael Hecht examined Christianity's negative response to suicide in her book, *Stay*. Hecht points to Phil 1:23–24 and rightfully says, "Even Paul, who was fixated on the afterlife, did not advise suicide."[7] Nor did Paul advise that Christians seek a martyr's death. Yet in the course of Christian history martyrdom became viewed in a more positive light than suicide. Chesterton reflects.

5. Hurtado, *Why On Earth*
6. Chesterton, *Orthodoxy*, 65–66.
7. Hecht, *Stay*, 49.

> The Christian attitude to the martyr and the suicide was not what is so often affirmed in modern morals. It was not a matter of degree. It was not that a line must be drawn somewhere, and that the self-slayer in exaltation fell within the line, the self-slayer in sadness just beyond it. The Christian feeling evidently was not merely that the suicide was carrying martyrdom too far. The Christian feeling was furiously for one and furiously against the other: these two things that looked so much alike were at opposite ends of heaven and hell. One man flung away his life; he was so good that his dry bones could heal cities in pestilence. Another man flung away life; he was so bad that his bones would pollute his brethren's. I am not saying this fierceness was right; but why was it so fierce?[8]

Chesterton concluded that the affirmation of martyrdom and the rejection of suicide were both done for the same reason. Both stances depend on the same principle that God created the world and gave the gift of life, therefore human life is worthy of preservation and is not for us to reject or throw away. As one Roman Catholic scholar summarized, the martyr chooses to accept death to affirm a principle of life, the Socratic principle that it is better to do right than wrong, or to reform communal life by bearing witness to the truth no matter what the cost. The suicide takes his life into his own hands and affirms that it is right to get rid of one's life under some circumstances, which involves a denial of hope.[9]

When Embracing Life is More than Optimism

Conceptually ancient Judaism separated the world from its divine source, unlike other ancient religions, seeing the world as finite and contingent, not eternal or divine. In other words, it did not have to come into existence. The fact that this universe exists at all is by God's decision and permission. Chesterton affirmed this when he said, "God was personal, and had made a world separate from Himself."[10] God designed and created our world to exist as something separate from his eternal being, even allowing the human race to live on this planet with a measure of freedom which can and has been abused.

---

8. Chesterton, *Orthodoxy*, 66.
9. Rev. James V. Schall, SJ, communication with the author, 24 June 2013.
10. Chesterton, *Orthodoxy*, 71. For God to create and bring into existence that which did not have to be brought into existence entails a personal choice. This is the opposite of necessity.

As we now live under conditions troubled by conflict and confusion, we find plenty of reasons to be pessimistic about this present age. Pessimism grows in our thoughts as we experience the distresses of the human race. Yet there is also something that counters our pessimism. It is not false optimism that helps us. Rather, we have an invitation to enter into spiritual fellowship with God. This is deeper and more enduring than optimism. This invitation is both for this life and the life to come. In this life much is hidden from our sight, yet we are promised a greater vision of God's glory and eternal purpose in the next. Therefore, in the light of our resurrection hope, God empowers us to make new choices. "The Christian optimism is based on the fact that we do not fit in to the world,"[11] that is, that we do not see the current state of affairs here as either totally right or set in its final form. Both nature and human community need to be repaired before this world can become anything like our permanent home. Because this is not our permanent home there is reason for hope. The discomfort we feel or emotional pain we experience cannot define us and make us unfit to live here. Furthermore, we may love this current world without trusting everything in it. We may live here precisely because it is not our final home and because we live in the light of our true home that is yet to come. This requires living in hope based on God's revelatory action in the history of ancient Israel, culminating in the life of Jesus Christ, whose promise to all the nations is still unfolding.

The Resurrection of Jesus Is the Sign of Hope for the World's Coming Renewal

Jesus of Nazareth embodies the meaning of this hope, assuring us the world will be made new in the future God is preparing. Our confidence is not a subjective optimism, but is based on the fact of his total life, with God's affirmation sealed by his death and resurrection in our space-time history. Through his triumph over the power of death we are given a sneak preview of the healing that is coming to all the world.[12]

---

11. Chesterton, *Orthodoxy*, 72.

12. There are large numbers of people who cannot hope in the coming resurrection day if they cannot accept that Jesus rose from the dead in space-time history. Is Christianity based on God's action in reality or on a fable? Ultimately, however, accepting the historicity of the resurrection is not enough if we stop there and do not pursue the meaning of the event, which is found in the context of God's messianic promises and the life of Jesus, and opens up opportunities to experience God through him in the

The resurrection of Jesus was utterly unique—the great singularity of the universe—yet in an important sense it was not an isolated event that can be atomized and separated from its context. This is because its significance cannot be understood apart from the person and character of Jesus of Nazareth. His earlier healing miracles pointed to the nearness of God's providential activity, present in his messiahship as he actively addressed victims devastated by suffering and loss. If read correctly, the miracles are not brain teasers for modern people to overcome, nor were they designed as thrills for ancient people. They were not at odds with reality but rather conformed reality to the Creator's saving purpose.[13] They were signs that pointed away from themselves to the reality of forgiveness, healing, and renewal for the people of Israel, with gentiles also benefitting when in contact with Jesus. These were preludes.

In my understanding, given ancient pagan or Jewish mindsets, the character of Jesus as presented in the canonical Gospels was humanly uninventable. If he did not exist and live and work as the New Testament Gospels say he did, no one could have imagined him. Not given

---

Spirit today. Insofar as there is personal interest but also difficult intellectual hurdles, the following resources may be of help. Craig, *Reasonable Faith*, is a good short introduction to questions about miracles and the historical reliability of testimony, which also includes chapters focusing on the early resurrection accounts; see also Habermas and Licona, *Case for the Resurrection*. Lengthier and more demanding works include: Allison, *Resurrection of Jesus*; Licona, *Resurrection of Jesus*; Eddy and Boyd, *Jesus Legend*; and Wright, *Resurrection of the Son*. Books of this size sometimes require constant reference to shorter outlines so the reader does not get lost in the woods. Wright relates that the resurrection event worked in tandem with Jesus's known character in order to convince his disciples that he was the Messiah of Israel, and that neither the Jews nor the gentiles spiritualized the resurrection to mean anything other than bodily resurrection. Allison does not side with all apologetics but finds grounds for the historicity of the resurrection event. Cf. Craig, "Dale Allison." Torrance, *Space, Time and Resurrection*, demonstrates the interconnectedness of Jesus's resurrection with every major theme in the New Testament. Torrance affirms that this ultimate event took place in our space-time dimension in relation to other ultimates, such as the creation of the world, the love of God, and the incarnation of God's Son, which altogether provides the framework for understanding the resurrection event itself. Additionally, the resurrection of Jesus has consequences for the future of humanity.

13. Concerning debates about the miraculous, see Earman, *Hume's Abject Failure*; Geivett and Habermas, *In Defense of Miracles*. The possibility of miracles is a separate question than whether a particular account is a report of an actual event, or whether it is accurately reported. However, these arguments offer reasons not to approach all historical accounts with an anti-supernatural bias. Scientists also offer reflections on the compatibility of an orderly universe with an openness to God's providential interaction: MacKay, *Science, Chance, and Providence*; Polkinghorne, *Science and Providence*; Pollard, *Transcendence and Providence*.

the worldviews of ancient times. What happened in his interaction with people, including miracles of healing, was the outflow of his own relationality with God. The resurrection is tied directly to Jesus's character and relationality with God, whom he addressed intimately (and transcendently) as "My Father." All his previous words, responses, and actions flowed from that relational center.

Because of who Jesus was in his relationship with God, he endured suffering and death, which was the opposite of any human expectation for someone divinely honored. Unexpectedly, he was raised from the dead. This unified miracle (life, death, resurrection) accompanies and fulfills the act of human reconciliation with God, which is God's intentional gift to us. In this death and resurrection, two sides of the same coin, is a sneak preview of what is to come when God renews the world. That will never happen for us because we are worthy, but because the renewal of all creation and the human family abounds to God's glory. The ascension of Jesus means that he remains connected to our present troubles and our destiny, ministering and ruling to bring us into the fullness of God's eternal purpose.[14]

Faith in this resurrection hope is why many Christian martyrs are able to forsake everything they hold dear, even life itself, in order to honor Jesus the Messiah. Those who love him still die for his name's sake. Their focus is on something other than themselves, and their ultimate goal is not to escape life but to bear witness to the truth. Likewise, for many of us who are not persecuted, faith in the resurrection hope is why we refuse to let pessimism speak the last word over our lives, why we cannot give in to suicidal thoughts. We can leave this world, if forced to, because we are made for God. And because we are made for God, we can stay in this world rather than depart, seeking divine support in days of misery or loss. If we are troubled in spirit or victims of crushing events, we can live in the light of the resurrection that is coming. We affirm the coming day when the reality of heaven becomes the reality of earth, and God's will is done "on earth as in heaven."

Living in the Light of the World to Come

To use a recent example, Mother Teresa saw emaciated people sifting through garbage dumps in Calcutta or Cairo, earnestly looking for

---

14. Baxter, *Ready*, 23–41.

cantaloupe rinds or scraps of food. Mother Teresa was not empowered to minister to starving people because she was an optimist. She knew the dark side of the world and at times endured horrible depression in her spirit, but she lived and worked without being guided solely by what she saw and felt within herself. She was guided by the future reality of the resurrection, by the light and truth of the world to come.

Mother Teresa had a friend, Mark Buntain, who also lived in Calcutta (renamed Kolkata) as an Assemblies of God missionary. Buntain built a hospital with funding from Canadian and American congregations, established a training program for nurses, and started soup kitchens for the destitute. Not content to live safely isolated from those who lived in abject poverty, he found people who were sick and uncared for, some too weak even to walk. They would sit or lie in the street, often covered with sores. Yet he would pick them up and carry them in his arms to his car, then have his driver take them to the hospital. Some of these were starving, and some actually had Hansen's disease (leprosy). He gently hugged them and spoke kind words in Bengali, in order to give them hope through compassionate care and medical attention.[15] Buntain was not guided by visible conditions but by the future reality of the coming resurrection. If God is going to remake the world in righteousness, then treating the poor and the broken with respect and kindness is living in harmony with the future rather than the present.

If God is going to remake the world in righteousness, then saying "No" to suicidal thoughts is one way you or I can live in the light of the future resurrection. Our lives can be guided by a reality that will one day heal and replace our temporary pain.

Yet perhaps Mother Teresa and Mark Buntain are somehow extraordinary. In case anyone thinks only rare people can live in the light of the world to come, like those who forsake comfort to work in harsh places, let me give an example from a more ordinary life. A Christian real estate agent recently saw a struggling single mom enter the business world as a competing realtor. As he observed how difficult it was for this new agent to garner clients, he felt led by God's Spirit to do something unusual. He consulted with his wife and they prayed together. Then he gave the new realtor two of his own good listings. Both opportunities quickly led to

---

15. Wead, *Compassionate Touch*. My family had multiple contacts with Buntain as well as his sister's family, which personalized and affirmed the picture presented by Wead.

sales. She gratefully pocketed the commissions, as he intended. This was a considerable gift because he too had a family to feed and support.

In the immediate moment, it cost him something to help her in this practical way. He was not guided by the greed and cynicism of our age, with its ruling principle of getting all we can for ourselves as quickly as possible. Rather, his gift was guided by the light of the coming resurrection, when God will show the true meaning of generosity and grace. How can we compare time and money lost today with the gift of a second life after death? Some things that look like sacrifices today are anticipations. When we live as if we really believe in this future we will probably look strange to a lot of people. This realtor who gave away two listings looked crazy to his coworkers. In similar but quiet ways, unseen by the vast majority, we might be used in God's plan to change the world, if only in our own small neighborhood. Then, like a pebble tossed in a pond, with outstretching ripples of grace, what began close to home can touch other lives and move out far beyond our range of vision.

14

Paul Tillich (1886–1965)

PAUL TILLICH'S THREE-VOLUME *SYSTEMATIC Theology* was a landmark in theological discourse after World War II. Some theological liberals of an older generation claimed that Tillich saved Christianity for them as an intellectual commitment, for Tillich spoke to both mind and heart in a compelling way. Others argued that his existentialism distorted his christological teaching, making it conform to philosophical idealism rather than to biblical affirmations of the incarnation and atonement. Reinhold Niebuhr once spoke of Tillich walking a tightrope between the boundaries of metaphysics and theology, observing that even pedestrians who cannot walk the rope themselves can recognize when a gifted acrobat takes a fall. However, debates about Tillich's philosophy and theology will not be presented here. We will only explore some of his insights into the human condition, especially observations on suicide and the ambiguities of life.

The Encroaching Threat of Despair

Our finite lives are lived out in such a way that estrangement, suffering, and loneliness are factors of human existence. Some forms of suffering are an expression of our finitude, while others are a result of estrangement. Our participation in community is always possible. Love drives us towards this participation, but rejection prevents it and leads to estrangement, which becomes a structure of destruction. Rejection can lead to hostility towards others, but also hostility against one's self.

"Destruction of others and self-destruction are interdependent in the dialectics of loneliness."[1]

In the structures of our existence, finitude always includes insecurity and uncertainty. For all of us, the courage to accept our finitude must come from an ultimate source, "the power of the dimension of the eternal." We have to look to the transcendent source of hope, for if we look to what is limited and finite to solve our problems then we ask more of something in our world than it can possibly give. If we look to anything limited for help and rescue, this misstep can become a destructive force that distorts our world. As a destructive force, it can be directed outwardly against those who represent a threat or directed inwardly against the fearful person in his or her own thoughts, moving him or her towards restless cynicism and the experience of emptiness. This type of move is always possible, either inwardly or outwardly, because there are structures of destruction within our finite existence. Yet Tillich adds, "Structures of destruction are not the only mark of existence. They are counterbalanced by structures of healing and reunion of the estranged."[2]

Evil is seen as the self-destructive consequence of sin. Structures of evil drive a person to despair. Despair is not merely a psychological or ethical problem, though it is both. Despair "is the final index" of the human predicament, the boundary line beyond which no one can go. Tillich borrows the description of despair offered by Kierkegaard in *Sickness Unto Death*, where "death" means beyond possible healing. In despair, people find themselves to be in inescapable conflict.

> It is the conflict, on the one hand, between what one potentially is and therefore ought to be and, on the other hand, what one actually is in the combination of freedom and destiny. The pain of despair is the agony of being responsible for the loss of the meaning of one's existence and of being unable to recover it. One is shut up in one's self and in the conflict with one's self. One cannot escape, because one cannot escape from one's self. It is out of this situation that the question arises whether suicide may be a way of getting rid of one's self.[3]

In this ongoing conflict, suicidal ideation has a wider significance than the number of suicidal acts can indicate. "First of all, there is a suicidal

---

1. Tillich, *Systematic Theology II*, 72.
2. Tillich, *Systematic Theology II*, 74–75.
3. Tillich, *Systematic Theology II*, 75.

tendency in life generally, the longing for rest without conflict. The human desire for intoxication is a consequence of this longing (compare Freud's doctrine of the death instinct)."[4] The desire for rest without conflict has affinity with George MacDonald, who thought that most suicides do not desire to end life, rather they desire to end some form of death. Yet there are other conditions to be considered.

> Second, in every moment of intolerable, insuperable, and meaningless pain there is the desire to escape the pain by getting rid of one's self. Third, the situation of despair is most conspicuously a situation in which the desire to get rid of one's self is awake and the image of suicide appears in a most tempting way. Fourth, there are situations in which the unconscious will to life is undermined and a psychological suicide takes place in terms of non-resistance to threatening annihilation. Fifth, whole cultures preach the self-negation of the will, not in terms of physical or psychological suicide, but in terms of the emptying of life of all finite contents so that the entrance into the ultimate identity is possible.[5]

This short summary shows there are multiple conditions and motivations that can underly a suicidal impulse, ones shared across cultural contexts. Tillich urged Christian theologians to rethink the question of the self-negation of life in view of these facts about the origins of suicidal ideation. "The external act of suicide should not be singled out for special moral and religious condemnation. Such a practice is based on the superstitious idea that suicide definitely excludes the operation of saving grace. At the same time, the inner suicidal trends in everyone should be considered as an expression of human estrangement."[6]

Yet, however successful suicide may seem as an attempt to escape the situation of despair on a temporal level, "it is not successful in the dimension of the eternal. The problem of salvation transcends the temporal level, and the experience of despair itself points to this truth."[7]

---

4. Tillich, *Systematic Theology II*, 75. Tillich links the longing for rest without conflict with Freud's death instinct.
5. Tillich, *Systematic Theology II*, 75–76.
6. Tillich, *Systematic Theology II*, 76.
7. Tillich, *Systematic Theology II*, 76.

The Strange Ambiguity of the Inner Life:

Arnold Bennett's novel *Clayhanger* tells the story of a young man in the Edwardian era who had responsibilities and family expectations placed on his shoulders at a young age, in a time of changing fortunes. By the end of the story, he is still young but has already experienced strain and disappointment. As he took over his father's business and assumed responsibility for his family circle, he knew instinctively that he was not going to do as well as his father. He had also learned that personal setbacks come when least expected. Yet all in all, at the novel's conclusion we read that "he braced himself to the exquisite burden of life."

The hopefulness in this expression seems unshakeable, like the brightness of spring sunshine. Yet we wonder how long it can last. What gives the hopeful attitude endurance in a life beset with problems? We know from firsthand experience many of the things that make life a burden emotionally, physically, financially, or socially. What, then, is woven into the fabric that helps us feel that life is to be cherished, even an "exquisite burden"? What makes us embrace this special privilege and not turn away from responsibility? And how long can we possess this inner strength and buoyancy of spirit before losing it? This is the subject for novelists who have deep insight into human nature, or for the kind of philosopher who can teach wisdom rather than merely analyze the logic of a sentence. For Tillich, the human person carries ambiguity.

> In the ambiguity of pain and pleasure, there is an anticipation of the ambiguity of life instinct and death instinct. The latter two phrases are questionable tools for grasping phenomena which are deeply rooted in the self-creative function of life. It is one of the contradictions of nature that a living being affirms its life and denies it. The self-affirmation of life is usually taken for granted, its negation rarely, and if the latter is taught, as in Freud's doctrine of Todestrieb (poorly translated by "death instinct"), even otherwise orthodox pupils rebel. But the facts, given in immediate self-awareness, prove the ambiguity of life as described by Freud (and seen by Paul when he speaks of the sadness of this world which leads to death).[8]

Here, Tillich affirms what Freud said about ambiguity in the inner life, about desires that concurrently move in two different directions. Freud acknowledged two basic instincts: Eros (the need to give and receive love)

---

8. Tillich, *Systematic Theology III*, 56–57.

and the destructive instinct. Freud's concept of the "death instinct" has been explored by many psychologists. Put in simple language, it refers to the ways a human person can have strange urges that are destructive and not life-enhancing. Psychiatrist Karl Menninger has written an accessible book on the subject, which has a lot to say about suicidal ideation as well as other manifestations of self-destructive attitudes and behavior.[9]

Tillich says the German word "Todestrieb" contains a richer nuance than the English phrase "death instinct" can convey. It is a conjunction of the German word for death, "Tod," with the word "Trieb," which can mean "urge" or "impulse," but also refers to the green shoot of a plant or tree, to something living that is small but growing larger. As a theologian, Tillich knew there were biblical references to foul or deadly growth within an individual human life, as well as within all social expressions of the human race, something competing with and opposed to growth in righteousness, wisdom, and harmony. He sometimes defined *Todestrieb* as the "drive for death." Sometimes this drive involves the appeal of returning to an earlier simplicity or comfort level, a move which does not always appear negative.[10]

Not all temptation comes from outside of a person's life, as from a friend's suggestion or invisible demonic influences. While these possibilities are considered in classical theology to be real possibilities, these are not the only sources of temptation. Speaking in traditional terms, there are temptations from the world, the flesh, and the devil. In Paul's usage "the flesh" represents the orientation of our total being in opposition to God, to the aspirations of our fallen nature. It is a metaphor rather than a physical reference. In Rom 7, Paul refers to carrying "this body of death." This burden was more than physical weakness and mortality. He meant all that happens in mood and outlook, desire and intention, under the distorting condition of sin.

---

9. Menninger, *Man Against Himself*. There are other theories of aggression that depart from Freud, but Freud touches on an ambivalence that is real: we may either be aggressive against others or against our own self. Cf. Pannenberg, *Anthropology in Theological Perspective*, 142–53.

10. Tillich, *Systematic Theology II*, 54. Part of this drive to get rid of oneself is the desire to escape the pain of the never satisfied libido (the desire to get rid of biological or sexual tensions), which remains unsatisfied even if used in an unrestrained way. This lack of satisfaction is a mark of deep human estrangement and a contradiction of created goodness, especially when we use another person for pleasure but do not want the other person for his or her own sake.

Paul actually spoke in the present tense about this problem, saying that it is because things are wrong within himself that he responds improperly to God's law, or intends to do good but does not actually do it, or does something bad that he really does not want to do (Rom 7:14–25).[11] In doing so, he spoke of himself as a mature Christian, not a spiritually immature one or beginning novice. The problem was not in the past, not something he had already overcome, but one that was ever present with him. Even with periods of apparent calm, our inner life can seem like a storm or battlefield at times. This does not mean we are abandoned by God.

Jesus's words about the principal source of personal corruption in Mark 7:14–23 are also important here, because they focus on the inner life, indicating that all aspects of human nature require redemption and transformation. Greed and jealousy, anger and resentment spring from within the heart, the inner reality of being human. Our will, imagination, attitudes, and desires are tainted to some degree. Much that is good and positive resides within, but not in unmixed purity. For this reason, we cannot romanticize our own feelings and trust only to our heart in all decision making. "Let your heart guide you" is neither classical Jewish nor Christian teaching. Emotions are important to consider, but not the ultimate determination of what is good or true. Human emotions and desires can be distorted, confused, leading us away from what is good for ourselves or good for others. As the prophet Jeremiah said, "The heart is more deceitful than all else and is desperately sick; who can understand it?" (Jer 17:9. Cf. Ps 14:1; Prov 12:20; Ezek 18:31).

Novelists from Victor Hugo to Cormack McCarthy show the harm we are capable of doing with or without much prompting by circumstances. The classic detective stories of Patricia Wentworth and Agatha Christie often portray situations where murder springs from the hearts of common, ordinary people, rather than criminal psychopaths and sociopaths with long histories of wrongdoing.[12] This was very intentional with

---

11. This is a widely accepted reading of Paul in Rom 7, though there are alternative readings: see Barclay, *Paul and the Gift*. The reference to spiritual struggle in the Christian's inner life can be derived from other passages in the Pauline collection, however one chooses to interpret the thrust and focus of Rom 7, so this summary does not depend on one passage alone. Charles Cranfield would also remind us that Rom 7 and 8 must be held together for a complete picture of the Christian life. The negative struggle is told in Rom 7 and the positive affirmation of the Holy Spirit's mediating assistance is told in Rom 8, and both are true simultaneously. Cranfield, *Romans*, 167–82.

12. This is done especially in Patricia Wentworth's Miss Silver stories and in Agatha

these two gifted writers, both Christians, because they shared the insight that common, ordinary people have the potential to do evil. Especially when provoked by the nasty actions of others, or enticed by their own vices and opportunities to enrich themselves. One underlying message that both Wentworth and Christie wove into their stories is that none of us can neglect the moral struggles we face within ourselves, not even at first onset when an impulse seems small and insignificant. Just as flowering plants can grow in a garden so can weeds that need to be uprooted. With some particular human feelings and impulses, resistance or spiritual assistance is required in order to enhance our humanity rather than diminish it.[13]

Tillich said preachers should stop talking about sins (plural) as immoral acts, because it gave the false impression that we could divide people into righteous or unrighteous, those who sinned and those who did not.[14] Sins flow from sin (singular), a state of being, a condition which all humans share. To make a new start, he advised using the word "estrangement" rather than "sin." We are estranged from God, the ground of being, and this makes estrangements between humans more acutely painful and pervasive as well. Without exploring all he said, there is one continuity here with the Protestant Reformers. They put the emphasis on sin as condition rather than sin as acts, for acts of sin and wrongdoing derive from the underlying condition.

The phrase "total corruption" means that sin pervades and touches every part of our lives and relationships, even though much goodness and giftedness is also present. Our corruption does not mean we are all as bad as we can possibly be. If that were the case we would all be like demons and life would be intolerable, for we would cease to be human in every way. The image of God is not totally absent in any of us. Something of the original created goodness can shine through in various ways by the providential and sustaining grace of the Holy Spirit. Each of us may do much good for which our neighbors thank us. Yet such is our condition that we cannot find God without God's help, and need miracles of mercy.

Christie's Miss Marple stories.

13. Of course human experience is more complex than gardening images convey. Sometimes there is a sense of alienation or a haunting sense of absence, an emptiness that needs to be filled (Augustine pointed to longings in which we are restless until God's presence fills them).

14 C. S. Lewis thought that the sins of the flesh are bad enough, but the sins of the spirit are worse. See Lewis, *Mere Christianity*, 102–3.

While I may not be as bad as I can possibly be, in every way I have the potential to be morally inadequate, ungrateful, or confused. Under certain circumstances of opportunity or provocation, I may choose to become extremely bad. A slight fever is not always an overwhelming problem, but it is not the same as a normal temperature and promises further problems if no cure is found.

In historic Christian theology, sin is primarily a dynamic, relational problem due to being separated from fellowship with our Creator, and so all of life, individual and social, is touched by it. Freedom requires that a new relationship with God be put in place, ultimately a new creation. Some contemporary critics of Christianity complain that we talk too much about sin and wrongdoing. Lest we feel any embarrassment, Bernard Ramm reminds us that all major secular thinkers developed secular doctrines of sin in their worldviews, because they recognized how pervasive and intractable the deeply rooted problems of the human race actually are. Hobbes, Spinoza, Voltaire, Rousseau, Kant, Hegel, Marx, Freud, Skinner, and Camus all had to say something about the twisted reality of humanity.[15] The condition of sin as a countering distortion of the exalted human condition, condoning neglect, erupting in aggressions and warfare, is too empirically verifiable to be neglected. From the Brothers Grimm to J. R. R. Tolkien, our folktales, dreams, and myths remind us that we live with both delightful and frightful possibilities all around us. Time and again we find confirmation that biblical revelation is realistic about the human condition. Christians also have a message of forgiveness and renewal that offers hope and light in the midst of darkness.

The Composition of Human Life Includes Spirit:

Tillich continues his anthropological discussion with reference to suicide:

> In every conscious being, life is aware of its exhaustibility; it dimly feels that it must come to an end, and the symptoms of its exhaustion not only make it conscious of this fact but also awaken a longing for it. It is not an acute state of pain (although this also may happen); it is the existential awareness of one's finitude which poses the question of whether the continuation of finite existence is worth the burden of it. But as long as there is life, this tendency is counterbalanced by the self-affirmation of life, the desire to maintain its identity even if it is the identity of

15. Ramm, *Offense to Reason*, 10-37.

the life of a finite, exhaustible individual. Thus suicide actualizes an impulse latent in all life. This is the reason for the presence of suicidal fantasies in most people but the comparative rarity of actual suicide. It makes unambiguous what, according to the nature of life, is valid only in its ambiguity.[16]

Tillich said that all "these factors have been considered without regard to the dimensions of spirit and of history." Any discussion of suicide apart from reflecting on the aspect of spirit will be incomplete. Any organic plant or animal experiences growth and decay, but in considering human beings, we cannot limit ourselves to such concepts, because the role of the human spirit must be taken into account. The human race has always known we are animals with physical needs but also that we are more than animals. From Plato to Freud, great thinkers about the human condition have acknowledged that the human being is spirit.[17]

While human life does involve physical and mental growth and decay, the role of the spirit is always interactive and relational. Thus, it is an important factor from infancy to old age. For Tillich, we cannot experience ourselves as human beings without being aware that we are "determined" in our nature by spirit, by spirit that both seeks to integrate what is within us and reaches out to what is beyond us. There is a dynamic to human life pertaining to the human spirit which makes us self-reflective, relational, and aspirational, fully able to dream and plan and cooperate with others. While we participate in life on one level as an animal, we are much more than animals because we are also spirit. Every human spirit may be encountered by the divine Spirit and receive affirmation and love in Spirit-to-spirit interaction, which, as James Loder has testified, can lead to amazing insights and transformations that provide mental and spiritual healing.[18]

Having Desires

Tillich wrote far more about spirit than can be told here. It seems important to add that it is not enough to say suicidal ideation is part of the

---

16. Tillich, *Systematic Theology III*, 57.

17. In conversation, Freud said, "Yes, the spirit is everything. . . . Mankind has always known that it possesses spirit; I had to show it that there are also instincts." Binswanger, *Sigmund Freud*, 81.

18 Loder, *Logic of the Spirit*. See also Loder, *Transforming*; Seamands, *Redeeming*, adds confirmation in a writing style more easily accessible.

contradictory aspect of human life, an impulse toward decay as opposed to growth, something latent residing within us. The human spirit plays a vital role, impacting both emotions and thoughts, impacting both our sense of self-identity and the meaning we make of our life in interaction with others. It makes a tremendous difference whether the human spirit is strong or weak to the meaning we make out of our relationships and life experiences. In pastoral prayer, we ask that the weak or wounded human spirit may be taken up and strengthened by the presence of the Holy Spirit, which ministers divine comfort and strength so that the human spirit is renewed in Christ's love and given its true range of freedom.

Furthermore, we can see that Tillich's willingness to read Freud and look for areas of agreement, not just disagreement, is instructive. There is room for dialog that complements both fields of study. This is not an apology for Freud, whose theories are laden with problems of their own, but a reading of Freud can accompany a wider critical reading in clinical psychology. Some of Freud's theories are strange and involve highly subjective judgments, now considered worthy of rejection or modification.[19] Yet we may still find areas of surprising affinity in some of his concerns and insights. For example, Freud helped people to understand their own desires in order to gain a greater mastery over them which was previously unattainable, a freedom that involved choice.[20] To this end, origins of desires were traced (if possible) and discussed in therapy. Freud did not think that all desires should reign supreme and be expressed without regard for the welfare of others. Understanding the origin of something, however, does not determine whether it is good or bad, harmful or beneficial. The classical tradition of pastoral care includes much advice about examining one's desires in order to make them objects of contemplation, prayer, and when appropriate, resistance and repentance.

Desires may be contradictory to each other or to our own best interest. According to prophetic and apostolic revelation (approached with hermeneutical care), some of our desires are contrary to God's design and highest intention for human life. Given this condition, we cannot urge people to follow their desires indiscriminately with a free reign, as

---

19. Crews, *Unauthorized Freud*, is a good beginning place. A longer study is Webster, *Why Freud Was Wrong*.

20. Freud affirmed this freedom as the goal of his therapy. He said, "after all, analysis does not set out to make pathological reactions impossible, but to give the patient's ego *freedom* to decide one way or the other." Freud, *Ego and the Id*, 40. A person who is successfully helped by therapy has enhanced capacity for choices.

though all desires were of equal value or able to enhance their welfare. Suicidal desires do not define who the person is or serve as true indicators of what the person should do, because, as with some other types of desires, these desires are not filled with integrity and truth.

There is an identity confusion when desires are seen as determining the composition and identity of a human life. This is why we must help people in counseling to see that desires are not what they *are*, not that which has the power or authority to define their lives, but rather desires are something they *have*. You are not your desires; desires are something you have. In your own meaning-making and self-understanding, when desires become something you have rather than what you are, they become dis-embedded from your understanding of self.[21] This means you can examine your desires in new freedom, choosing for them or against them. You can bring them into God's light in prayer. You can hold them close and cherish them, or reject and fight against them as unworthy to direct your life and shape your dreams and personal commitments. This freedom is essential to the fullness of human life because it makes new choices possible. Even Freud, as a psychological pioneer and person who had no time for religious faith, worked towards the goal of helping patients discover this freedom.[22] Freud cannot be our theological guide, for his ideas about the origin of religion are dismissive of God's reality—and when analyzed are unconvincing.[23] Freud simply posited his atheism as fact, and refused to explore the possibility of revelation, or how humans would actually respond if created for spiritual yearning and awareness of their Creator. But as an anthropological guide, he does see that the fullness of human nature, insofar as it was known to him, requires a freedom that includes choices, even a choice for self-control rather than its abandonment.

---

21. For the concept of being "embedded" in an inadequate form of meaning-making, see Kegan, *Evolving Self*. For a short summary, see Kegan, "There the Dance Is," 403–40. For an in-depth discussion of the transformation of meaning-making which has relational, spiritual, and emotional dimensions, see the works by Loder.

22. Freud, *Ego*, 40. A person who is successfully helped by psychotherapy is made capable of choice for or against pathological reactions.

23. McGrath, *Intellectuals Don't Need God*, 94–100; Plantinga, *Knowledge and Christian Belief*, 41–44. For a critique of Freud's use of anthropological evidence to support his theory, see Schmidt, *Origin and Growth of Religion*, 103–15. Vitz argues that Freud failed to establish a connection between belief in God and neurotic childhood experience; conversely, there is detailed clinical evidence "that rejection of God can be a consequence of unconscious neurotic needs." See Vitz, *Sigmund Freud's Christian Unconscious*, 220–21.

Is it Harmful to Suppress or Reject Personal Desires?

Yet when we talk about desires, we often find evidence of a common misunderstanding. When many people hear Christian pastors preach or counsel people to deny a desire that is harmful or sinful, they think they are being told to repress a part of their life. This bothers people who commonly think that to deny or reject something which they desire is to repress it. Yet this is not the case. It has become a common belief on a popular level in North America, almost a mantra, that "repressing" desires is unhealthy and may even lead to severe psychological problems. Unfortunately, what is at work here is a major confusion about the meaning of suppression and the meaning of repression. Armand Nicholi taught psychiatry at Harvard Medical School, offering a popular course comparing Sigmund Freud and C. S. Lewis on ultimate issues.[24] Nicholi says Lewis understood the difference between repression and suppression.[25] This is an important distinction which needs to be reviewed.

Lewis said, "Repression is when something is thrust into the subconscious (usually at a very early age) and can now come to mind only in a disguised or unrecognisable form."[26] Freud famously reminded us that what is repressed must come out one way or another. Yet suppression is not repression because it is the conscious control of one's impulses. "When an adolescent or an adult is engaged in resisting a conscious desire, he is not dealing with a repression nor is he in the least danger of creating a repression."[27] Nicholi says that by confusing repression and suppression, "many in our culture concluded that any control of sexual impulses is unhealthy. Lewis argued that this is nonsense. In reality, lack of control is what is unhealthy."[28] Surrender to every desire can lead to infidelity, lies, sneaking, concealment, and physical disease in the sexual realm, to say nothing of relational and emotional problems.[29]

Likewise those who have not learned to control their problems with anger or other destructive impulses are often a menace to others during times when they are under acute stress. Furthermore, angry outbursts do

---

24. Nicholi, *Question of God*. Nicholi's important comparison is enlarged by Terry Lindvall, "Freud and Lewis on Jokes, Humor and Laughter."
25. Nicholi, *Question*, 136.
26. Lewis, *Mere Christianity*, 101–102.
27. Lewis, *Mere Christianity*, 102.
28. Nicholi, *Question*, 136.
29. A reworking of Lewis, *Mere Christianity*, 100.

not generally minimize or dissipate the feeling of anger. It is difficult to see how the absence of control can lead to a better human society. This concern applies to the problem of suicidal ideation. Those who cannot exercise control over impulses are in danger of a weaker response when impulses move in a destructive direction or when frustration mounts in their daily lives. (Pannenberg raises this concern, below.)

15

Karl Barth (1886–1968)

KARL BARTH IS OFTEN mentioned in any short list of great theologians. Many today rank him with Irenaeus, Athanasius, Augustine, Thomas Aquinas, Martin Luther, and John Calvin, considering the breadth and depth of his theological output.

Barth's Letter to a Suicidal Prisoner

When already famous as a professor and prodigious author, Barth also did more humble works of ministry without fanfare. For example, he went regularly into the prison at Basel and preached to the prisoners. This "congregation" responded to his direct speech and proved a more receptive audience than anticipated.[1] One prisoner wrote Barth and indicated that nothing helped him overcome his despondency. He said he considered taking a "final step," which Barth understood to be a reference to suicide. Barth wrote in reply, dated December 20, 1961:

> Since you obviously want something from me, you cannot be serious in expecting me to judge you harshly. But can I give you any supporting counsel?
>
> You say you plunge deeply into the Bible in vain. You say you also pray in vain. You are clearly thinking of a "final step," but you shrink back from it. Have I understood you correctly?

---

1. See a collection of some of these sermons in Barth, *Deliverance to the Captives*.

> First, regarding your prayers. How do you know they are in vain? God has his own time, and he may well know the right moment to lift the double shadow that now lies over your life. Therefore, do not stop praying. It could also be that he will answer you in a very different way from what you have in mind in your prayers. Hold unshakably fast to one thing. He loves you even as the one you now are. . . . And listen closely: it might well be that he will not lift this shadow from you, possibly will never do so your whole life, just because from all eternity he has appointed you to be his friend as he is yours, just because he wants you as the man whose only option is to love him in return and give him alone the glory there in the depths from which he will not raise you.
>
> Get me right. I am not saying that this has to be so. . . . But I see and know that there are shadows in the lives of all of us . . . which will not disperse, and which perhaps in God's will must not disperse, so that we may be held in the place where, as those who are loved by God, we can only love him back and praise him.
>
> Thus, even if this is his mind and will for you, in no case must you think of that final step. May your hope not be a tiny flame but a big and strong one even then . . . for what God chooses for us children of men is always the best.
>
> Can you follow me? Perhaps you can if you read the Christmas story in Luke's Gospel, not deeply but very simply, with the thought that every word there—and every word in Psalm 23 too—is also meant for you, and especially for you.[2]

This response to a despairing man is both instructive and surprising. Barth constantly sees something we did not see and says something we did not expect. Rather than say he really doesn't have it so bad, Barth agrees that the prisoner's life may actually seem intolerable. He then embraces rather than removes this problem. God may choose to keep someone in a state of despair in order for God to be loved and worshipped by a depressed person. God may want to be loved by someone living in a hard and difficult situation. God may not want to be loved and worshipped only by those who are happy, or by those who have an easy life.

Perhaps Barth's words do not seem to comfort at first sight, but they may have sustained the prisoner more than any other approach, by the realistic acknowledgment that he was in a difficult and lonely place. In this regard, Barth took the man very seriously, and any person with a wounded spirit wants to be taken seriously rather than handed trite, superficial phrases. What we say about propinquity in our discussion of

---

2. Erler and Marquard, *Karl Barth Reader*, 87–88.

the Psalms applies to Barth's approach with this person. When someone's mood can be matched or entered into there is a momentary feeling of being understood, of not being alone with one's pain, to the point that this can bring a temporary release of pressure, even a lifting of a dark mood. In addition, Barth held out to him the possibility of hearing God's unique call, a call to love and honor God from a position of difficulty. Many other people could not answer this divine call, but this man was uniquely qualified to respond from his life as a troubled prisoner. In so doing, Barth taught him to take God quite seriously in his personal context.

Barth closed the letter by pointing him to Scripture, and asked him to read it as though God were speaking directly to him. Not everyone has learned to do this, and there is a danger that sometimes when people do this they might get carried away in flights of personal fancy. But in a pastoral care situation, it is important to connect a person to the Scripture with encouragement to listen for God's voice applying the text in a direct and personalized way. Here is an affinity between Martin Luther and Barth, for, as a preacher, Luther often paraphrased a verse in order to help his listeners understand that they were being addressed at that very moment, that they should both hear and respond to this particular word of God. Although it was originally spoken long ago, now they should hear it as though God were speaking a new and fresh word directly to them. Barth asked the prisoner to read Luke's Christmas story and hear the promise of the angels as though it were personally spoken to him, as though he were one of the shepherds that night. And then do the same with the twenty-third Psalm. John Calvin said to read the Scripture by putting your eyes in your ears. Listen to what the Holy Spirit is saying through this text. Barth urged this man to listen in such a way that he heard God speak promises into his life. Promises of rescue, protection, help, and blessing.

In his pastoral care, Barth was committed to a theology that highlighted God's reconciling and renewing grace. Simultaneously, because of the full humiliation and horror of Christ's death in atoning love, he could never devalue that gift of grace by encouraging a presumptuous sin. Neither would he presume to know the outcome of God's judgment for a particular individual. God's sovereignty is holy freedom. God is both free to judge the sin of suicide in holiness and free to forgive the sin of suicide in holiness. Thus, it could not be a matter of indifference whether someone commits suicide, for presumption would hold God's forgiveness or God's judgment in contempt. While Barth attempted to sympathize with the prisoner's personal struggle with despair, he firmly stated, "In no case must you think of that final step."

Caution Against Judging the Motive of Suicidal People

Barth cautions the pastor or counselor not to hasten to conclude that all who consider suicide do so out of a desire for self-murder, or as those who desire to disobey God. When people are in great distress and do not know which way to turn, they may not even understand themselves enough to explain what is going on inside their thoughts and feelings. As spiritual counselor James Loder once said, "Sometimes we do not even know how to pray, because we do not even know what we want God to do. We do not always know what we want."[3] Yet in such times, God knows us better than we know ourselves. If this can be said in general of people who pray, regardless of what contributes to their confusion or lack of self-understanding, how much more can it be said of people who are suicidal? We do not want to make a virtue out of the confusion, only point out the danger of using a quick diagnosis to identify the suicidal wish and equate it with rebellious thoughts. Barth warned against making this equation because it assumes too much. Good people can be tortured by wondering whether God is really with them, for them, or against them. Some feel isolated and rejected. "A man assailed and afflicted is hid from all others and sometimes even from himself. He is alone with God, and tortured by the terrible question whether God is really with him and for him."[4] There are inner afflictions which pastors and moralists may only dimly perceive, which is why we cannot think we know what happens between the afflicted person and God.[5]

Even when Barth is willing to define the action of suicide as a violation of the commandment prohibiting murder, he cautions against a simplistic assessment of a suicidal person's motives. If our own motivations are sometimes hard to clarify, how can we be sure we understand someone else's motives? The deepest desire may not be equated with the desire for self-murder, however we classify the end result. Sometimes conflicting motives surge within us.

---

3. Koonz, "Prayer and the Cure," 66–74.
4. Barth, *CD* 3/4:404.
5. Barth, *CD* 3/4:404.

Can an Individual Receive Divine Approval for an Act of Suicide?

Not all suicidal intent has the primary focus of self destruction. In some special situations, a person's intent might be to die as a self-offering. There may be cases where God gives one the freedom to choose death as a self-offering, but in that case it will not involve self-assertion or an expression of autonomy, which Barth refers to as "false sovereignty." One thinks especially of cases where an individual sacrificed his or her life in order to save other people. An example from the Netherlands during World War II is the father of Corrie ten Boom. Casper ten Boom was elderly when he was arrested for hiding Jews and other refugees. Seemingly out of respect for his age, a Gestapo officer promised him release from prison, on one condition. If Mr. ten Boom would give his word not to protect any more Jews, he would be free to go home that very day. What was the answer? "'If I go home today,' he said evenly and clearly, 'tomorrow I will open my door again to any man in need who knocks.'"[6]

He was spiritually free to answer with integrity, free to live or die according to the will of God. His arrest was already due to the fact that he had rescued and successfully hid eight people when his house was raided. The decision to give his life was already made and lived out with the fullest possible integrity as he acknowledged God's sovereignty over his life and family. He carried his cross (Mark 8:34). Even so, he did not feel free to commit suicide to avoid suffering in prison. Nor did his daughters seek suicide as a way out of their hellish concentration camp experience.

Casper ten Boom did die in prison. His daughter Betsy also died. These are not the only type of examples of the freedom to die, but they are likely close to what Barth had in mind. They are examples of non-combatants who took specific actions knowing they would probably end in death. Barth also considered that Samson may have ended his life in peace with God, but he considered such an example an uncommon exception to God's will for us to live, even when life involves difficult surrenders and self-sacrifice.[7] Sometimes it requires more self-sacrifice to stay alive and give helpful service in a difficult situation. For example, Betsy ten Boom lived for a while in a concentration camp and shared her food with other starving inmates rather than consume every morsel

---

6. ten Boom, *Hiding Place*, 128.
7. Barth, *CD* 3/4:411.

herself. Betsy also lived to give words of encouragement (She comes to mind, though she is not Barth's example).

However, if there is an exception, when God might direct someone to die and when it is not a denial of faith, then it will arise in specific historical situations and not be something that can be classified in advance in abstract and theoretical discussions. As when someone dies to prevent others being tortured, there are possible situations where a Christian might perceive a divine permission to die. We should be very careful then to practice listening to God so that we discern God's voice and properly distinguish it from other voices and influences. Barth closes this line of thought with a warning.

> If a man kills himself without being ordered to do so, then his action is murder. God may forgive him, but it is still murder, so that none can will to perpetrate it with uplifted head if he has faith in the gracious God who forgives sins.[8]

Perhaps the greatest need Christians have today to consider and apply Barth's warning is in reference to the debate over assisted suicide. As a society, we will continue to face the question of how to administer nursing care to the elderly so they can fulfill their days in dignity with minimal pain, honoring their humanity regardless of their utility as contributing members of society, yet without keeping them artificially alive and usurping the divine decision about when life should end. For centuries, Christians built hospitals and ministered to the sick and dying.[9] Will we have a prophetic and visionary word to speak today even when we (as denominations) no longer control the hospitals we once established? Christians cannot avoid the hard task of addressing this issue. We will continue to be asked, through selective use of anecdotes and information in the media or through legislative efforts, to allow or assist those who choose to die before their bodies and minds completely fail. Will we reason from biblical principles, or will pragmatic and emotional concerns predominate?

Ethical discussion will not always be very effective in our churches unless our people are taught to think about aging, incapacity, and avoidance of pain from a theological perspective. Here we have a lot more work to do in practical theology. James Loder, James Packer, James Houston, Michael Parker, Will Willimon, and Mary Baird Carlsen have

---

8. Barth, *CD* 3/4:412.
9. See "Hospitals and Health Care" in Schmidt, *How Christianity Changed*, 151–69.

already made valuable contributions.[10] Hard intellectual questions and moral dilemmas may suddenly become very personalized as the road of life takes a sudden turn. How do we remain faithful and thankful for the gift of life when we can no longer see its luster, having lost both ability and strength? What is the right response as our memory fails? The loss of memory is so painful because memory forms our identity and holds together personal connections. How can we honor and glorify God when the aging process is destructive and frightening? Churches today must give serious thought and prayer to both youth ministry and aging ministry. Aging ministry must go beyond the chaplaincy model of ministry, one that merely provides comfort to the helpless and aged through hand holding and prayer. We do not have easy answers concerning end of life issues, but acknowledge that all our days belong to God.

When Barth said we should not assume we have automatic permission to end our life, his caution is in harmony with two thousand years of Christian teaching and emphasis. Yet he also said people in hard circumstances need to turn to God for their ultimate guidance. How one discerns the direction and guidance of God without seeking affirmation for one's own preferences is left unstated, but the note of warning is present regarding actions based on false assumptions.

God's Gracious Permission to Live: When the Command Cannot Help

In chapter 3, we initially presented Barth's position on suicide. He does not see it as an unforgivable sin, but he also said that no one has a right to take his or her own life. We cannot decide whether our own life is a success or a failure, whether our existence is tolerable or intolerable. No human is authorized to be his or her own judge or take his or her own life.[11] Life is on loan from God and should be used in God's service. God can take life back, but until that moment it must be lived for God's purposes. Our freedom to live may seem like a burden, but we do not have permission to destroy our

---

10 See "Beyond 65" in Loder, *Logic*, 316–37; Packer, *Finishing Our Course*; Houston and Parker, *Vision*; Willimon, *Aging*. Carlsen, *Creative Aging*, is not theological but is important for dialog with practical theology, because she focuses on the importance of personal narrative and analyzes the way people change their meaning-making as they age. Personal narrative and meaning-making can be transformed by the Holy Spirit regardless of age or circumstances, as Loder emphasized.

11. Barth, *CD* 3/4:404.

own life. Suicide, then, is the misuse of our God-given freedom to live. It may be done as a form of self-justification or self-glorification, or done as an expression of despair. Regardless of the motive, it may be seen as a form of self-murder. But "even suicide in this sense is not as such unforgivable sin."[12] Yet, "God's forgiveness is no excuse, much less justification, for sin."[13] The sin of suicide is often a form of rebellion against God. How then can we help someone see the reprehensible nature of suicide?

It is Barth's conviction that we can only help someone on the basis of the gospel and faith, not on the basis of law or a moral code. Any so-called command against committing self-murder seems like an empty prohibition to a despairing person, even though it be taken from the Bible. Yet which passage should one use? In the Bible there is no direct prohibition of suicide.[14] To a person assailed by suicidal thoughts, moral arguments and prohibitions do not carry weight or ring true. The empty void seems to surround one's life and engulf everything.

Because despairing people may consider suicide out of noble motives rather than base ones, attacking their motives is not generally helpful either. The light of our reasoning and admonition does not easily penetrate the darkness, but God's light brings the announcement that we may live. Barth asks that we not confuse permission to live with a command to live. It is permission to live that frees us to live and diminishes the darkness of despair, not a command to live.[15] We are free to live, not obligated to live. "Life is the freedom which is bestowed by God. To will it is to will what we are permitted."[16] (To a suicidal person we might say, "God graciously gives you permission to live.") But in order to recognize that we are free to live we must not see our lives as autonomous. Rather, we must see our lives as lived under the providential care of God and therefore in relationship with God.[17] Because we are surrounded by God there is an unfailing supply of forgiveness and hope, and help in time of need (Barth liked to say "the angels are on our side").[18]

---

12. Barth, *CD* 3/4:405.

13. Barth, *CD* 3/4:405.

14. Barth, *CD* 3/4:406. C. S. Lewis came to the same conclusion (as shown above in chapter 6).

15. Barth, *CD* 3/4:406–7.

16. Barth, *CD* 3/4:407.

17. Barth, *CD* 3/4:407.

18. Barth, *CD* 3/4:408.

16

C. S. Lewis (1898–1963)

CLIVE STAPLES LEWIS TAUGHT English literature at Oxford and Cambridge universities. He wrote *The Chronicles of Narnia* fantasy series for children, which made him internationally famous, as well as books that help modern people understand Christian belief, such as *Mere Christianity*, *Miracles*, and his fascinating study of temptation, *The Screwtape Letters*. Because Lewis's books and articles on Christianity were so highly esteemed, a number of readers began to look to him for spiritual guidance. He received letters from all over the world, many more than he could answer. One of his correspondents was an American poet and college professor named Sheldon Vanauken.

A Cautionary Word for Sheldon

Sheldon felt that he and his wife, Jean "Davy" Vanauken, had shared a truly radiant love. After her death, he felt he could not continue without her. He had thoughts of suicide as a means to join her, which was expressed in one of his letters to Lewis. They shared mutual respect and had developed a sympathetic intimacy in their earlier correspondence, which Lewis built on in order to address Vanauken's revelation. We come into this lengthy letter where Lewis wrote that the marriage relationship cannot be an end in itself: it is made for God and is to exist, two people as one, for God's glory and then, additionally, for the benefit of children and neighbors. Perpetual spring, shared only between two people, is not allowed to go on endlessly, for it is not the ultimate goal. Lewis responded to what Vanauken wrote about his relationship with Jean, including the fact that he was jealous of God because he could not love her as perfectly as God:

> You have been treated with a severe mercy. You have been brought to see (how True and how very frequent this is!) that you were jealous of God. So from US you have been led back to US AND GOD; it remains to go on to GOD AND US. She was further on than you, and she can help you more where she now is than she could have done on earth. You must go on. That is one of the many reasons why suicide is out of the question. (Another is the absence of any ground for believing that death by that route would reunite you with her. Why should it? You might be digging an eternally unbridgeable chasm. Disobedience is not the way to get nearer to the obedient.)
>
> There's no other man, in such affliction as yours, to whom I'd dare write so plainly. And that, if you can believe me, is the strongest proof of my belief in you and love for you. To fools and weaklings one writes soft things.[1]

Vanauken reflected, "After this severe and splendid letter I loved Lewis like a brother. Like a brother and father combined."[2] While the whole letter touches on many points, our focus is on Lewis's concern about Vanauken's thoughts of suicide. Here, Lewis was not trying to console so much as instruct as a spiritual director. In intense grief for the loss of his wife, Vanauken had thought to manipulate the timing of his own death in order to join his wife all the sooner in a blissful reunion. Lewis said two important things in his response. The first touches on God's purpose, not Vanauken's. God's purpose must take precedence. In my understanding Lewis was not saying that God decreed her death, but something closer to: God may have a reason for you to endure this season of grief, or rather, God may bring good into your life during this season of grief. Lewis refused to romanticize suffering or grief, neither did he spiritualize it to make it redemptive in and of itself.

---

1. Vanauken, *Severe Mercy*, 211–12.
2. Vanauken, *Mercy*, 212. Vanauken's entire story should be read for the context of this letter, as well as his telling what it meant to him in the years following.

Suffering Is Not Good in and of Itself

What matters most is whether we seek God in order to interact with God in the midst of our suffering. Even if our prayer must first take the form of complaint, the importance of seeking God's response to our suffering has biblical precedent. This is seen in Job's protest in the midst of suffering or Martha and Mary's complaint after Lazarus's death (John 11:21, 32). In Lewis's anthology of George MacDonald, we find this insight: "Complaint against God is far nearer to God than indifference about Him."[3] Lewis recognized that it is possible for the complaining sufferer to want God, for a person to draw closer to God in voicing complaint than in pretending a submissive piety.

> There is something holier about the atheism of a Shelley than about the theism of a Paley. That is the lesson of the book of Job. No explanation of the problem of unjust suffering is there given: that is not the point of the poem. The point is that the man who accepts our ordinary standard of good and by it hotly criticizes divine justice receives divine approval: the orthodox, pious people who palter with that standard in the attempt to justify God are condemned.[4]

Submitting to God's will does not mean we should like the suffering or call it good. In our weakness and inability to hold God's hand, we acknowledge that God holds on to us, in spite of our pain and anger. And we ask God's presence to be near and God's name to be honored in and through our suffering, or in spite of our suffering. If God has unfinished business with us, we ask that it be completed to the benefit of our soul. However, to say that God is good and we should have faith in God is not the same as saying that pain is good. Lewis wrote elsewhere, "I answer that suffering is not good in itself. What is good in any painful experience is, for the sufferer, his submission to the will of God, and for the spectators, the compassion aroused and the acts of mercy to which it leads."[5]

Lewis knew something which James Loder was to explore later in depth as a Christian therapist. When we cannot circumvent the pain of this life and invite God's presence within it, then it may become the locus of God's redemptive activity. Welcoming and seeking God in the midst

---

3. Qtd. in Lewis, *George MacDonald*, 167. The quote originally comes from MacDonald's *What's Mine's Mine*, published in 1886.
4. Lewis, *Christian Reflections*, 70.
5. Lewis, *Problem of Pain*, 110.

of suffering may even transform the meaning of the tragedy for the person involved.[6] Lewis suggested to Vanauken that he had been focused on spiritual growth together with Davy, but now there was opportunity also for spiritual growth in her absence. Avoiding this painful time when you are severed from her does not help you move toward God. God can fulfill a purposeful work in your soul if you allow him to do it, even now when you are painfully alone. This possibility should be explored rather than stifled or cast aside by a suicidal death. Yet nothing Lewis says means that suffering or loneliness is good and sent by God, but rather that God can bring good into it and lead you through it to something more, even eternal life.

Secondly, Lewis pointed out that the way to join the obedient is not through a final act of disobedience. To think that a reunion is automatic under such conditions is to be presumptuous. For Lewis, suicide that is not a noble sacrifice for the sake of preserving other lives, as when a soldier gives his life in order to protect his squadron or when a mother covers her child in a fire, is nothing less than disobedience to God. This is a sin that he does not think God takes lightly or overlooks in indifference, hence his warning that there is no ground "for believing that death by that route would reunite you with her." This is not equivalent to saying there is no forgiveness for the sin of suicide. It is rather an acknowledgment that our placement in the next world is in God's hands, not ours. We are not allowed to dictate, control, or manipulate that which will come our way in the world to come. Here we see an affinity with Barth's affirmation that we cannot presume upon the grace, mercy, and judgment of God. If in faith we place our lives in God's hands, leaving the decision up to our Creator to determine the length of our days, so we also must allow God to determine the timing of celestial reunions.

---

6. See Loder, *Logic*; cf. Loder, *Transforming*.

17

Dietrich Bonhoeffer (1906–1945)

AS A YOUNG THEOLOGICAL lecturer in Germany, Dietrich Bonhoeffer was a founding member of the Confessing Church which opposed Nazi ideology.[1] In August, 1936, he was forbidden to teach at the University of Berlin. In 1939, he went to New York, where friends urged him to remain, but instead he returned to Germany when war was imminent out of a sense of duty to help his people. He joined the German military intelligence organization Abwehr, which had the task of protecting Germany from foreign espionage. Bonhoeffer's involvement with the Abwehr kept him from being drafted and enabled him to have personal contact with some members of the opposition to Hitler. In careful cooperation with others in the Abwehr, Bonhoeffer helped German Jews escape to Switzerland.[2]

During this time Bonhoeffer began to write a book on ethics. When he discovered the extent of Nazi atrocities through access to Abwehr information, he no longer believed he could die "with clean hands" like the early Christians who died passive deaths. He knew that he had to resist, even if there was no guarantee resistance could be effective in a police

---

1. He also came to criticize the Confessing Church for protesting governmental dictates to the church without voicing an equally strong protest over mistreatment of the Jews.

2. Some of Bonhoeffer's statements in the early 1930s lacked full support for Jews who were subjugated by the Nuremberg Laws, but he later realized his mistake (Klenicki and Neuhaus, *Believing Today*, 58–69, especially 60–61). The sincere correction that Bonhoeffer offered was not done with words alone. He also took dangerous risks for the sake of others, transporting Jewish refugees to freedom in Switzerland. If he had been caught he would have suffered arrest much sooner.

state.³ He was arrested in 1943. Later, when the identity of the "Canaris group" of anti-Hitler organizers was discovered, Bonhoeffer was put to death upon Hitler's order that all participants in Admiral Canaris's plot be killed. After the war, Bonhoeffer's unfinished work on ethics was published posthumously, which included a short discussion on suicide.

Life Is a Gift

In Bonhoeffer's view, human beings are not like animals who must carry their lives as a compulsion which cannot be thrown off. The human is free to either accept the life given at birth or reject it. In this great freedom, we can go in more than one direction. The life of our body is a gift that is to be preserved, but it may also become a sacrifice that is offered for a higher good. This freedom is not without a reason or a focus, for this is ultimately a freedom to live to God.⁴ But this powerful freedom can be misused by us.

The history of the human race is one of struggle for survival and other successes, and sometimes defeat turns one's thoughts to the possibility of a self-inflicted death, to rob blind fate of a victory. When a person grieves great losses or thinks one's life is ruined, a sense of regaining leverage seems to be offered in suicide. This action may require courage and be a sign of asserting strength rather than cowardice or weakness.⁵ In some cases, it may involve self-expiation of guilt or shame for a life that seems to have failed.⁶ While many suicides originate in a condition of despair, some may originate in a desire for self-justification, even as a grasping for atonement.⁷ When confronted by an act of suicide, our hor-

---

3. Historian Joachim Fest presents the very limited role Bonhoeffer had, mainly discussing ethical questions, without participating in any effective assassination plans. See Fest, *Plotting Hitler's Death*.

4. Bonhoeffer, *Ethics* (2005), 197.

5. Bonhoeffer, *Ethics* (2005), 197.

6. Bonhoeffer, *Ethics* (2005), 198.

7. Bonhoeffer, *Ethics* (2005), 198. Editor Clifford Green explains that "Selbstmord" is properly translated as "self-murder" rather than "self-inflicted death/suicide/self-killing." The German language had three different terms to describe a voluntary death, and he deliberately chose the term that placed him in conversation with a thousand years of Christian theological tradition. He did this with respect for Christian ethics and did not think human actions were morally neutral. He worked with the term that had been given the most reprehensible connotations. While recognizing that not all suicides can be called "self-murder," he was willing to take the worst-case scenario and examine it in the light of the gospel. See Bonhoeffer, *Ethics* (2005), 37–38.

ror is not merely the horror of death, nor the moral iniquity of the deed. There is a loneliness in the deed that unsettles us.[8]

The sin of suicide is not that it affronts human morality or human sensibilities, but it is wrongful as "the sin of unbelief" before the living God.[9] Lack of faith cannot be judged purely as a moral state, for it can accompany both noble and base deeds. However, there is a disastrous confusion in thinking that suicide can release us from the hand of God. God is God over us in life and God is God over us in death, whether or not we wish to affirm this truth. Therefore, God must determine our destiny, and every person should place his or her end of life under God's control. "Only God knows the goal toward which a life is being directed. God alone wishes to be the one who justifies or rejects a life."[10] Suicide is wrong because it is an attempt at self-justification and a denial that over each life God must reign as God.

Many Christians Have Died Sudden Deaths Without Repenting of All Their Sins

Bonhoeffer denies that an individual has a greater right over his or her life than God, but also says that the impulse to save lives by declaring suicide unforgivable is wrong, and we can surmise that it is wrong because in a different way it also disregards the reality of God. Here there is an affinity with Samuel Johnson (see chapter 10 above). Bonhoeffer particularly disagrees with the argument often used by Christians that "suicide rules out the possibility of repentance and, therefore, also of forgiveness." He is not indifferent to the importance of repentance in the life of every person, but in the end, the argument is incomplete because there is no adequate theological reason why the last moment of life is the only decisive factor.

"Through sudden death, many Christians have died with unrepented sins. This argument overvalues the final moment of life."[11] Beware of setting too much store on the last moment of life (see Barth's agreement with Bonhoeffer in chapter 3; and John Warwick Montgomery's basic agreement in chapter 19.)

---

8. Bonhoeffer, *Ethics* (2005), 198.
9. Bonhoeffer, *Ethics* (2005), 198.
10. Bonhoeffer, *Ethics* (2005), 198.
11. Bonhoeffer, *Ethics* (2005), 199.

Because our lives belong to God, none of us need to justify the existence of our lives, least of all to other humans. It is God who gives our lives their value, not wealth, prestige, specific work, or the approval of a loved one. Bonhoeffer also says, "It is a remarkable fact that the Bible nowhere explicitly forbids suicide, but that again and again it appears [often but not always] as the consequence of the deepest sin" [as with Ahithophel and Judas].[12]

> The reason for this is not that the Bible approves of self-murder, but that instead of prohibiting it the Bible wants to call the despairing to repentance and grace. Those who stand on the verge of self-murder no longer hear a prohibition or command; they can hear only the gracious call of God to faith, to salvation, and to turning back. The despairing cannot be saved by any law appealing to their own strength; this only drives them into more hopeless despair. Those who despair of life are helped only by the saving act of another, the offer of a new life that is lived not by their own strength but by the grace of God. Those who can no longer live cannot be helped by the command that they must live, but only by a new spirit.[13]

Bonhoeffer affirms the effectiveness of the freeing power of grace, and finds that using the command of law is not helpful when dealing with a wounded spirit. As we saw above, Barth made the distinction between a command and permission to live. The suicidal person is often so weakened in spirit that he or she cannot respond to commands, exhortations, or personal appeals. Ultimately, spiritual healing is required and a more gentle approach can prove helpful.

An Act with Hidden Motivations

Because of the spiritual and mental components of human motives and actions, which are hidden from our gaze, suicide must be seen as an act of solitude in such a way that "the ultimate decisive motives almost always remain hidden. Even when preceded by some external catastrophe, the inner, deeper reason for the deed escapes the outsider's understanding."[14] Having reached the limits of human knowledge, we must suspend

---

12. Bonhoeffer, *Ethics* (2005), 199–200.
13. Bonhoeffer, *Ethics* (2005), 200.
14. Bonhoeffer, *Ethics* (2005), 200.

judgment. We cannot always know the underlying motive when a suicide is committed. Does the motivation arise from freedom to make one's life a sacrifice? Or is the core problem the abuse of this freedom for the purpose of self-murder? In a variety of examples which Bonhoeffer considers, it is very difficult to say that the motive has to be self-murder. Among these, Bonhoeffer thinks of the prisoner who takes his life out of fear that he may betray his country, exposing friends to harm and danger under torture, who thereby chooses to preserve other lives through self-sacrifice. Is this not a free offering of one's life though done under circumstances of duress? He mentions the sufferer from incurable disease who sees that his extensive care will bring about the material and psychological ruin of his family, using his own decision to free them from such a prospect. Bonhoeffer is aware of appropriate moral objections to such drastic actions, which the Bible does not specifically authorize, yet he believes total condemnation is impossible.

We cannot be sure we know the motive or cluster of motives that are preeminent in the mind of the suicidal person. Such uncertainty makes complete moral condemnation extremely difficult to justify. He gives other examples that blur distinctions between the principle to preserve life and the principle to offer one's life as a sacrifice. During the horror of a sinking ship, a Christian feels an unquestioned duty to give the last place on a lifeboat to another person even though it ensures his own death. In combat, a Christian might feel called to shield another person's body from a bullet or hand grenade. While the individual's own decision is a contributing cause of death, it seems obvious these actions may be performed without a thought of self-murder. At other times these actions may include mixed motives, and then we cannot always be sure which motive predominates. For this reason, we must leave the person in question to God's perfect judgment and refrain from condemnation.

Even though Bonhoeffer thinks a purely moral judgment on suicide is impossible, from the human point of view, the ultimate possibility of surrendering one's life into the hand of God via suicide does not mean that there is somehow a right to suicide. God does not give an automatic free pass. In all we do, we should seek to honor God. Of course Bonhoeffer knows that not everyone who commits suicide believes in God or takes God into consideration. And it is the case that an atheistic ethic cannot offer legitimate grounds to oppose suicide. "The right to self-murder breaks down [is nullified] only before the living God."[15]

Battle conditions or a sinking ship provide external motivations for giving oneself away sacrificially and ending one's life. In addition to outward circumstances, there are also internal motivations which operate with intensity. These internal troubles are more often the personal battleground we face, especially when confronting our weaknesses and fears. The Christian is liable to these inner disturbances as well as the atheist—especially regarding the believer's own negative spiritual assessment. "Hatred of the imperfections of one's own life, the experience of the contrariness of earthly life in general to being fulfilled by God, and the resulting sorrow and doubt about any meaning in life at all–these can lead to dangerous hours."[16] As an example, he pointed to Martin Luther's admission of spiritual fights with depression, doubts, and discouragement. (From multiple seminary contexts, which Bonhoeffer was familiar with on two continents, there have been repeated incidents of suicides among both faculty and students. Pastors and people with theological interests are not immune from deep depression.) For the Christian facing interior problems, Bonhoeffer said, "Only the comfort of God's grace and the power of Christians' prayers can help in such temptation."[17] Grace allows a person to continue living under God's forgiveness. Yet Bonhoeffer knew that even devout Christians succumb, and ended the discussion by saying, "And who would say that under this most severe temptation the grace of God cannot embrace and bear even failure?"[18]

---

15. Bonhoeffer, *Ethics* (2005), 202.

16. Bonhoeffer, *Ethics* (2005), 202.

17. Bonhoeffer, *Ethics* (2005), 202–3. The editors say he had Eberhard Bethge's prayer in mind, which supported him during a very low moment, 203 note 109.

18. Bonhoeffer, *Ethics* (2005), 203.

18

Modern Continentals

Jürgen Moltmann (1926–2024), Wolfhart Pannenberg (1928–2014)

Jürgen Moltmann (1926–2024)

Jürgen Moltmann was a German Reformed theologian. He is primarily known for his theological affirmation that God wills to suffer with the human race in our sufferings, while at the same time promising us a future without suffering.

On the topic of suicide, Moltmann agrees with the movement away from calling it murder or self-murder. Here is reflection on a funeral service from his early pastoral ministry.

> When I was a young student pastor in Bremen, I had to take the funeral of two students who had taken their own lives. I did not bury them as "murderers" or "self-murderers," but I did not penetrate their motives either. Such a decision often brings us up against an insoluble riddle, and we must respect the mystery these people take with them to the grave, probably intentionally. But we must be all the more attentive to warning signs, which are often unconscious cries for help.[1]

---

1. Moltmann, *Ethics of Hope*, 96. Moltmann also had extensive personal encounters with depressed people as an eighteen-year-old prisoner of war.

At the same time he refuses to view suicide as normal because it is an action directed against life, "and life is in all circumstances deserving of protection." Furthermore, suicide appears to be a free act based on a free decision, but in reality it is not a free act, not a voluntary death. "No one kills himself as a supreme act of freedom. Suicide is generally the outcome of a lack of freedom which sees no way out."[2] Because no individual is completely autonomous, living solely in relationship with herself or himself, but in multiple social relationships, no person's life belongs only to herself or himself. This means that every death, including suicide, touches the lives of parents, wives and husbands, sisters and brothers, children and friends. Some of these can be plunged into deep grief following a suicide.

At the end of this discussion, he relates a wartime example of a high-ranking officer who committed suicide to protect his family from cruel reprisals after the failed assassination attempt on Hitler's life. "If we cannot interpret suicide as either 'self-murder' or 'voluntary death,' we can perhaps understand it in many cases as a matter of self-defence. . . . Persons with depression take their own lives in order to avert unendurable psychological pressure from within," but in most cases we cannot completely penetrate to the motive in the decision.[3] For this reason, we need to treat the suicidal death with respect and without heaping reproaches and accusation onto the victim, because there is a mystery here into which we cannot penetrate with accuracy.[4]

Should We Encourage the Helpless to Die?

With reference to death on demand for the elderly who suffer, this is not necessarily a matter of suicide, especially when the people who ask for death no longer have the strength or capacity to carry it out. This wish often arises from self-defense against some unbearable condition, or in response to "unreasonable life-prolonging measures." Those who assist

2. Moltmann, *Ethics of Hope*, 96.
3. Moltmann, *Ethics of Hope*, 97.
4 If the language of mystery is held under suspicion due to Moltmann's universalism, it should be pointed out that his conclusions can be supported by those working with other theological commitments, including those far more classically orthodox on matters of eschatology: see chapter 19. Barth and Bonhoeffer thought it impossible to penetrate into the relationship between suicidal victims and God's presence, to discern motives accurately, and understand the self-experienced isolation of these souls prior to death.

such people see themselves not as accessories to killing but as accessories to a natural death. Such people may act "in service to life, of which dying is quite simply a part." Yet if someone administers poison, then this is "an act at the service of death." Moltmann sees an act that allows someone to die a natural death as ethically justifiable, but not an act of poisoning.[5]

Furthermore, suicide should never be suggested to the old. The retired and elderly should never be made to feel that they are "superfluous" or a burden to others. Rather, we should see that God does want the healthy and the competent to share and experience community with the helpless. We are not meant to live only for ourselves and those who can do something for us in return. "The demand that suicide should be suggested to the disabled, the incurable ill and the old is blameworthy because it is cynical. It relieves 'the healthy and competent' of solidarity, sympathy, and active neighborly love."[6] We are not truly free and autonomous when we choose to live without neighborly love.

Wolfhart Pannenberg (1928–2014)

Wolfhart Pannenberg was a preeminent theologian in the second half of the twentieth century. In his book on anthropology, Pannenberg discusses recurrent problems in human community which may have a bearing on suicide.

Aggressive Attitudes and Behaviors Are Not Good

After a review of Kierkegaard's analyses of dread and despair, Pannenberg looked at modern research into aggression. Pannenberg does not side with those who think that aggression is part of a normal outworking of the human instinct for self-preservation or self-expansion, as something pertaining to ego development, as if that would somehow make it innocuous and give people a perfect right to react against restrictions. Modern efforts to justify aggressive personal behavior towards others are unjustified, no matter how much a person's weak ego may need bolstering. This insight that aggression should be contained and not permitted against others has ramifications for both penal law and education. Pannenberg notes that permissive education has theories and practices

---

5. Moltmann, *Ethics of Hope*, 98.
6. Moltmann, *Ethics of Hope*, 98.

which actually encourage aggressive behavior, which has contributed to the rise in aggressive behavior rather than the decline of it.

Aggression is not merely the result of frustration, for while this can spring from frustration, there are other sources that feed anger and resentment as well. The theory that says the removal of constraints "on the striving for self-assertion should in fact lead to the disappearance of destructive aggressivity" is wrong and harmful. "Wherever aggressive behavior is tolerated or even rewarded, it spurs imitation."[7] Furthermore, self-development requires self-conquest. In this Pannenberg is supported by the earlier work of René A. Spitz on early childhood development. There is no normal growth in ego development unless the infant experiences frustrations and incorporates them into personal memory through experience and endurance, learning that there is life beyond these moments that delay gratification or bring unwanted stress.[8] Freud had earlier emphasized the necessity of failure as a key element in personal growth. What remains true for the earliest years of the developing ego remains true for growth from youth to adulthood. Self-development should be sought through self-conquest, rather than allowing personal energy to be used for destructive purposes.

Pannenberg says there is still room for recognizing that some aggressive behaviors are linked to frustrations of the ego instincts. Anxiety does play a key role, as Kierkegaard saw, whether or not we join him in identifying anxiety as the original sin. Anxiety can precede actual forms of aggression as well as follow outbreaks of aggression. There is a "universally present existential anxiety that precedes any actual aggression and takes the form of a vague realization of the vulnerability of one's own existence and of the threats to it."[9] Personal experiences full of frustration may suddenly intensify this "primordial existential anxiety." When this happens, there are two common human responses. "This may lead to aggressive behavior, but it may just as well make the person choose flight and depression."[10]

---

7. Pannenberg, *Anthropology in Theological Perspective*, 147–48.

8. Spitz, *First Year of Life*.

9. Pannenberg, *Anthropology*, 149.

10. Pannenberg, *Anthropology*, 149. Pannenberg cites in support of this statement Rolf Denker, *Angst und Aggression*, 89.

Aggression Against the Self and the Sin of Egoism

Aggressive behavior is not always connected to frustration, but generally cannot escape some connection with a pervading anxiety. In anxiety, we often enclose ourselves in on our own limited resources rather than reach outward to God for help and assistance. "While anxiety is the basic form in which sin manifests itself in human self-consciousness, both (destructive) aggression and flight depression are also to be seen as expressions of human sinfulness."[11] Awareness of personal flaws and incompleteness, including moral failure, can feed aggression or depression.

All too often, the consciousness of guilt and failure is linked to "elements of aggression against the self," and suicide is "the extreme form of self-aggression." Augustine gave reasons for rejecting suicide. His three main reasons were that suicide is a form of murder, that suicide is an expression of despair of receiving God's mercy, and that suicide allows no time for repentance. Pannenberg says that all of Augustine's reasons "do not connect suicide with the psychological analysis of sin as egoism and concupiscence." Concupiscence is larger than the question of sexual gratification, for it means a pervasive attitude towards the world (especially other people) that demands it provide pleasure, comfort, and security, using everyone and everything to one's own advantage. Pannenberg enlarges on this point.

> And yet the connection between pride and aggression against the self is an obvious one. The proud cannot easily tolerate the awareness of their own nonidentity and existential failure. The inclination of the proud to identify their own existence with the perfect attainment of their destiny and to ignore the difference made by their own imperfection facilitates the passage from consciousness of nonidentity to self-hatred. This shows that aggression against the self is just as much an expression of sin as is aggression against others.[12]

Pride as false arrogance can play a role in suicidal ideation, particularly when circumstances and failures infringe upon the kind of life and reputation the proud person would choose, resulting in loss of control. While consciousness that such pride is sin should lead to repentance that brings the individual's life before God for forgiveness and restoration, the inner struggle can turn in the opposite direction. The very consciousness of

---

11. Pannenberg, *Anthropology*, 150.
12. Pannenberg, *Anthropology*, 153.

sin can serve a negative role rather than a positive one, plunging one into self-recrimination and aggression turned against the self, especially when a person does not seek the restoration which only God can provide. Such restoration does not serve the purpose of putting us ahead of the pack and into positions of importance, but moves us toward our eternal destiny.

Also, God may use a broken servant even more than a whole one, as it were, and for this reason it is not for us to decide when God is done with us. Therefore, in all self-examination, we have to beware of distortions that can misguide and eventually destroy us. We must surrender even our consciousness of sin, failure, and inadequacy into God's hands as we seek to conform to God's overall plan for our lives. Pannenberg sees our lives as a journey with a destination, and reminds us that we cannot travel this road through life without God's assistance, especially given our awareness of inhibiting inner flaws. When we review the evidence of our lives, all the sad losses and glaring broken pieces, we need to be reminded of the truth: "Your life is hid with Christ in God" (Col 3:3).

19

Diverse North American Evangelicals

J. Vernon McGee (1904–1988),
John Warwick Montgomery (1931–2024),
R. C. Sproul (1939–2017),
Jack Cottrell (1938–2022)

J. Vernon McGee (1904–1988)

JOHN VERNON MCGEE WAS ordained a Presbyterian pastor at the outset of his ministry, but eventually became the pastor of a large non-denominational church. He developed an extensive radio ministry called "Thru the Bible," and his particular gift was explaining and simplifying difficult passages. In his expositions, he usually gave his reasons for various interpretations or doctrinal and ethical positions in short, precise statements. In his rather direct approach, he also affirmed in print that suicide is not an unforgivable sin.

He stated that for a Christian to commit suicide is to commit a sin. He noted that a person who dies by suicide does not have time to ask for forgiveness. How then can he or she be forgiven? He answered, "Well, I think there are many Christians who die with unconfessed sins. They will have to answer for them at the judgment seat of Christ." He added that Christ Jesus is the only provision for all sin, confessed or unconfessed. In his humane and understanding way, McGee said, "I can understand that a Christian may think he has gotten into a situation where there is no way out." A person can be so down that suicide seems like the only alternative. Furthermore, Christians are not immune to the problems with which all people grapple, including problems with mental breakdowns or catastrophic illness. McGee concluded, "I would not sit in judgment upon a professing Christian who does this because, to begin with, the minute he commits this act he is out of your hands and out of my hands. We cannot pass judgment on him. And I know this: if that person is a child of God, he is saved. I don't care what you say, he is saved if he is a child of God."[1]

McGee also shared a vignette from one of his pastoral counseling experiences. During his first pastorate, he was relaxing on the front porch on a hot summer day, when a man came without an appointment and sat down, took out a large revolver and declared, "If you can't give me a good reason why I shouldn't kill myself, I'm going to commit suicide." The young pastor was totally surprised and instantly troubled. He was unsure what to say, but as he silently thought and prayed he noticed that the gun was very rusty. So he said, "If you can show me that you would solve your problems by taking your life, I'd be willing to get you a better gun than you've got there so you can do a better job of it." This provoked the man and McGee added, "You don't solve your problem by taking your life; you merely complicate and multiply your problem."[2] You multiply your problem by extending it into many other lives, from those who find you to those who must support your family or take care of your business, to those who grieve your loss and cannot be consoled. McGee was then able to offer encouragement in other ways once his visitor turned away from his suicidal intention. Then, in his most direct way, McGee pointed the man to his need for Jesus Christ.

John Warwick Montgomery (1931–2024)

John Warwick Montgomery was a Lutheran theologian, historian, and legal scholar. As an apologist, he lectured and debated in many university settings on the question of God's existence and the historical case for the resurrection of Jesus Christ.[3] He also worked extensively in the

---

1. McGee, *Questions and Answers*, 50.
2. McGee, *Questions and Answers*, 51.
3. Montgomery, *History, Law, and Christianity*, provides a lawyer's case for the

area of international human rights. In the early 1980s, he founded the Simon Greenleaf School of Law (now Trinity Law School) in southern California and served as Dean, while simultaneously hosting a call-in radio program called "Christianity on Trial."

As a college student, I listened to this program and called in to ask about suicide, stating that a relative committed suicide using a gun (indicating that death came instantly), and wondered if there could be any hope for God's forgiveness when there was no time for repentance afterwards. This is a question that Christian people ask repeatedly in contexts of suicide. In my case, the question arose from my grief and concern over my cousin Don's suicide during our teenage years, as well as the other neighbor whom I told about in chapter 1. Here is the impromptu response Montgomery gave in live air-time.

> In a situation like that, God can see into the person's heart. God can see what the person's actual condition is. God could see, for example, what would have happened if he had not been successful in the suicide attempt, and would therefore have had to face what he had done. And the Lord would determine whether this suicide was actually saying to the Lord, "I'm sick of my relationship with Christ, I don't any longer want that kind of thing. I'm relying on myself, and I intend to destroy myself."
>
> Or whether the person is simply depressed and would certainly, if he had the chance, come to his senses and repent of it. We can't tell that, because we can't look into the person's heart. The only unpardonable sin in Scripture is the sin of refusing the grace of God in Christ. And the refusing of the grace of God comes only when a person volitionally chooses to go his own way, and doesn't bring this to the cross of Christ to cover it.[4]

Montgomery does not automatically exclude the suicide from salvation. He does not see suicide as the unforgivable sin because there is not biblical grounds for identifying it as such. Nor, on the other hand, does he think every person gets an automatic free pass. God alone knows the condition of the human heart, something we cannot know simply because the last action committed was suicide.

Biblical references to the human heart are designations of a person's inner life, especially the mind, the will, the imagination, and the desires. It is always difficult to know the core quality of another person's

---

resurrection.

4. Montgomery, *Christianity on Trial*.

character. This point was underscored when the prophet Samuel had to select one of Jesse's sons to be anointed as the next king of Israel. The men who looked like good candidates were all rejected by God for that role. "People look on the outward appearance, but the Lord looks at the heart" (1 Sam 7). This is the difference. God can see what we cannot, especially the truth about another person's life and all the contributing factors that have made it so. We cannot look at the outward appearance of a suicide and understand with certainty the condition of that person's heart in the final moment, which means we cannot automatically interpret the act of suicide as a rejection of God or a rejection of grace. Does the dying person turn towards Christ or turn away? Does the dying person seek an end to pain and simultaneously seek forgiveness? God alone knows. Therefore we must leave judgment to God and not presume to disqualify anyone from eternal life based on their final moment.

Think of a different question. What about people who have never heard the gospel about Jesus? Can they be saved? Montgomery acknowledges the Bible does not ask or answer this question directly. Yet we are told "God desires all people to be saved and come to a knowledge of the truth" (1 Tim 2:4). With this verse in mind, Montgomery says,

> This surely means that no one will miss out on salvation unjustly. One thing is perfectly clear: a fallen race can never be saved by its good works or human effort; only a relationship with Jesus Christ, the Savior, is the way to heaven (John 14:6; Acts 4:12). Perhaps, at the moment of death, those who through no fault of their own, have not heard the gospel–or who through prejudicial circumstances have never been able to consider the gospel seriously–will be confronted by the Christ and be able, on the knife edge between time and eternity, to accept or reject Him.[5]

Perhaps also the suicide will be confronted by the Christ at the moment of death and be able, "on the knife edge between time and eternity," to accept the one who offers life and salvation. There is much that is hidden from us, but God desires all people to be saved, including the suicide. No one will be lost unjustly. Montgomery's answer to this question may be applicable to suicide.

---

5. Montgomery, *Defending the Faith*, 60.

Affinities with R. C. Sproul (1939–2017) and Jack Cottrell (1938–2022)

Others who do not think a suicidal death must require the victim to be lost include such diverse people as R. C. Sproul (Reformed) and Jack Cottrell (Restorationist Movement).[6] Sproul taught at Reformed seminaries, engaged in prison ministry, and shared Montgomery's interest in historical theology and apologetics. In one of Sproul's books, he offers short answers to common questions he encountered in classroom discussions and other ministry settings, including one about suicide. Sproul begins by saying, "I think it is possible for a person who has committed suicide to go to heaven."[7] He considers people who live under the impact of acute depression, and asks, "Can we say who is culpable for their behavior or who is not?" Looking on from the outside, we cannot know whether suicide is an act of confusion and desperation or deliberate rebellion against God. Sproul thinks suicide is a sin, a wrong choice, and in some cases may be a final act of unbelief, yet says, "I don't think we can assume that this is the mental state of everyone who actually commits suicide."[8] Importantly, he also says, "I know of nothing in Scripture that identifies suicide as the unforgiveable sin."[9]

Jack Cottrell was a professor at Cincinnati Christian University, and did not share Sproul's affinity with Calvinism, but on this question agrees with McGee, Montgomery, and Sproul. He does not identify suicide as the unforgiveable sin. What about 1 John 1:9 and the impossibility of repenting after suicide? He says this verse is more than an admonition to repent of specific sins.

Cottrell does think, however, that if a suicide is an act of defiance against God's lordship, then the individual may end up separated "from the grace of God and the hope of heaven. More commonly, though, the sin of suicide is actually an act of desperation and not a deliberate rebellion against God. As with most other specific sins, it does not automatically separate one from the grace of God, even if there have been no specific repentance and confession relating to it."[10]

---

6. Sproul, *Good Question*, 291–92; Cottrell, "Suicide and Forgiveness," 157–59.
7. Sproul, *Good Question*, 291.
8. Sproul, *Good Question*, 292.
9. Sproul, *Good Question*, 292.
10. Cottrell, "Suicide and Forgiveness," 158; cf. 21, where he makes it clear that he is not a universalist.

He disagrees with the view that suicide automatically sends a person to hell, because he sees this as based on a wrong approach to 1 John 1:9, "If we confess our sins, He is faithful and righteous to forgive us our sins and to cleanse us from all unrighteousness" (NASB). To turn this verse into a declaration that every time we sin we lose our salvation until confession is made is to misunderstand the doctrine of justification by faith which is found in the New Testament. Cottrell sees 1 John 1:9 as referring to the overall and life-long acknowledgment that we are sinners in need of redeeming. This is in contrast to the person mentioned in the verses immediately before and after, 1 John 1:8 and 1:10, who claims to have no sin in need of cleansing (cf. Luke 18:9–14).[11]

Therefore 1 John 1:9 is more than an admonition to repent. In the prayer of daily repentance, we recognize that we never outgrow our need for forgiveness in this life, and acknowledge God's gracious umbrella of forgiveness with thanksgiving.[12] Elsewhere, he says this provides a keener sense of grace operating in our lives, "because Christ has paid the debt owed for that sin."[13] It is appropriate for us to pray that God will strengthen our faith, and "that God will continue to apply the atoning blood of Christ to us."[14] In such a prayer, we recognize our ongoing need for forgiveness. We live as a forgiven people by faith in Jesus, "apart from the record of our good works and our sins at any particular time (Rom 3:38)."[15] (God does not save us by grace in order for us to keep our salvation valid by law.[16]) We do not lose our salvation each time we sin, and this entails that suicide does not automatically remove us from God's forgiveness. He concludes by saying, "Any person who is contemplating committing suicide needs serious help, but if the person is a Christian, the false threat of guaranteed condemnation to hell is not the answer. If that sad act happens anyway, at least those of us who are left behind can grieve without being in despair over their eternal salvation."[17]

---

11. A summary of Cottrell, "Suicide and Forgiveness," 155–56.

12. "We live our lives, day in and day out, performing good works and bad works (sins), while remaining under the gracious umbrella of justification through our faith in Jesus." [Cottrell affirms we do not re-enter a state of lostness every time we sin.] "Persistence in sin can cause our faith to die, but individual sins are not the equivalent of apostasy." Cottrell, "Suicide and Forgiveness," 152.

13. Cottrell, "Suicide and Forgiveness," 110.

14. Cottrell, "Suicide and Forgiveness," 156.

15. Cottrell, "Suicide and Forgiveness," 159.

16. Cottrell, "Suicide and Forgiveness," 126.

17. Cottrell, "Suicide and Forgiveness," 159.

It is helpful to read these theologians in context and benefit from their full discussions. In this short comparison, McGee, Montgomery, Sproul, and Cottrell were conservative evangelical theologians from different backgrounds, all of whom affirmed biblical inerrancy and cannot be accused of waffling with their own communion's understanding of historic Christianity. They were not universalists, for they thought the alternatives of heaven and hell are real possibilities in eternity. In their considered study of the Bible, they each concluded that suicide is not an unforgiveable sin, not on the ground of suicide alone, yet in no way did they think it should be treated lightly or encouraged. They understood that it could be a sign of rebellious unbelief in some cases, but certainly not in every case. They did not presume to know the final thoughts of any person, nor the judgment of God. They found room to hope in the grace and kindness of God for many victims of suicide.

20

Roman Catholic and Eastern Orthodox Views

OUR EXAMINATION OF THE Roman Catholic approach must deal with the popular understanding many people have about Rome's theological stance, both Roman and Protestant. Here we want to look at Rome's official stance in its most up-to-date form. This is done to correct the common misunderstanding which exists in the minds of many people: that there is no hope for salvation if one commits suicide. We shall also discover a common thread in the Roman position with the Protestant theologians in our survey. Our chief area of concern involves questions of sin and grace, particularly the possibility of forgiveness for suicide.

Does the Official Roman Catholic Position Teach That All Suicides Are Damned?

In our canvass of several Protestant theologians above, we see that a common thread of agreement is that suicide is not automatically considered an unforgiveable sin. With one or two exceptions, there is general agreement that God's grace covers this sin. However, the question may arise whether we have skewed these theological reflections by ignoring the contribution of Roman Catholic theologians. This, we want to make clear, is not the case.

Firstly, chief among Roman Catholic theologians are St. Augustine and St. Thomas Aquinas, both of whom are represented in our historical survey (see chapter 6 above). Augustine did seem to think some people who committed suicides would not likely be forgiven, but not only on account of their mode of death. Furthermore, he refrained from saying that all suicides are unforgiveable. Aquinas also refrained from teaching outright that the sin of suicide was unforgivable. Closer in time was the Roman Catholic G. K. Chesterton, who spoke so eloquently against suicide. Neither did he pronounce it unforgivable (see chapter 13).

Secondly, what matters most for Roman Catholics is not the particular theologian who said this or that, but the official teaching of the church. Frequently I have met people, including many Roman Catholics, who have the impression that the official Roman Catholic teaching is that all suicides go to hell. This is not the official position. Furthermore, in 1983, the Vatican removed barriers which previously had prevented suicides from receiving church funerals and burials in sacred ground.

Official Teaching

For the official position, we must go to the *Catechism of the Catholic Church*, the authoritative exposition of the Roman Catholic faith approved and promulgated by Pope John Paul II, prepared by a commission presided over by then Joseph Cardinal Ratzinger, who later became Pope Benedict XVI. The official teaching is clearly and succinctly presented in this authoritative edition which is translated into English. The important points are detailed in very clear language.

First, God is the sovereign master of life. Everyone is responsible for his or her life before God. "We are obliged to accept life gratefully and preserve it for his honor and the salvation of our souls. We are stewards, not owners, of the life God has entrusted to us. It is not ours to dispose of."[1]

Second, "Suicide contradicts the natural inclination of the human being to preserve and perpetuate life. It is gravely contrary to the just love of self."[2] The historical influence of Aquinas is strongly evident, for as we saw above he said, "suicide is contrary to the inclination of nature, and to charity whereby every man should love himself."[3] Therefore, the catechism says suicide is "contrary to the natural law and to charity." Then it enlarges on the affront to charity by adding that suicide, "likewise

1. *Catechism*, 550.
2. *Catechism*, 550.
3. Aquinas, *Summa*, 1463.

offends love of neighbor because it unjustly breaks the ties of solidarity with family, nation, and other human societies to whom we continue to have obligations."[4] Because suicide is not an expression of love towards self or neighbor, it cannot be an expression of love for God, but rather its opposite: "Suicide is contrary to love for the living God."[5]

Third, due to the grave nature of this sin any collusion in suicide, any cooperative help that is offered a suicidal person "is contrary to the moral law."[6] There is little wiggle room here.

Fourth, only God can judge rightly concerning a suicide, for God knows the underlying causes that disturb and threaten life: "Grave psychological disturbances, anguish, or grave fear of hardship, suffering, or torture can diminish the responsibility of the one committing suicide."[7]

Fifth, a very important question is asked: is this sin forgivable or unforgivable? Is there grace for the person who committed suicide? Listen to the officially approved answer: "We should not despair of the eternal salvation of persons who have taken their own lives. By ways known to him alone, God can provide the opportunity for salutary repentance. The Church prays for persons who have taken their own lives."[8]

In this succinct presentation, we see the strong emphasis on living life to God's glory, a clear teaching that mitigates against the practice of suicide. We also see an acknowledgment that God's grace may be applied to the person who committed suicide, with an emphasis on trusting in God's provision of grace for this sin after death. According to this way of thinking, those who need an opportunity for repentance after death may be given that opportunity in the exercise of God's freedom and power. It is natural to assume the Roman theologians have the concept of purgatory in mind, with many long-held associations. What are we to think of an opportunity to repent after death?

---

4. *Catechism*, 550.
5. *Catechism*, 550.
6. *Catechism*, 550.
7. *Catechism*, 550.
8. *Catechism*, 550.

Thinking with or Without the Traditional Concept of Purgatory

If Roman Catholic theology is right and there is a purgatory after death, then purgatory is ultimately a blessing that moves people in a heavenly direction. But for evangelicals who do not accept the teaching, it may be said that time in purgatory is not necessarily required if God should choose to provide a different context for repentance or a quicker application of forgiveness and purgative healing. For example, it is possible the opportunity may come the moment we meet Jesus after death and are allowed to see him "as he is" (1 John 3:2). The God who can purge sin and error in a long stretch of time (the idea of purgatory) can surely purge in an instant, the way God can resurrect the body of any person who has died and do so in an instant. If God can do the one thing instantaneously, then so can God do the other. Without undue speculation on how God might provide grace and bring it home to the person in question, we can simply affirm, in agreement with Rome, that God is free to forgive sinners because of Jesus Christ. The healing and reconstituting of souls is determined by God.

The idea of purgatory has a long history and embraces the idea of spiritual purification after death. Without a full examination of the history of this idea, including the way it has hindered an Eastern Orthodox as well as Protestant reunion with Rome, we note that some Roman Catholic theologians are reexamining and reinterpreting purgatory to mean the moment or point of intersection between life and death. This is different from the traditional belief that purgatory, for most baptized sinners, would require a great length of time and considerable misery in the process of soul purging. Insofar as a few Roman Catholics are moving in a new direction, they may discover affinities with some forms of Protestant theology. As Donald Bloesch says in examining Ladislaus Boros's reinterpretation, "The encounter with Christ at death is our purgatory when we are received into the divine presence through the purifying power of divine love. This converges with the traditional Reformed view that the souls of believers are purified of sin at the moment of death or immediately after death (cf. Rom. 8:18, 23, 30; Heb. 12:23; Rev. 14:5)."[9]

We cannot probe the mystery to any degree of satisfaction, but should hesitate to declare that no one can be saved after the point of death, for that declaration would take the decision out of God's hands.

---

9. Bloesch, *Essentials of Evangelical Theology*, 219–20.

Insofar as Rome faces the possibility of redemption beyond the point of death for someone who committed suicide, with or without traditional ideas of purgatory in mind, there is an affirmation of hope for salvation. Not an assurance that takes the decision away from God and makes it automatic, but a reasoned and prayerful hopefulness. Hence the affirmation, "We should not despair of the eternal salvation of persons who have taken their own lives." Thus we see that suicide is not considered an unforgivable sin in official Roman Catholic theology.

This conclusion harmonizes with the vast majority of theological reflections we presented above. Protestant theologians such as Martin Luther, Dietrich Bonhoeffer, and Karl Barth did not see suicide as an unforgiveable sin. Thus those of us who preach the possibility of grace at a funeral service today cannot be accused of waffling on questions of sin and forgiveness. We are not selling out to the "spirit of the age" or forsaking the orthodox teaching of the Bible. We are not the first ones to say that suicide is not necessarily unforgiveable, especially when we say that God's grace is greater than the power of human sin and death. Yet we should not let ourselves run eagerly forward to offer false hope either, for that can be perceived as an expression of fear or a superficial platitude offering cheap grace (something devalued by disrespect). In the absence of a life of faith, we should not claim to know God's ultimate decision in judgment on a particular person. We may speak of the possibility of forgiveness and grace without claiming more than we know. We are never called to give false hope because that is not compatible with the comfort of the Holy Spirit. Any word of hope we have to speak at a funeral must point to Jesus Christ, our atonement for sin and disobedience, who is for us the face of God incarnate.

Eastern Orthodoxy

Priests in Greek Orthodox and Russian Orthodox churches (henceforth Orthodox) generally avoid speaking about a deceased person's eternal placement. This seems appropriate. They do not indulge in affirming or indicating, directly or indirectly, whether a departed person might go to heaven or hell. This is an important point because they have never abandoned the affirmation that both heaven and hell are real destinations, however impossible they may be to define or describe at this time. Orthodox priests do offer prayers for the dead and ask for God's mercy, but seek to honor God by not trespassing on God's freedom to judge in righteousness or forgive sinners. So they are usually most hesitant about declaring or celebrating the departed person's eternal destination, and this caution generally applies to all funerals. Yet practice does not always match theory.

In one sense, they do seem to intrude human judgment, however, because they generally refuse to offer a full liturgical service for a suicide. This form of public censure comes from a long tradition of discouraging suicide which goes back for many centuries. Sometimes the church authorities will not allow a funeral or burial service even where the suicide was an Orthodox Christian. At the same time, parish priests can ask permission of the bishop to offer a shorter service that includes prayers for the suicide, the same as they can ask permission to offer a service for someone who died of other causes but was not of the Orthodox faith. So there seems to be both a holdover of ancient attitudes, mostly negative, and a new openness to minister to the needs of the suicide's family with a public service, even a shortened one. Part of this modern shift in practice is due to the recognition that frequently suicides are the result of personal despair, overreaction to life trauma and disappointment, or recklessness that can be a manifestation of addiction or mental illness. In some cases, when human infirmities are looked on with empathy, the underlying cause appears to have weakened or virtually removed a person's will (agency).

Therefore, due to increasing awareness of the complexity of the underlying spiritual or mental condition of a suicidal person, there is a new openness to refrain from judgment and allow funerals. With the explicit blessing of the bishop, after consultation, a parish priest may conduct a regular memorial service for an Orthodox person who has ended his or her life. One priest said this is done with the understanding that the suicidal impulse was an "attack that added insult to injury against them." Here is an affinity with Martin Luther, who said that some people are attacked from the inside of their being just as others are attacked on the outside by robbers. There are also a few Saturdays of Souls in the Orthodox calendar, something like our western All Souls Day. These are times when prayers are said for all the departed, prayers which include specific names for any local congregation. Here, family members and neighbors may be prayed for, both Orthodox and non-Orthodox, as well as people who committed suicide.

Words That Point to God's Infinite Presence in Finite and Empty Places

The aftermath of any suicide is usually a time of crisis for surviving family and friends. At such times, Orthodox priests are often asked the same questions as Protestant pastors or Roman Catholic priests, because Christian people think and wonder along the same lines: "Can there be forgiveness when there is no time left for repentance after the act of suicide?" One priest in my local community responds to this question with an older Russian proverb, "God is between the bridge and the river."[10] This is meant to be a reminder that God was not absent in the moment when the suicide happened. There is no gap in space or time in human experience which God's presence does not fill (Ps 139:7–16; Rom 8:35–39), not even the gap between the bridge and the water. This is not a carte blanche assurance of forgiveness, but a very important reminder that we must leave the decision about forgiveness to God.

A Pastoral Letter

Over time, there has been a growing recognition that a variety of factors may influence a person's decision to commit suicide, including conditions that weaken the human mind and will, as well as recognition that the pastoral focus cannot neglect the survivors who require support in their grief. Early in the twenty-first century, a "Pastoral Letter on Suicide" was circulated to the priests after approval by the conference of Orthodox bishops. Here is an excerpt:

> First, we must remain mindful that the primary focus of the Church and its pastoral ministry in cases where a suicide has taken place is on the living, the family and friends of the deceased. We should maintain a certain humility while remembering that the state of the suicide victim is and must remain in the hands of God. Those left behind carry a great burden—of hurt, guilt, and often shame—with the realization that their loved one has taken his or her own life. They look to the Church and, especially, to the parish family, for strength and hope regarding the deceased, and for the support and love they themselves so urgently need. In addition to their personal pastoral response, clergy should direct grief-stricken family and friends to crisis

---

10. I owe this reference to Father Silouan Thompson.

> counseling resources in the area, which can complement the healing ministry of the Church.
>
> Second, as we have studied this issue, it has become clear to us that far more cases of suicide than have previously been recognized involve spiritual and/or physiological factors that significantly compromise a person's rationality and freedom. While not removing moral culpability from all suicide cases or changing our general stance against suicide's moral permissibility, we affirm the deep relationship between physical and spiritual factors in human agency and we acknowledge that, in most instances, the complex web of causes contributing to a suicide lies beyond our full understanding.
>
> Finally, because of the complexity of suicide, both in terms of determining causes and in terms of ministering to those most affected, the parish priest should always consult with his diocesan hierarch in order to discern the proper course of action, the general pastoral recommendation being that a church burial and memorial services could be granted unless there were an absence of significantly diminished capacities.

As the letter began with a review of biblical passages and the history of Orthodoxy's theological stance, which strongly affirms the sacredness of life, part of the conclusion returns to the theme that we also have a sacred connection with those who grieve in the aftermath of suicide.

> In his beautiful description of the Church as the "body of Christ," St. Paul writes, "If one member suffers, all suffer together; if one member is honored, all rejoice together." (1 Cor 12:26) The suicide of an Orthodox Christian is a tragedy that is suffered by the entire Church. As hierarchs of the Orthodox Church, we are acutely mindful of the need to maintain a perspective on suicide that is consistent with our identity and mission as the unified body of Christ.[11]

Icons and Prayer

Eastern practices have long been a mystery to western Christianity. One chief misapprehension on the part of evangelical Christians is that the Orthodox (Greek, Russian, Serbian, et al.) venerate icons to the point of worshipping them. This is not actually the case. Icons are religious

---

11. Canonical Orthodox Bishops in the Americas, "Pastoral Letter on Suicide."

images of biblical saints or saints from the patristic era, whose character and spiritual strength, or basic story, has been passed down as an example to the faithful. Icons are not used as the objects of worship but as aids to prayerful contemplation and the worship of God. Icons are images purposefully made unrealistic so that they become like lenses of spectacles, something used to see through rather than something to look at. The eastern Christians use icons as reminders to think about God and contemplate God's reality and truth, and in so doing, human thoughts are not meant to terminate on the icon itself but on that which the icon represents, namely God's work in the lives of Bible heroes, the holy family, and the saints. Thus, the praying person becomes open to God's Spirit working also in their own lives. This prayer time is about self-humbling, waiting and seeking, and being open to God's grace.

Theologian Nikos Nissiotis used to lecture on the distortions of perspective and the statuesque posture of the faces and figures, so contrary to realistic art and advances in perspective made by Renaissance art. These strange ways of drawing are done on purpose to shift attention away from the human portrayal and assist the praying viewer in thinking about the divine presence. Because this is the true purpose of an icon, they should never be seen as commercial or decorative art.

In presenting the insights of Professor Nissiotis, James Loder summarized by saying that icons are "designed so as to focus the viewer's attention beyond the icon to the reality they signify. As self-mitigating symbols and images, icons vanish as three-dimensional objects when the divine appears. As pictures they become windows for the divine presence. Thus contemplatives attend to an icon until they are met from the other side by the divine presence."[12] This in turn can help them look again at their world and circumstances in God's presence, with the Holy Spirit helping them re-envision or re-compose their life, purpose, and place in the world. This means that the use of icons in prayer may offer an opening for spiritual renewal and inner healing as well as guidance and insight. This is a potential but not an assured result.

Some icons are pictures of symbols which represent God's inner Triune nature. In each case, they are pictures which assist the mind and heart to focus on God's truth and look beyond distracting daily realities which interfere with prayer. The right use of an icon as an aid to prayer is foreign to many of us, but is not improper and may be beneficial.

---

12. Loder, *Educational*, 224.

None of this means that, even with proper use, respect, and devotion to God, icons become sources of insight or conduits of healing mercy. No more than reading the Bible is a guarantee that each time the Holy Spirit must illuminate the soul with some special personal message. God may choose to use such a method, but God is free not to if in providential wisdom a time of silence and waiting is required. All of which means there are no guaranteed paths to receiving a spiritual encounter with the living God. With this in mind, let us consider the following story that was brought to the attention of psychotherapist and theologian James Loder, after hearing the Nissiotis lectures. In his own context of spiritual counseling, a woman came to him who had felt drawn to death.

A university student from Taiwan felt overwhelmed by a broken love affair, the death of someone close to her, and a broken parental home that could no longer give her emotional support. She was very talented and intelligent, but her spirit was so weakened that her internal structure of strength seemed to collapse under the strain. She felt empty, exhausted, and unable to live. In this state of mind, she determined to commit suicide, but for some reason had an inner compulsion to clean her room first.

> As she did so, she came across an icon—an image of the face of Christ before which the devotee burns incense. Struck by the presence of the forgotten icon, she decided to pray and ask God's forgiveness before she took the overdose of sleeping pills. But as she performed the ritual on her knees, she began to contemplate the face of Christ behind the wisps of smoke that rose from the incense. Soon the image vanished and she found herself once again in Christ—that is, viewing herself as Christ viewed her, valuing herself from the standpoint of his love for her. When she finished, she rose up feeling joy in her heart and a desire to live. Moved in this way by Christ's Spirit, she dumped out the pills. The iconic image had become transparent, an imageless image, and now instead of seeing the little icon as part of her despairing world she saw the world through Christ's eyes. His vision of the world had become her own vision.[13]

Christ does not need to become a visible presence in order to heal the wounded human spirit, but visible symbols (icons, crosses) and visible reminders (including the living congregation that gathers for worship) can assist us in turning to Christ. This is one area where more conversation needs to take place between eastern and western forms of

---

13. Loder, *Educational Ministry*, 225.

Christianity. We may not always be aware of all the things that can support our individual or collective faith. Under times of persecution which lasted for centuries in the Middle East, for example, visible symbols and simple rote-learned confessions, prayers, and responses were used by God in many places to prevent the church from disappearing altogether.

Summary of the Historical Survey

In a long review of major theologians across denominational lines, we discover that they neither encourage suicide nor see it as a sin in a separate category by itself. Suicide is not a form of death that automatically places one beyond the reach of God's grace. Hopefully, these insights, taken separately or as a whole, assist pastoral care and theological reflection.

The official Roman Catholic teaching does not say that suicide is the unforgivable sin. Rome teaches people to pray for the departed to receive the fullness of God's grace, and encourages prayer for their surviving family members as well. While evangelical Christians are not historically in agreement with praying for the dead, nonetheless the Roman affirmation that God is free to save people who committed suicide cannot be discounted when making theological comparisons.[14] Significant thinkers in other branches of Christianity have arrived at the same answer, even if by other routes. None feel they understand it all. Suicide remains a mystery to us, but not one that can automatically undo the work of God in Christ for the salvation of sinful and broken people.

No one wants to offer false hope or unsound theology. In fields of scientific study, medical care, or psychological therapy, practice has to be grounded in sound theory. In harmony with this insight, pastoral care has to be grounded in sound theology. That is the reason why this theological survey has gone across generations, consulting some of the great minds and faithful servants in the history of the church. Taken as a whole, the majority of those in our survey never endorse suicide, yet do not give a counsel of absolute despair regarding salvation. In many cases human suffering tears down internal order and even devout Christians can descend into confusion and despondency, but there is another life that defines our hope. To be "in Christ" is our hope. We live by faith in God's promise that *in him* we are justified and sanctified, not in ourselves.

---

14. Regarding evangelical scholarship on the question of purgatory, see Wright, *Surprised by Hope*, 166–174.

Section Three

*Contemporary Samples
of Christian Reflection*

21

Sermon for Michael Foster by Canon Dr. Vigo A. Demant

IN THIS CHAPTER, WE discuss the important role that hope plays in human life. The beliefs and ideas we hold about God inform our hope, open doors to new possibilities, and encourage looking to spiritual resources. Therefore, we cannot discuss the presence of hope or the loss of hope only in psychological or medical categories. Humans are relational creatures and hope is tied to spiritual and relational contexts, to the inner strength and meaning-making potential of the individual person, and to the interaction between human spirit and Holy Spirit.[1] Therefore we cannot talk about hope in a Christian context without talking about everything needed to sustain hope, including one's sense of community.

Hope and Hopelessness

Theological work, whether done by pastors or other people, concerns the attempt to speak about God and human conditions as appropriately as possible based on biblical revelation and insight. With any sudden death, people think about the choices and actions that led up to it. Did the swimmer get cramps or intend to die? Questions can come to mind on the part of the preacher or listening congregation at every funeral. Here we ask, what does Christian theology say about hope? How is hope maintained

---

1. Loder, *Logic*; Carlsen, *Creative Aging*. Meaning making interacts with both our emotional and mental aspects of being human.

when God seems silent and far away? What does our theology say about the loss of hope? When we look on a suicidal death, do we equate losing hope with losing faith?

For any individual, the loss of hope is devastating. In the course of my early pastoral ministry, I knew adults who vividly remembered European refugee camps during and right after World War II. One woman recalled her childhood between the ages of six and ten, when everything her parents owned was reduced to what they could place in a suitcase. Hunger was hard to deal with, as the search for food became a constant daily struggle. There was fear about the future and uncertainty about missing relatives. The faces of brutal soldiers, frightened civilians, and lost and desperate people at food lines became etched in her memory. The very hardest thing to endure in that horrible time, however, was seeing her mother lose hope. That scared her to the core of her being because it felt as if her mother had already died. In Vigo Demant's sermon, the loss of hope is presented as a contributing factor to suicide. When something is so essential to human survival as hope, what contributes to its terrible loss?

The loss of hope becomes overwhelming when persons assume they will never recover their sense of safety, trust in others, or reason to keep fighting for a better future. If the reason for living is lost, life itself does not seem worth holding onto. Hope may be intangible, but it is essential to human survival. Edward John Carnell put it very simply when he said, "Some people despair. They are so weary of living that they kill themselves. A few of these people have sick minds, but most of them simply lose hope."[2] Losing hope is not the same as mental weakness, though the person who has lost hope will not respond to rational arguments as though they count for very much. The loss of hope is a spiritual affliction and must receive a spiritual cure. Canon Demant's sermon significantly points out that losing one's hope is not the same as losing one's faith. We should not lose sight of this very important distinction when talking to people who are grieving after a suicide.

On the subject of losing hope, I would only add that losing the feeling of hope is not the same as losing one's ground for hope. Whether we feel it or not, God's love is *for* us in Christ Jesus (2 Cor 1:18–20). God's promise of atonement for sin and resurrection after death is based on a foundation that is secure in God rather than in human feelings. The gift God promises cannot be lost just because we no longer feel sure about it,

---

2. Carnell, *Kingdom of Love*, 14–15.

or recognize our unworthiness to receive it. A ship can float on the water based on its own sturdy construction and proper ballast, not because of how passengers feel about riding on it. Our feeling of hopelessness is a form of suffering, but does not require God to remove the hope of our salvation. Nothing we hope for in Christ Jesus depends on how we feel about it, but rather on the trustworthiness of him who loved us and gave himself for us (Gal 2:20).

V. A. Demant also clarifies that not all suicide is a rejection of God, though it may be a failure to completely trust in God through a particular set of circumstances. In the inner life of the suicidal person, it may seem that hope is gone, but losing one's hope is not necessarily the same as losing one's faith. One may be suicidal without any intention of rejecting God's grace. In the despair of the moment, a person might be engulfed by an overwhelming desire to end pain, but that is not exactly the same as turning away from God. There may be no intention of renouncing one's faith in Christ, however much it seems impossible to entrust one's circumstances into God's providential care. We are reminded once again that only God can judge righteously, for only God knows the thoughts, desires, and inner workings of every wounded soul. Only God knows how to redeem those who have failed, many times in life or in the final hour, to fully trust in God's providential care and sustaining grace through all tribulations.

The circle of God's faithfulness to each one of us must always be drawn as a greater circumference that entails within it the smaller circle of our inadequate faith. The wider circle of God's faithfulness engulfs the smaller circle of our weakness and inconsistent faithfulness. We may yearn to please God more but fail to do so. Even so, God's commitment to us is greater than our inadequate response to his love. Nothing can separate us from the love of God (Romans 8), including the pain in our souls.

Who Was Michael Foster?

Because there was a specific context for Vigo Demant's message, a word or two may be in order about the victim, because he was well known then but less so now in the passing of time. Michael Beresford Foster was a scholar working at Oxford University as a lecturer in philosophy. His first book, *The Political Philosophies of Plato and Hegel*, was well received.[3] He also

---

3. Foster, *Political Philosophies*. This still received favorable reviews over two

published important articles on the history of science in the journal *Mind*. He wrote *Mystery and Philosophy* as a response to the prevalent logical positivism that was used by some intellectuals in an attempt to undermine the Christian faith of students.[4] Foster worked in a rigorous discipline and was not ashamed to be identified as a Christian in such a notable academic climate. Because of his quiet witness, many students came to talk with him who were not assigned for tutoring. When he took his own life at age fifty-six, his friends were dismayed. As Kathleen Bliss reported his death, she included these reflections on suicide:

> To the popular press, this was another intellectual with a hidden kink overbalancing; to the non-believer, one more instance of the inadequacy of Christian faith to defend its exponents from ultimate despair. To any close-knit fellowship, especially to one bound together by a common Christian faith and loyalty, an event of this kind in its midst inflicts a blow which cannot be measured in the ordinary terms of loss, though is present and keenly felt. The measure is also one of failure. It is not enough for Christians to say there were signs of mental illness; "it is all quite explicable; we must accept a medical view—he was sick, and we didn't realize how sick." The medical explanation needs a larger context if it is to satisfy Christian conscience. When and where community was strong, suicide was rare. Its high incidence in modern life has at least some of its roots in loneliness as a spiritual and mental thing. To a frightening extent, we human beings sustain one another in life by things more than bread. To be 'one body in Christ' is to acknowledge our interdependence on the ultimate source of all life in Him. It is not enough to have a "personal faith" it must be faith lived "in the body."[5]

Bliss's concern about the loss of community is very relevant to our present time. After recounting aspects of Foster's life, she concluded by saying, "Many people will all their days carry the memory of this gentle, kind, and deeply disturbing man and count themselves glad to have known him. He brought peace wherever he went; may it be his at last."[6]

---

decades after its initial publication.

4. Foster, *Mystery and Philosophy*. Philosopher Diogenes Allen wrote of this book, "An uncompromising contrast of Christianity and analytic philosophy, with a brilliant presentation of the nature of mystery in Greek and Christian thought. The finest single response to analytic philosophy." See Allen, *Philosophy for Understanding Theology*, 278; see chapter 11 for a review of the origins of analytic philosophy.

5. Bliss, "Michael Foster," 258.
6. Bliss, "Michael Foster," 258.

Vigo Demant's Sermon for Michael Foster

The following sermon was preached by Revd. Dr. Vigo August Demant, Canon, and Regius Professor of Moral and Pastoral Theology at Oxford University.

Sermon for Michael Beresford Foster, who died 15th October 1959, preached in Christ Church, Oxford, on Sunday, 18th October 1959.[7]

> Christ Church mourns today over the loss of one of its senior members, Mr. Michael Foster. Whatever may be said of him later and better, on this first Sunday after his death a tribute is due to his memory. He was known and loved and respected not only by his pupils, by his academic colleagues and the domestic staff of the College, but also by many members of the University outside these walls, as well as by men and women of the general public. What is more, this esteem very often grew out of an immense gratitude which many, both young and older, feel they owe to Michael Foster for his understanding, his sympathy, and for the trouble he took in helping them spiritually or intellectually, or with just deep personal concern for their problems.
>
> Those of you here to whom he may be only a name, must therefore forgive us for using this sermon period in order to voice briefly what we feel we have lost so suddenly. Indeed, it may not be so difficult for a general congregation to allow us this domestic privilege, because, as I hope I may help you to see, there is a sermon to be found in Michael Foster's life and teaching and struggles.
>
> All who knew him well, and mostly those who found their Christian faith through him or had it strengthened, were aware that his own faith—which he came to latish in life after a period of agnosticism—was maintained only through a recurring struggle against practical doubt, and this is what made him such a wonderful kindler of faith in others. You know, there are two types of Christians who have conveyed to their fellow men the resources of Christian faith, and the Lord uses both types in His own way. One type seems favouritely blessed by Almighty God; their faith is a steady, unruffled, strong assurance which carries them across the dark patches leaving no deep spiritual scars. Such were in modern times men like John Wesley and Archbishop William Temple.
>
> The other type is used by God, almost unmercifully it seems to us; they cannot relinquish the faith to which they have

---

7. Used by permission.

committed themselves, but for them it is not one of "the consolations of religion," it is a heroic struggle to hold on with the will to obedience and discipleship, when often their thoughts and feelings seem to say they are God forsaken. John Henry Newman was, I think, one of these, and so was Bishop Charles Gore. These men acquire a seminal and robust kind of certainty, all the stronger for the pressure of practical doubt, especially doubt of their own acceptance by their Lord and Master.

Michael Foster was one of these. I was privileged to have his confidence from time to time in moments of deep depression which afflicted him. The roots of that recurring melancholia were never clear to me or perhaps to him; and it would be impertinent and irreverent to probe too deeply. I can only say that I have a terrible sense of failure, in that I was only able to restore his confidence for limited periods. I think it is a testimony to the depth and reality of his faith that it gave him over and over again a desolating sense that he was betraying it. Of the three theological virtues, he had faith and charity in abundance; but somehow there frequently occurred a hitch just where faith spills over into the virtue of hope.

Perhaps, if he had met wider Christian influences after his conversion, he would have been able to see his repeated dejection as part of the dark night of the soul, which when first met seems as if it means that God has taken Himself away from us into a far country, but when understood becomes a means of assurance that God holds us in our very being in spite of leaving our thoughts and feelings bereft of a sense of His presence.

I would say that Michael Foster came by a hair's breadth only short of complete sanctity; he had all the marks of holiness but just missed the joy of the saints. Yet, note how the Lord used him. In the two days since he died I, and at least one of my colleagues on the Chapter, have received messages of condolence from people—odd people about town and university dons here and elsewhere—who say that they owe their faith and their soul to him. Isn't it as if, in a way, the Lord sometimes laid upon him the doubt and desolation he was removing from others, like the suffering servant?[8] He was taking their burdens upon himself,

---

8. The servant passages are found in Isa 42:1–4; 49:1–6; 50:4–9; 52:13–53:12, with references to the servant generally followed by words of God's affirmation. Whether or not the original reference was to the suffering of the nation of Israel or to a suffering representative of Israel, such as an obedient prophet, the fourth song is particularly interpreted by Christians as having an ultimate reference to the suffering of Jesus Christ. Not all assign it the category of predictive prophecy, however, for some see it as typological, which means that the New Testament writers began with the life of Jesus

and in his great humility, frequently thinking that he himself was the castaway.

I was about to describe him as a heroic soul, but he would not have liked that, for he tells us in his book *Mystery and Philosophy* that heroism is not a Christian virtue. The heroic man prays, "Lead me into temptation so that I may test out the power of the good in me," he quotes from Bonhoeffer.[9] But the Christian prays, "Lead me not into temptation," the fiery trials which I may not be able to stand. If then we may not call him a heroic soul, we can certainly say that his was a sacrificial life; he gave to others what he could not all the time ensure for himself, namely that assurance that he was accepted of God.

This man endured the Cross in himself; he could have avoided that by relinquishing his commitment to Christ. He was one of those on whom tribulation comes "because of the Word," as our Lord said in explaining the parable of the sower.[10] But, unlike the men whom Jesus there described, Michael never shirked the tribulations by going back when he had once put his hand to the plough.[11] That is how the Lord uses some of his most faithful servants. As for most of the rest of us, for whom our faith is a calm certitude or a shallower and painless contentment–well! We may be thankful that God has used us mercifully, and we have our own kind of ministry. But we are not of very much use to Him; we haven't suffered enough in our faith. We get the blessing which Jacob received without having had to wrestle with the Angel of the Lord.

We must then thank God for this sacrificial life. I would have conventionally said that it has been cut off too soon. But a letter I received corrects me, and I now see with greater insight. It is from a lady in this university, and she puts the matter in a different light. She writes, "Rather it seems to me that it was a great grace that allowed someone as heavily burdened with

---

and then searched the Scriptures for similar patterns of ministry, witness, suffering, restoration of hope after a time of despair, or restoration of life itself. In all the swirl of current scholarly discussion, it is not to be doubted that Jesus derived his own identity and sense of mission from these passages, as well as Dan 7. He is uniquely responsible for linking the Messiah's mission to personal suffering. Jesus of Nazareth also taught that his obedient servants must be prepared to suffer for his sake: Mark 8:34 and Luke 9:23; cf. Phil 3:8–10.

9. Bonhoeffer, *Temptation*, 9–10; cf. Foster, *Mystery*, 71–84.

10. This reference to personal tribulation is from the parable of the sower, Matt 13:3–5, 20–21.

11. Luke 9:61–62. A good short explanation of this passage is Bruce, *Hard Sayings of Jesus*, 161–63.

unresolved sorrows as Michael Foster was, to continue so courageously and faithfully for so long."

He must have been one of the best loved university teachers in the whole country. We loved him here, though he tried us sometimes by turning a direct practical problem into a tense moral dilemma. He was at the disposal of pupils and outsiders who came to him for guidance and got it. He was also at the mercy of unhappy people with a grudge against life or a grudge against others, and he agonized over whether perhaps they had not been victims of injustice. Here again is the sacrificial life in action.

I have touched on these solemn and religious aspects of our dear colleague's life, and I know that he would wish me to say these things now, which if they had been said in his lifetime, it would have been telling secrets.

There are other things. Of his work as a teacher of philosophy I am not the man to speak, nor is this the place. But two aspects of his work strike me as adding to the picture of his mind and personality. A good many years ago, Michael Foster wrote some articles in a philosophical journal on the origin of the scientific impulse in Western civilization, and connected it with the world outlook brought about by the influence of the Bible and Christian theology. This apparently paradoxical thesis has been quoted over and over again by others who have shown its importance by building upon it.[12] But Michael never seemed to think they were of much importance or value, and did not take up the matter again.

The second thing I have in mind is the way Foster would handle a purely secular subject like political theory, respecting its autonomy as a secular discipline, and at the same time making clear that a Christian thinker must see its meaning as a worldly matter in the light of God's providence. He never brought in religion as a pinch of piety to sweeten up worldly

12. Foster, "Christian Doctrine of Creation"; Foster, "Christian Theology." These seminal studies showed that Christian theology was integral to the rise of modern science, having an indispensable part in developing and promoting the right conceptual mindset and favorable conditions for its growth and public acceptance. Foster was in agreement with some things said earlier on this subject by Alfred North Whitehead, but expanded on the information and contended for recognition of Christianity's truly positive role in the development of science. Many scholars specializing in the history of ideas have carried Foster's work forward since the time of his death, including Reijer Hooykaas, Stanley Jaki, Christopher Kaiser, Harold Nebelsick, and T. F. Torrance. Sociologists Alvin Schmidt and Rodney Stark have also focused on Christianity's role in securing the foundations and development of modern science. T. F. Torrance stated that Foster's role was groundbreaking.

concerns. He sought to place secular things like government or science—those which belong to this age, this saeculum between creation and the last day—to place them in a framework fashioned by God. Michael never encouraged people to go about being pietistic when they were meant to be scientific or political. But he strove to suggest that secular things were an essential element in God's world.

Today is the Feast of St. Luke the Evangelist, who gave us the Third Gospel and the Acts of the Apostles. He tells us in the preface to his Gospel what he was after. It was to give to his readers—personified as one, Theophilus, lover of God—to give them an assurance that the faith they were living by was grounded in evidence which could be tested. He did it by finding out and collecting all that was known about the Christ. Luke himself had not been an apostle or an eye-witness, but he went for his information to those who could testify. Thus he gave us what is in some ways the fullest, best written, and most moving account of the strange happenings which started our faith.

Michael Foster too wanted students and scholars to find the same kind of assurance in testing what they believed, and this was to be done, not by running to the Bible or theology or the Church between times, but by pursuing the things they were studying as if the pursuit were a vocation. His own life was a vocation, and a costly one to himself.

To God's gracious mercy we commit him;
           and may light eternal shine upon him.

Editor's Reflections

Canon Demant spoke to mind and heart in this beautifully written and meaningful sermon. Before a congregation that included many who personally knew the victim, Demant held out the most negative and frightening aspects of Foster's affliction, then helped them hold together both the nature of his affliction and his faith. Did Michael Foster have doubts? Did the doubts compound his depression or vice versa? Yes, there were doubts and bouts with despondency. God seemingly used his struggles with doubt to empower his sensitivity to those working through their own serious doubt. Did Foster lose his sense of hope? Yes, at times and in the end, but without losing his faith. It is possible he was a suffering servant, like that of Isa 53, who did more for God through his suffering than many do for God who enjoy riches of happiness, wealth and comfort.

When a pastor can speak the truth about the victim's affliction, if done with modesty and sensitivity, the listeners are often empowered to trust the preacher on a basic level. A trust develops because they sense real understanding about the human condition, and a sincere empathy for the particular person in this tragedy. It is not always easy to do, but connecting an affliction to the victim's faith carries more power to lift and heal wounded hearts than can be imagined. Professor Demant had genuine material to work with on both counts, based on his personal knowledge. He did a masterful job tying together important factors that may not have been obvious to everyone in the congregation. Beyond the question of how Michael Foster may have viewed his own life, the preacher went into the deeper waters of how God may choose to use one's life, even the life of a contemporary suffering servant. Your life may be lived in faithfulness to God without being fully aware of all the ways in which you serve God's purposes, even when your life includes pain, fear, confusion, and distress.

22

A Suicide, A Funeral, a Sermon by Will Willimon

SURELY YOU PREACHERS WILL back me up when I declare to seminarians, "The funeral sermon is the chief theological test of your preaching."

In funerals, we must either put up or shut up. On many Sundays, we can get away with a presentation of the Christian faith as American self-help with a spiritual tint, savvy life coaching, unctuous focusing upon our vaunted wounds, or a moral nudge to buckle down, follow our better angels, and work justice in the world, since God's isn't. But when death has done its worst and then smirks, "There, what do you have to say about that?" we preachers show why the church needs us.

The world's sentimental platitudes ("She'll live on in our memories," "Everything happens for a reason," "He's gone on to a better place") are pitiful, insufficient bromides in the face of death. No wonder that we preachers are intimidated by having to concoct a funeral sermon. If the church has nothing to say in response to death's dealings, then why listen to us about anything?

Paul said we do not grieve as those who have no hope (1 Thess 4:13). The funeral sermon demands an answer: What is our hope, our peculiarly Christian hope, that refuses to give Paul's "final enemy" (1 Cor 15:26) the last word?

Good pastoral leadership of the funeral begins with clarity about the question, "Who's a funeral for?" Pastoral care for grieving family and friends who are in the immediate crisis of grief. Yes. But a funeral goes off the rails if conceived only as an act of pastoral care for a family in mourning. It's a service of death and resurrection for the community: those who may not be in an acute crisis of mourning but who are dealing with past loss and preparing for future losses (that is, all of us), those who, living in a death-denying culture, lack the theological resources for honestly thinking about mortality and finitude (just about everybody in the room). As a word the church says to the world, the service is potentially prophetic, evangelistic. "Hey world, Jesus Christ has given us the means of talking truthfully, publicly about the unmentionable. Jesus Christ, the only one who ever made it out of the tomb, gives us something better than the world has to say."

I doubt that any of you preachers will disagree with my contention that among the toughest of funeral sermons is the one demanded at a service for one who has walked down the lonely path of suicide. Facile "Celebrations of Life" wilt before the dreadfulness of self-inflicted dying. In few pastoral contexts is a congregation's question "Got any word from the Lord?" more challenging.

Tom Smith (I'll name him): aged 50, spectacular success in business, married, father of two teenaged boys. One morning, after bantering with his wife about groceries, he went into his garage and hanged himself.

The Smiths were members of a Presbyterian church, but, like lots of people, hadn't gone much since COVID. As a friend of the family, I attended the service of death and resurrection on a gray winter afternoon. Sure, I grieved for the family in their shock, loss, and, I suspected, even anger. But I had a special place in my heart for the pastors and the task that lay before them. The community has been shaken to its core by this death, wracked by all sorts of questions and speculation. Now the church gathers, demanding that its pastors say something in the face of this unspeakable sadness that dares not speak its name.

The service and the sermon will stick in my mind for a long time. What I heard from two skilled pastors, Meg and Jarrett, judged the shakiness of my own funeral leadership and is a model for those of us who are faced, as all of us preachers are sooner or later, with having to say a word in the face of one of the most difficult kinds of death.[1]

Pastor Meg's opening welcome determined the course of the service:

---

1. The pastors were Meg Peery McLaughlin and Jarrett McLaughlin, serving University Presbyterian Church, Chapel Hill, North Carolina (names and sermon extracts used by permission).

> In life and in death we belong to God.
> We must start with that gospel truth. It is the only thing that will carry us through this.
> We gather today in sure and certain hope of the resurrection to give thanks for the life of Tom Smith.
> We gather to express our sadness at his death. We do that together, so that his beloved family, Susan, Jim, and Joe would not have to bear that grief alone.
> We do all of this in the presence of God who has made promises to Tom and to us, promises that can be trusted: that God is our refuge and strength, a very present help in trouble;
> that the eternal God is our resting place and underneath are the everlasting arms.
> . . . And my dearest friends, God keeps God's promises. They are steadfast and sure. Even now.
> Especially now . . . I know that it may feel impossible to know what to pray, what to say to God right now. And perhaps the words that you do have, you feel might not be church appropriate.

Meg took little of the congregation's readiness to listen for and to speak to God in worship for granted; she knew that it was important to step up and lead, and to clearly articulate the purpose, the intent, and the legitimate expectations worshippers might have for this service:

> Hear me when I say everything you bring into this sanctuary is allowed, we need not hold anything back from the One who knows it all already. In church we tell the truth. And we trust that God hears the prayers we scream or stumble to get out. And when we can't muster any prayer of our own, we lean on the community around us.
> So let us pray together an Irish Prayer, as we sing hymn number 450, Be Thou My Vision.

Christian? In most funerals I attend, and in too many that I have led, pastoral attempts at comfort, assuaging of grief, and psychological support take precedence over truth. Death, particularly death by suicide, casts us preachers (judging from many funerals) into an almost irresistible temptation to euphemize, obfuscate, and prevaricate. In doing so, we sell our great gift of distinctively Christian hope for a mess of psychotherapeutic, sentimental pottage, offering care that's not really care, hope that's false. As unpleasant as the truth may be, there's no getting through grief without truth-telling about the reality of our loss, about a merciful

God in whom is our only hope. How refreshing to hear a pastor warn (or reassure?) upfront, "In church we tell the truth."

Then Pastor Jarrett prayed:

> God, we are here. Love has drawn us in its tether to this place to surround this family with our loving care; to seek comfort for our own troubled hearts; to honor the life and express our sadness at the death of Tom Smith.
>
> Truth be told, we're also unsteady on our feet, so we are also here to lay hold of some bedrock promises. We cling to the words of Jesus, who said, "I am the resurrection and the life."
>
> . . . We are here to remember these promises for ourselves, and to claim them for your servant and child Tom. We pray this in the name of Christ the first born of the resurrection. Amen.

Afterwards I learned that pastors Meg and Jarrett scripted every word they spoke in the service. Though they led with warmth and conviction, directly addressing the family and congregation, they left nothing to ad-lib or extempore improvisation. Respecting the gravity of the situation, the challenge of offering pastoral care to family and friends in their particular grief, as well as the need for a clearly articulated statement of peculiar Christian hope, they carefully premeditated the whole service, word-for-word.

There followed two friends who spoke "Words of Remembrance," heartfelt, warm reminiscence of Tom, though their words were redundant and predictable. Was I the only one in the congregation—as Tom was praised for his love of his boys, his joy in sports, his kindness and hospitality—who thought glumly, "and Tom chose to leave, rather than stay here with us"?

Jarrett introduced a reading of Ps 139 with,

> Tom was a seeker . . . reading and seeking deeper understandings of God. . . . My prayer is that at the end of all that seeking, Tom understood himself as the one who is sought—that there is nowhere we can go that God cannot find us, and hold us in loving care.
>
> O Lord, you have searched me and known me.
> You know when I sit down and when I rise up;
> You discern my thoughts from far away.
> You search out my path and my lying down
> and are acquainted with all my ways.

"Tom was a seeker": appropriately personal, naming, claiming the unique personality and discipleship of the deceased, yet quickly moving to a theological characterization of the departed as "one who is sought." Only a God who delights in seeking and saving can help. That's a biblical truth there's no way of knowing without being told it by the psalmist or a preacher.

Meg then read Jer 31:31–34, and Rom 8 as prelude to her funeral sermon.

Words of Hope

Joe, you told me your dad loved coats and blankets; to be wrapped up in the cold. He hated hot weather, maybe because he grew up near Chicago. The Triangle isn't the coldest place Tom could have chosen to live, but . . . Susan had a job there.

. . . Tom loved his family, this family. Having grown up without a strong relationship with his own father, parenting Joe and Jim was the joy of his life.

Today we honor and celebrate that love—how Tom sat on the sidelines to watch you boys play ball, how he loved to travel with you, and share meals with you.

A foodie to the core, he was the kind of man who when given the option between McDonalds and nothing, would choose nothing.

. . . And now we are here, on a rainy cold day, bracing for the days ahead without him.

[Meg begins her sermon with touchingly human, specific memories of Tom. The warm blankets that Tom enjoyed are truthfully contrasted with the "rainy cold day" of the funeral as family and friends brace themselves "for the days ahead without him." Fine mix of comforting, cheerful memories with somber truth. Run-of-the-mill funeral sermons would leave things there and think they had accomplished the purpose of the proclamation. A family left holding a few fond memories as if our remembrance is sufficient consolation for "the days ahead without him." But not for Pastor Meg.]

One of the scripture passages I chose today are words from the prophet Jermiah, who speaks of covenants and law.

This is what Tom spent his days in, of course, contracts and law and agreements between parties. But even had Tom made a living another way, I'd still be reading this, because what the prophet says is that God writes God's love down.

Writes it down so it's plain to see. So anyone can come back to it. God writes love on our very hearts.

[Nice connection of a lawyer who loved to read and write with the words of a prophet about a God who loves to write. Then, it's as if citation of the Scripture gives the preacher the gumption to speak even greater truth. Again, candor.]

Tom wasn't an easy man to know. He was quiet. Reserved. His social circle wasn't wide, but it was incredibly deep.

Tom was in his head a lot.

[Back to the writing of prophet Jeremiah as a way of illuminating the life and death of Tom.]

Maybe that's why he had this unique habit. Tom always carried around a little notebook. And he'd forever be writing in it.

He read something he wanted to remember, he treasured something from a conversation, he had an idea pop into his mind, he wanted to recall the name of a good bottle of wine, or a place he'd like to travel to see.

He'd also write about you. He'd note that you were interested in this or that, and then he'd send you an article about it 18 months later. He wrote it all down.

Surely this is one way that we can see that Tom was made in God's own image. For God knows the importance of writing things down. Of making note of what is most important. Of keeping the words close. Of having them there to go back to when you need them most.

And what God chooses to write, church, is the very promise of the Gospel: that God will be our God no matter what. That we will be God's beloved people no matter what.

We don't have to learn it or earn it—or even understand it. It simply is true: We belong.

It is written down. Here. In us.

[Tom's quirks and habits, his life and death, as opportunities to highlight "the very promise of the Gospel." Meg's voice gains intensity as she stares the congregation in the eye and forcefully speaks truth, specifically gospel truth about life, death, and life beyond death:]

So, listen to me. Tom Smith's life is not defined by his tragic choice last Friday morning. Not defined by his too-soon death. Not defined by his mistakes, his burdens, his regrets.

Tom Smith is God's beloved child. That is who he was, and who he is. Even now.

Tom was baptized as a child. . . . I don't know what the baptismal font looked like there. I know what ours looks like. Susan, you and Tom stood by this one when Jim and Joe were baptized. [Baptismal memories from a happier time. Subtle, but so appropriate the connection of baptism with death and resurrection.]

Most baptismal fonts have eight sides. You may remember, in the story of creation from the book of Genesis, that God created the world in seven days, including the day God rested.

So you might think the font should have seven sides, for those seven days of creation. In ancient Christian tradition, the eighth day signified the New Creation; the time when, through Christ, all that is wrong will be made right, all that is broken will be reconciled, all that is injured will be healed, all that is hurt will be mended. All greed gone. All shame erased. All tears wiped away. All things, everything, made whole, made new. [Eschatological promise. I love it when mainline, liberal preachers risk eschatology.]

It is a day God promises for all of God's children. Tom Smith is one of those children. He is God's beloved child. [Having honestly alluded to some of the painful facts of Tom's life and death, the preacher honestly, decisively, tells the truth about God.]

Just as you are. Just as you all are. And in just a bit you will walk out of here into the cold, so put on your coat, [back to the earlier image of cold and warmth] and trust that though your heart is broken in grief, [honesty about the pain] on it is also written the gospel truth. [In the end, in death, our sole comfort is that which is "the gospel truth."]

God's love is written on your heart.

In my experience of this sermon, I felt Pastor Meg achieved just the right interplay of unabashed affirmation of Christian eternal verities ("Listen to me.") and honest, affectionate recognition of the loss of a specific beloved, confusing, human life. By God's grace, Tom's ending might not be the end.

There followed "Amazing Grace," rendered by bagpipes [I love Presbyterians.], an affirmation of faith, and closing hymn.

Pastor Jarrett Then Spoke a Prayer

Lord, what are we supposed to say to you? What are we supposed to say at all? We open our mouths and nothing comes out—or whatever does come out feels clunky and clumsy. We are speechless. So perhaps we will simply let our tears do the talking for us?

. . . We're confused and unsure how to feel. We're stricken, we're sad, we're scared, we're angry—it changes with each passing moment and sometimes we are all of these at once.

We're left wondering about how we weren't done loving him.

We're perplexed by all the questions that have no easy answers.

What we will not say is that any of this is okay.

We will not pretend that it makes any sense. And we refuse to say that it's your will.

So perhaps our prayer is that you would speak to us, God. And please, please start by saying that you hurt. You hurt for Susan, Jim, and Joe. For this brokenhearted family and for all who surround them in loving care this day.

But keep speaking, God. Speak comfort to our ache, and bring comfort into being through the gifts of community. Into our bleak confusion and sadness, speak light.

When community encircles Susan speak comfort, when teachers and coaches and friends draw close to these boys—speak love.

Speak forgiveness where regret weighs heavy and where moments are replayed on repeat in search of something to regret; where there are things we wish we hadn't done or things we wish we had. Speak grace.

Above all speak resurrection: new life, yes to Tom, now, who finds embrace in your loving arms, but also to each and every soul who feels a little less alive inside. Speak newness. Speak hope. Speak resurrection.

And then give us ears to hear you.

Even if we cannot soak in what you are saying, even if we can't at this moment believe it, help us to sense your presence at the edges, trusting that with your voice there speaking, we have some glimmer of trust that we are not alone.

[I very much liked this concluding return to Meg's sermon's theme of speaking, and hearing, fruit of close consultation and care between the preacher and the liturgist.]

God, with you we are never alone.

Finally, O God, we pray that our grief not smother our gratitude: for even through our tears we can picture him scribbling something in his field notes and tucking away some sliver of knowledge. We celebrate this man who sought out a wider world through the unlikely friendships he cultivated.

We give thanks for this foodie who loved to set the table for one more.

... Help us hold onto these images of Tom Smith, just as you see in him all that was good and kind and faithful. Help us trust that he is at home with you now and forevermore.

We pray all this in the name of Jesus Christ, who when we couldn't find the right words, gave us these to say together: Our Father, who art in heaven.

[In this pastor, the great Reformed tradition of public prayer continues.]

A tragic suicide, a well-crafted, biblically accountable service, a skillful, faithful sermon; encouragement for us preachers.

23

Sermon for a Teenage Boy
by Eric Peterson

Editor's Introduction

As a young pastor, the first suicide incident I worked with was a nineteen year old boy who felt devastated when his girlfriend broke up with him. He took a gun and aimed it at his chest, his eyes swimming with tears. When he pulled the trigger, either because of the angle or because his hand was shaking, the bullet narrowly missed his heart but punctured a lung. In the shock of finding himself shot but still alive, he suddenly realized he wanted to live. Before he passed out from physical trauma and loss of blood, he got to a phone and dialed 911 (a few years before cell phones were common).

I mention this to show that some teenage suicide is not contemplated in advance, does not involve planning or prolonged brooding, but rather is based on a sudden impulse acted out in a spur-of-the moment decision. In moments of great distress, a teenage person's reason can be overwhelmed by emotion and temporarily unbalanced. Things can be done quite suddenly without forethought. Some actions are totally destructive in a final sense, as in a suicidal act which cannot be undone. This type of suicide is different from the brooding, depressed young person who contemplates suicide for a long while and plans out the details of how, when, and where it will be done. In this first case, thankfully, the boy was very fortunate to have botched his suicide attempt, a failure that is rare with males. His was a beautiful failure because he got a second opportunity to live. In the instant after he was impacted by the bullet, he knew his mistake and realized that life was a gift he did not want to throw away. A number of family and friends gathered in the hospital to give him support and encouragement. In this case there was no funeral.

In another case where I helped with a funeral, the boy was very successful in keeping his plan to destroy himself a secret, carrying it out in a private location where he could not be found in time for an intervention or resuscitation. In this case, death was not based on a sudden impulse. As with the case Pastor Eric Peterson describes below, it rocked his family and neighbors. High school classmates displayed great emotion for days and disrupted their normal routines in many ways. While an overflow crowd was anticipated, rightfully as it turned out, we were asked by school officials not to hold the service at the school gymnasium. A great emotional display of love and grief, with the whole school participating, has in some other cases triggered copycat suicides. This happens when another young person with personal problems seeks to create additional tension and drama through a second act of suicide: his or her own. In general, it may not be desirable to hold such a service in a school gymnasium, although there are situations where no other location seems practical because of crowd capacity.

Because of concern over the problem of copycat behavior, we held the service in a church setting, but would not allow a slide presentation showing numerous photos of the young man. As painful as this denial was to the family, we had been advised by grief counselors that it was necessary to take this precaution. This may have been excessive worry on our part but it was difficult to determine in advance. The mother expressed disappointment but the father agreed with our decision. In hindsight, it seems we could have allowed a few slide pictures without an excessive amount of drama, and this probably counts as one of my pastoral mistakes in the early years of my ministry. We could have found some middle ground. But this is also an example of a time when I knew I was in over my head and did not know which way to go. As pastors, we ask for guidance but make mistakes, and some mistakes are only seen in retrospect. These tragic funerals are no exception. As pastors, we seek wisdom in prayer and counsel, then do the best we know how to do, trusting in God's providential care and mercy.

The following sermon was given at a suicide funeral in a large auditorium. Eric Peterson serves Colbert Presbyterian Church in Washington State, and knows many teens who attend family worship and youth meetings. In the following, he presents the context and the sermon for the suicide of a teenage male whose family did not attend his congregation, with his name changed to protect privacy.

Pastor Eric Peterson's Context and Pastoral Concerns (in His Own Words)

I received the call from a sheriff's chaplain, asking me to tend to a family in our neighborhood who had come home to find that their middle child, a son, had committed suicide. Brad was a popular young man, a star football athlete, and would have graduated from high school the following month. But he suffered from a severe case of sleep apnea and he was very depressed and sleep deprived, causing a significant impairment in his judgment, leading to what was, apparently, a fairly impulsive act that ended his life.

The school administration and I shared a common concern over copycat behaviors. In the days following Brad's death, there was an enormous outpouring of emotion and energy which dominated the campus environment. Adolescents seem to have a fascination with death, and when it is coupled with the kind of power that can immobilize (or mobilize, depending on how you look at it) an entire community, suicide can be an attractive option for students who otherwise have no power and little popularity. One of my goals in leading this funeral was to dissuade anyone contemplating suicide, either then or in the future.

Although there were many adults in the gymnasium that day, the audience I was primarily speaking to was the twelve hundred students who were reeling emotionally and trying to make sense of the kind of tragedy that most had never yet come even close to experiencing. Frankly, I overstepped my personal confidence level when I tried to reassure the community that Brad's new home was with God in heaven, partly because I wasn't clear about his commitment to Christ, and partly because such judgments are God's alone. Ultimately, I opted to address the mistake of suicide and to emphasize (and personally rely on) the grace of God.

A Service of Witness to the Resurrection

Opening Remarks

We are here to celebrate Brad _____'s life this afternoon. And we'll have ample time to do that in just a bit. But I want to be clear that we are not here to celebrate his death. In this life that we have been given, we are also given a lot of freedom to make a lot of decisions about how to live. But the Bible is clear that the giving and taking of life is God's business, not ours.

Brad's life was and is worth celebrating. But his death was tragic. It was a huge mistake. And it should not have happened. When I stood at his grave site earlier today with his family, I told them that our visit to that cemetery was grossly premature; we were standing there about seventy years too soon. That, I believe, is nothing if it's not a tragedy.

And I am quite sure that Brad, given a second chance, would have made a different choice. If he could now see the effects of his decision to end his life, I think he would be deeply remorseful, and, given a second chance, I think he would most certainly have chosen otherwise. And while we don't know everything that was going on in his mind and his body, we do know that he wasn't feeling well and he wasn't thinking clearly. He wasn't thinking about how much his decision was going to hurt you all. All he could think about at the time was finding some relief—a way out of his pain.

This room is full of a wide range of emotions right now. There is deep sadness combined with profound gratitude. There is anger and there is the kind of pain that can't even be described. And Brad caused it. Because he made a terrible mistake. We've all done that from time to time, haven't we? Made mistakes that were the cause of other people's pain? Usually, we can say that we're sorry, receive forgiveness and go on with our relationships. But this is the one choice, the one mistake that can't be repented of. Because he's gone.

But that doesn't mean that we can't forgive him for what he did.

I'm not worried about Brad's relationship with God. The fact is, God forgave Brad before he even took the action that ended his life. The Bible says that while we were yet sinners, Christ died for us. Because God precedes us with grace he has forgiven Brad for taking the life that was given to him.

But I am concerned about your relationship to Brad. And so it's our turn. We need to forgive him for his decision which has so disordered this school, disrupted your lives, and devastated this family. Can you forgive him for that? I'd like to ask that we do that right now. Let us pray.

Prayer

Gracious God, we have arrived in this place today to confront and deal with an enormously difficult and painful thing, and we need your help. We need courage.

In our hearts and in these halls there are holes—empty places.
At the _____ home there is now an empty bed.
In the locker room there is an empty football jersey.
In a matter of weeks there will be some empty space on the prom floor, and an empty seat at graduation.
Because of that emptiness there is love that will never be enjoyed.
There are children who will never be born, friendships that will never be made, work that will never be done. Because he's gone.
And we come to this place, so full of people, full of a weird and wild mixture of feelings. Some of us are so sad our hearts ache. Some of us are simply in shock, and we can't even believe we're here; it's all so surreal. And some of us are good and angry, indignant that we're here at all, having to deal with this. Brad has done this, and we'll never be quite the same ever again.
But Lord, we know that you have already forgiven him. And so we now begin the long process of forgiving him as well. Grant us the grace to forgive where and when we've been hurt. Teach us to forgive as freely and as generously as you forgive each of us, through Jesus Christ our Lord. Amen.
(Scripture reading: Exod 15:2–3, 11–14)

Resurrection Hope

I've been carrying around Brad's Bible with me this week, thumbing through it from time to time. I have it here. It's a marked up Bible and it appears that he had a fairly comprehensive understanding of the Scriptures from beginning to end. But I was having a hard time understanding why certain passages were highlighted. And then it came to me. Yesterday, while on a long bike ride, I realized that, with just a couple of exceptions, the verses he had drawn a circle around picked up on the twin themes of the suffering of Christ, and the triumph of God.

The crucifixion of Jesus is an example of the first. The song of Moses that we just listened to is an example of the second. The suffering of Christ, and the triumph of God.

These may well be the two most important things for us to realize as we navigate our ways through this life. There is suffering, and we all share in it. And there is victory over it because God is in control. And it is a victory that he extends to all of us who believe.

The fact is, none of us is immunized from pain and suffering. Nobody is insulated from difficulty. We all experience it and share in suffering. Bad things happen. Sometimes we suffer the consequences for our own bad decisions. Other times it seems that we are victims of random acts of pain that have no clear cause; it doesn't always make sense. The sooner we come to terms with that, the earlier we accept the fact that all living things undergo suffering, the better we'll be able to live, and live well. Life involves some real pain. Exhibit A is identified by a cross; it's something that Jesus willingly endured, and it's something, the Scriptures insist, for us to bear as well.

But suffering isn't the last word. There is a greater reality at work in this world that has power over all pain, all difficulty, all fear. It even has power over death. It is, of course, the power of the resurrection. And when we are grafted into the body of Christ we are given the power to ultimately be victorious over sin and suffering and, yes, even death.

God did not take Brad. This was not God's will for Brad. God's will for Brad, as it is for all of you, is that you live a long and a holy life. Your lives—every last one of them—are absolutely precious. The worth of your individual lives would be impossible to overestimate. Each of one of us has been created in the image of God and God has a purpose for all of us. Brad's choice, unfortunately, circumvented God's will for his life. God did not take Brad. But God has, I assure you, received him into his presence. For in matters of life and death God always gets the final word. And his is a word of grace, a word of mercy and forgiveness. A word of life. Eternal life. Resurrection Life.

This is a tender journey we are on together. And for all of us there will be moments, if not whole seasons, of suffering. It just goes with the territory of being human and of living in a world in which sin yet abounds. But because of the suffering that Jesus absorbed in his very body, we know that we are never alone in our pain. And because God raised Jesus from the dead, we know that God's grace always triumphs over the biggest mistakes we can make and the deepest pain we might endure.

It doesn't appear that in his reading Brad got all the way to the end of his Bible. But if he had, he would have read about a promise that is recorded in the book of Revelation that "God will wipe away all tears from their eyes. There will be no more death, no more grief or crying or pain. The old things have disappeared" (Rev 21:4). That's a promise offered to both Brad and to you.

Let us, then, keep our hearts and our minds, our very lives focused on the One who is our help in ages past and our hope for many, many years to come. He is Jesus Christ, the author and perfecter of our faith, the one who triumphs over sin, the one who comforts us in our sorrow, and the one who is victorious even over death both in this life and in the life to come. In the name of the Father and of the Son and of the Holy Spirit. Amen.

Reflecting on Eric Peterson's Sermon

(1) Naming the problem and preventing it from becoming a barrier that hinders ministry between neighbors.

One important thing Pastor Eric Peterson did was to identify Brad's death as a suicide. His purpose was not to beat up on Brad or attack his memory, but to name it and keep it from becoming the unmentionable secret. By publicly mentioning the fact of suicide, permission is given for everyone else to acknowledge it, so this part of their painful experience can be brought out into the open and addressed. This also gives freedom to friends and neighbors to minister to the family after the service without tiptoeing around the reason for their deep-seated grief. The mention of suicide, however, does not have to be brutal or prolonged. It can be done simply and briefly.

For example, "Her death was a death by suicide. We don't need to labor the point, just acknowledge it. We are here today to honor her life. I mean that. We can celebrate her life even though we cannot celebrate her final choice. But we can love her memory and cherish the time we had with her." While there is nothing eloquent in this wording, many have appreciated such a direct, blunt approach, so long as it is done with a kind tone of voice and without either hype or embarrassment. As I have learned, to do so at the outset of the service has helped ease the tension in the room, based on feedback from many people in different contexts. By doing so, you certainly are not revealing a secret in most cases, but rather helping remove an invisible barrier that keeps people from coming forward and giving support to the family.

(2) The need of the survivors to forgive the person who committed suicide.

Another reason this serves as a good example is because of what Peterson did with the people. He addressed their need to forgive Brad. A suicide is so painful that the mourners most often have a lot of anger mixed together with their sorrow, because the pain inflicted on them, if you will, was inflicted by the avoidable course of action taken by the victim. So, for example, a brother or sister can see this death inflict pain on their mother, and hate the dead person for making such a hurtful, self-centered choice.

There are some people involved in pastoral care and chaplaincy work today who want to change the way we speak about suicide, so that we do not say that anyone "committed" suicide. They think that is too hurtful for the family to hear. While their hearts may be full of concern, I think this approach is misguided. An action was committed by a person who first made a choice to do it. The family knows this as well as anyone else. It is quite normal, though not necessarily healthy, for family members to be filled with anger about that choice and action. They generally believe they are justified in their anger, and therefore we cannot overlook or gloss over their reason for anger. If we pretend the victim of suicide did not make a personal choice, we lose credibility and are easily tuned out when we speak. If we address that choice and the resulting pain and anger on the part of the surviving family and circle of friends, then we can offer the best spiritual response that opens the door to healing. Peterson addressed their anger when he said they needed to forgive Brad in prayer.

Forgiving is not always a one time event. For many people, it is a process that must begin but takes time to complete. It does not mean we forget the tragedy or think someone's hurtful action was morally acceptable. What forgiveness does include is giving up our right to be angry as we hand the matter over to God. We may be tempted the following day to retrieve our right to be angry, holding on to it, and then have to pray again for God's help to give that up more completely. The prayer for forgiveness may have to be repeated many times. While the prayer at the service certainly did not end all need for personal forgiving, especially for those most closely affected by Brad's death, it did show the way forward. There is teaching power in having the assembly of people say this prayer together or affirm the pastor's prayer on their behalf. It reinforces in the minds of many participants that there is a need to forgive. When they once again feel anger in their sorrow for Brad's death, or a need to forgive in a different context, they have a model to guide them as they think and pray.

Today, fewer young people are raised in praying homes, and this kind of public lesson is needed. Pastor Peterson did it in a timely and respectful way, and thus ministered to the people's deep spiritual need. Perhaps it also helped some in the audience be more open to hearing his message. I see a lot of wisdom in including this prayer in the public service. But it was more than a lesson about prayer and forgiveness. It was a powerful moment that I am sure God used to actually bring spiritual healing to many people. It was a moment when some people were released from intense pain because they were released from anger. (Some might have received help to forgive in other directions as well. To be set free from an angry spirit is a miracle that spreads blessings in many directions.) Furthermore, it may have sent a strong signal to a disturbed teen, a potential copycat suicide, reminding him or her that to commit suicide is to deeply wound those around you. It is far from being glamorous drama. There are reasons why suicide is wrong and those reasons need to be recognized. All in all, the public was invited to participate in an important prayer which works meaningfully on more than one level.

(3) Addressing misconceptions about God.

Even people raised all their lives in the worshipping context of a church can have flaws in theological understanding. This does not mean they are bad people, only that there may be a great disconnect between what a pastor teaches and what they apprehend about God or the Christian life. For example, upon the occasion of his retirement, a pastor shook hands with many people after his final sermon. He had served the congregation for over twenty years and repeated the central themes of Christianity time and again, including the great doctrine that we are justified (put in the right with God) through faith in Jesus Christ. A man who had attended regularly came to shake his hand, saying with a warm smile, "Well, Pastor, like you always said, if we're just good we'll go to heaven." The pastor was shocked but replied, "I have never said that."

Preachers who strive to communicate with precision cannot always understand how the disconnect takes place, but it does. Confusion is out there and we have to be aware of it. Another anecdote shows how it arises in a crisis context. More recently a young man was shaken because someone close to him was in a coma from a heroin overdose. He said, "How could God do this?" Well, did God force one person to sell heroin, then force another to buy it and inject it into his veins? No, God did not "do this." God gives us freedom, a frightful amount of freedom, and there are often consequences for misusing this gift. In this illustration from an actual moment in ministry, the man had grabbed hold of one biblical affirmation, the almighty power of God, and forgot everything else, including the fact that God grants freedom and holds each individual responsible for his or her actions. So in the end, the grieving man did not conclude there was a problem with drug abuse or a life out of control, only that "God took him." Perhaps initially, this confusion appears useful to us, because it seems easier to blame God than the one we lost, but in the long run it is not helpful. When we distort the way we see God in our own minds, we might not welcome God's presence, cutting ourselves off from the resources the Spirit of God wants to provide to help, comfort, and strengthen us.

Comments like "Why did God do this?" also contribute to more confusion on the part of other grieving friends. This was a problem Peterson was aware of and addressed publicly, giving a short but necessary correction. Many teens and adults have ideas that are only half-thought out. Many are not church attenders and get exposed only to popular religious ideas expressed by parents or peers. Some people do have sound ideas and approach an understanding of God that more readily harmonizes with biblical teaching. Far too many others operate with very naïve, simplistic, strange thoughts that only distort their mental picture of God, lending to confusion or a sense of estrangement. Peterson briefly addressed one of these misconceptions by saying, "God did not take Brad. This was not God's will for Brad." Here was a simple but necessary reminder that God allows us to live in a risky world, where harm and tragedy are possible, but that is far different than God decreeing and orchestrating a tragic event. God did not "take Brad" in the sense of forcing him to commit suicide and die young, bringing pain to those near him. "God is not the author of evil." We cannot teach everything in one sermon or answer all questions. But a short and simple phrase can redirect many people and correct an error: "God did not take Brad."

The preacher's ability to discern and address one or two theological misunderstandings comes from interaction with the people around a certain tragedy. While attending to a family and providing pastoral care to relatives and teenage friends before the service, if the pastor's antenna is up and he or she hears some of the things which indicate a basic theological confusion, then it must be weighed in the balance with all the other things that need to be addressed in a short message. If one person voices a confusion, however, it is very likely that some other people are thinking in the same way. When you address the question, however briefly, with a clear answer in your message, you give other people the ability to repeat the answer and speak more appropriately should that confusion be voiced again in private conversation. Often it takes a congregation or larger circle of people to help someone work through a question, but they are looking to you for guidance.

Dare We Speak a Word of Grace?

Pastor Peterson admits a fear that he spoke too positively about Brad's position in the next world, and that is understandable. It is so hard to get the right balance. Those who decry suicide as a terrible sin sometimes leave the impression there is no forgiveness for it. Those who emphasize God's grace may leave the impression that they operate with an all-embracing universalism that does not make a human response to God in trust and obedience seem very important. Both are pitfalls. We should always be cautious of consigning any departed person to a place in eternity because the decision is not ours. We cannot speak presumptuously. At the same time, where the gospel has been introduced in the context of a person's life, we may focus on the reach of God's grace without encroaching on God's final judgment. We may celebrate the power and presence of the Holy Spirit at work in someone's life who has heard the gospel and responded positively, however imperfectly, to the offer of salvation.

Peterson, I think, was trying to honor the vast range and depth of God's grace, saying in bold and clear language that God's grace may be applied even to the case of suicide, even to Brad. He rightfully connects his hope not to a nebulous idea of God, a form of positive thinking, or a wishful universalism, but to the suffering, death, and resurrection of Jesus, who atoned for the sin of the world. Thus, in a Christ-centered way, he emphasized the Shepherd's faithfulness that carries a wounded sheep home, which is greater by far than our weak, inadequate discipleship. While on the one hand he boldly proclaimed God's grace, he also said a word of law that needed to be heard: "This was not God's will for Brad." It is a serious thing to violate God's will: there are children who will never be born, friendships never to be made, work never to be done.

When a pastor seems to err on the side of grace rather than speak a word of condemnation, we need to keep one of Martin Luther's insights in mind: it is always easier for the devil to undermine a word of grace than a word of condemnation. The human heart is more prone to believe the negative, condemnatory word than the promise of forgiveness and eternal life. In difficult settings, as with other days, preachers do not always get the right emphasis or say the right words with complete precision, which is why we must rely on God's strength and covering mercy before, during, and after a funeral message. Every preacher must speak in harmony with his or her doctrinal commitments and do a credible job of interpreting and applying biblical messages, but even when we've done our best, in the end we must say, "We are unprofitable servants."[1]

Ultimately one's theological position on major doctrines will guide and set the boundaries for what is said in a crisis context, especially the doctrines of sin and grace, union with Christ, faith, and justification. The sample sermon we are examining comes from a pastor steeped in the Reformed tradition. Preachers working theologically with the teaching of the Reformers believe that God justifies sinners. We will never obtain perfection apart from our union with Jesus Christ, who is the only completely righteous human being who ever lived. As such, he is God's gift to us. We must each throw ourselves on God's mercy because our human righteousness is tainted with impurity and is, even at best, incomplete. The promise of the New Testament is that we can be put in the right with God, we can be justified, through faith in Jesus Christ. Justification is given to us as a gift, as is sanctification, in union with Christ. While our obedience does not lead to forgiveness, God's forgiveness makes possible our living more obediently in gratitude. Faith and repentance are important in living the Christian life each day, anticipating the freedom

---

1. Luke 17:10, KJV.

of living in harmony with God in the world to come. Insofar as we experience faith today, however, our trust is not in ourselves but in the faithfulness of the one who reconciles us to God.

As a summation of New Testament teaching about the church in the present and in the future, Martin Luther and John Calvin both taught that the person who has faith in Christ is *simul justus et pecator*, simultaneously sinful yet justified. Simul justus et pecator does not mean we are indifferent to sin or condone it, for we fight many battles with wrongful desires, but it does mean we are realistic about the presence of this problem in the earthly life of the Christian. For this reason, we conclude that no Christian teenager or adult comes to God at the point of death as a perfected person, with all one's sinful nature eradicated from his or her life. God justifies sinners and incorporates each one *in* Christ, including those who die in old age from health complications, or die young in a car wreck, mountain climbing accident, or by suicide. We have no grounds for saying the way we die is the deciding factor in eternity.

If we live and die as children who are simul justus et pecator, on this side of heavenly renewal, then the act of suicide illustrates the earthly condition we struggle with, but cannot define the heavenly position of our adoption and incorporation into the savior's righteousness and victory. Therefore, we should pause before we ever think suicide has greater power to decide a sinner's destiny than God's actual justification of sinners.

24

Talking About Suicide in Reference to Societal Issues

A Sermon by Will Willimon

Hard Topics Need to Be Addressed

WITH MORE THAN FIFTY THOUSAND suicides a year in the USA by the late 1980s, James Clemons thought there should be less silence on this subject in the churches. Whenever he asked people if they had ever heard a sermon on suicide, the answer was usually "No." Whenever he asked pastors if they had ever preached a sermon on suicide apart from a funeral service, the answer was usually "No." So he published a book of sample sermons that address suicide. He thought this was important because it might save lives. Clemons believed that the pulpit was an effective means for pastoral care as well as religious instruction. He was supported by psychiatrist Lucy Davidson, then a consultant on suicide to the National Center for Disease Control. She understood that pastors and church-related counselors are often the first to be sought out by suicidal persons when they want help, and that it makes sense for them to address this topic apart from a funeral context. She argued that it was a myth that "talking about suicide will only plant the idea."[1]

---

1. Clemons, *Sermons*, 28. Concerns that theological questions need to be addressed

The time to talk more in depth about suicide as a topic, of course, is not during your funeral message. For example, if you want to make a sociological argument about something in modern society that is contributing to the rise in the suicide rate, you need to find a more appropriate venue than when people are gathered in grief to pay their final respect to a deceased friend. This is a question of wisdom in selecting what to put into your message and what to leave out. No funeral message can cover all the points you may want to make any more than it can include all the personal stories and memories people want shared.

The rate of suicide is higher today so Clemons's concern is not outdated. Topics like suicide are rare in Sunday sermons or educational settings. As a result, people in many churches do not enter into full discussions about any aspect of the problem, nor learn how to think theologically about it or respond appropriately to people suffering in a context of suicide. Because it is very difficult for any person to wrestle with, it is often avoided. This only makes congregational ministry harder in tragic circumstances. Some public reference may give more people freedom to explore the topic openly. People already have unspoken attitudes and questions, and some will find it a relief to be able to bring them into the open in the context of their faith community. If the Sunday sermon is too constrained time-wise or because children are present, then an adult class can be helpful with a give-and-take discussion following.

Hard topics need to be addressed when the listeners are not overwrought with emotion at a funeral. Serving as Chaplain at Duke University in 1998, Methodist theologian Will Willimon addressed the trend to promote the acceptance of assisted suicide. While he could not cover every question in one message, he said enough to stimulate thought and debate. Today adults over 75 have the highest suicide rate in the USA compared to other age groups.[2]

Will Willimon's Sermon "Suicide Is Not a Private Matter"

"Suicide Is Not a Private Matter" was preached by Will Willimon on March 29, 1998, the Fifth Sunday in Lent.

---

and some practices modified in the Church of England are raised in Parsons, *Suicide and the Church*.

2. Statistics are annually reported by the Centers for Disease Control and Prevention.

"I want to know Christ, and the power of his resurrection and the sharing of his sufferings by becoming like him in his death. . . . I press on to make it my own, because Christ Jesus has made me his own" (Phil 3:10, 12).

We are following, in Lent, Jesus down a lonely road, down the road toward his death. He did not want to die. In Gethsemane, Jesus prayed that "this cup might pass from me" (Matt 26:36–42; Mark 14:32–39; Luke 22:39–42). He did not want to suffer. What human being does? And Jesus was fully human. And yet he went to the cross, not because it wouldn't hurt, not because he had some romantic desire to die dramatically, but because, in Jesus's words, "Not my will but thine be done."

Jesus vividly displayed that his life, even his, was not his own. His life was owned by God, caught up in the purposes of God. Commandeered.

We are created to be social. "It is not good for humans to be alone" (Gen 2:18) were the words by which we first came to God's mind. We are intended for community. Our lives are not our own but rather interconnected to the larger purposes of God.

Wandering in a cemetery, in a small Southern town, I saw a gravestone to some dead celebrity of the past. "He was a self-made man," proclaimed the tombstone to the world.

What a curious designation for a human. Self-made.

Underlying liberal democracy's philosophy is this notion. We are self-made, on our own, autonomous, self-sufficient. What a curious view of humanity.

Who here is totally free from a web of relationships, standing alone? If you are, I feel sad for you, very sad. *Creatio ex nihilo*, created out of nothing, cannot apply to human beings. The modern notion that I am my own creator is a terrible fiction, which means at its core, I am alone. I am therefore free to do as I please. No wonder, in this society, everyone seems to me a stranger, a competitor. When the Supreme Court justified abortion on the basis of our right to privacy, I thought it silly, even for Justice Blackmun. The taking of the life of a fetus based upon my right to be by myself?

But then I realized that the Supreme Court was right. We have no higher value, in life and in death, than privacy, the right, in the words of Justice Brandeis, "to be left alone." Thus the Court forged a nice link between privacy and death. The fetus, being utterly dependent upon another, is subhuman, for humanity, by definition, consists of being utterly independent, autonomous, self-sufficient.

Next, down the slippery slope, came "physician-assisted suicide," upheld by the Ninth Circuit Court of Appeals as a guarantee of personal liberty. The Supreme Court unanimously reversed the lower court this past June, though I can't imagine why. The reasoning might be that suicide is legal, permissible, as long as it is done alone, without assistance from a doctor or anybody else.

But does anyone live or die alone? Aristotle condemned suicide as an act of injustice against the state, which seems bizarre to us, except that Aristotle felt that the state was the highest good, being the highest community, and citizens had no right to deprive the state of themselves. Aristotle believed that we are social by nature, created for community, born with a web of claims from others laid upon us. We are in society for a reason greater than ourselves.

Is not this the human meaning of death, and why we so greatly, and justly fear and avoid death? Death is the ultimate loneliness, that time when at last we are left alone. Death is the ultimate abandonment. We get a foretaste of the pain of death in those times of despair and dereliction, when we cry as Job (Job 19:14), "my kin have abandoned me, and my fellows have forgotten me." Jesus quoted Ps 22:2 from the cross when he cried, "My God, my God, why have you forsaken me?" In choosing death, in suicide, we attempt a preemptive strike on death, attempting to take these matters into our own hands. We wish to die as we have lived—alone, autonomous, since we believe that the essence of our humanity is in our self-sufficiency. We call this "death with dignity," that is, death where we call the shots, where we make the choice of killing ourselves, which, when you think about it, is an odd definition of freedom.

I recollect the woman who said with bitter irony, "The government now tells women, 'Congratulations, we are going to allow you to destroy your fetus so you can be free.' This is freedom?"

Whereas formerly death was that ultimate reminder that our lives are not our own, to do with as we please, a final word that we are not in control, now death is transformed into another fantasy that, "This is my life and I can destroy it as I please."

Of course, no one advocates physician-assisted suicide except for those who are "terminal," which means all of us, for who isn't? If we are all on our way to death, and if death is the ultimate loss of control, therefore the ultimate loss of human significance and dignity, then what reason is there not to terminate life at any time in life?

In his classic study, *Suicide*, Emile Durkheim asked why suicide rates had risen so sharply in modern, relatively affluent, industrial societies.[3] His answer was his theory of anomie, that sense of being disconnected to others, not part of any web of relationships, that sense of loneliness when we feel that we are nothing more to this world than expendable producers, or expendable consumers. Is not this the rationale behind many appeals for assisted suicide? "She is no longer living a productive life." In this economy, when someone can no longer either produce or consume, what reason is there to live?

Comedian Dennis Miller recently referred to suicide as "thinning the herd."

I find that the greatest fear most people have of aging is not that they are moving closer to death, but that they are at greater risk for dependency. "I don't want to be dependent upon my children," they say. It is revealing that we fear dependency, the need to reach out in need of the care and concern of others, even more than we fear death. Admittedly, in this society, there is good reason to wonder if when it comes our time to be dramatically dependent upon others, there will be anyone there to care. Why was I not surprised that the *Duke Chronicle* praised Dr. Kevorkian for his work, elevating him as a hero? I for one—when I become dependent, incapacitated, needy—would not want to place my fate in the hands of the editorial board of the *Chronicle*!

Don't you worry about a society that tells us, when we are tempted toward self-destruction, that we are on our own? In those dark nights, when we are least self-sufficient, least able to choose and to decide, is when we most need the love and concern of others. We live in a violent, death-dealing world, and we need others to overcome our murderous tendencies. The first murderer, Cain, asked, "Am I my brother's keeper?"

As Christians, we believe that we have been charged by God to love and to care for every human life, especially the most vulnerable lives. In a society where productivity and consumption are elevated as the supreme human virtues, those who are "non-productive," "dependent," and "needy" deserve our special attention because they are the ones who are most likely to be disposed of by this society because they live as truthful reminders of who we really are, and we can't stand the truth.

We ought to intervene when any of our sisters or brothers is tempted toward suicide. We ought to use every means at our disposal to attempt to

---

3. Durkheim, *Suicide*.

dissuade them from this act. One of the reasons we will use is that they, in their unique, God-given humanity, are valuable. They are loved and loved deeply and ought not prematurely to deprive us of their presence by taking their own lives.

You ask, "Is it fair to ask some terribly suffering person to go on living?" Life is suffering, in differing kind and degree. I admit that I am a terrible bearer of pain. Yet if it becomes my lot in life to suffer, the Christian gospel bids me to see my suffering as opportunity to witness to others that life is worth living, as long as God gives life, that even in pain, there is a reason to go on. A person who endures terrible suffering is not disposable and unwanted. Indeed, such a person becomes a prophet, testifying to the rest of us that the goal of life is not hedonistic pleasure and comfort but rather courage, love, and endurance in the confidence that God gives life, God owns life, and only God may take life.

From seriously incapacitated, sick people I have been given virtues I would not have had had I not known them. I have been taught patience, joy in the little things of life, and courage. The bravery and perseverance of some who are seriously ill threatens the rest of us who are made to wonder if, when we are called to suffer and come close to death, we will have the spiritual, intellectual resources to triumph.

It is tragic that many who are near the end of life are considered burdens and obstacles to our self-fulfillment and are made to feel unwanted, unloved, made to feel as if they now have a responsibility to take matters in hand and become their own executioners. Once it was bad enough to be suffering from a terminal illness. Now, you not only have to suffer, but you are made to feel as if you owe it to your family and to the national debt to go ahead and take your life and stop being a drain on national resources.

"Not my will, but thine be done," that is our last, best prayer.

Willimon's Notes

[Willimon's notes are presented as well because they were attached to the printed handout of his sermon in the original context:]

I am indebted in this sermon to an article by David Novak, professor of Jewish studies at the University of Toronto, in the August/September, 1997 issue of *First Things*.[4]

---

4. Novak, "Suicide Is Not."

In 1997, the Lutheran Church—Missouri Synod issued *That They May Have Life*, in which the church stated the following.

> Human life is not an achievement. It is an endowment. It has measureless value, because every individual, at every stage of development and every state of consciousness is known and loved by God. This is the source of human dignity and the basis for human equality. It must therefore be asserted without exception or qualification: No one is worthless. . . . Will all be counted as neighbors, or will some be regarded and treated as strangers and cast beyond protection? . . . American society is steadily becoming a society of strangers, obsessed with personal rights and severing the ties of duty, compassion, and love to the weak and unwanted.
>
> American culture has come to favor those who can stridently assert their autonomy and choice in a struggle for political power. As a result, America has become an inhospitable, even dangerous, place for those too weak to compete effectively in this contest of rights—the young, the elderly, the dying, the handicapped.
>
> American society has adopted a distorted definition of freedom. Freedom focused only on the self and its rights. Freedom from the bonds of community. Freedom from duties of parents to children. Freedom from the obligations of generation to generation. Freedom from the responsibility to sacrifice for others. Freedom from even a sense of empathy.
>
> The ultimate and inevitable outcome of this new freedom is the individual's private, autonomous power to choose life or death, for self or even for others. . . . The church must also speak for the elderly and the sick who are near the end of earthly life. Many who are considered burdens and obstacles to the self-fulfillment of others and made to feel unwanted, unloved, and rejected appear ready to become their own executioners, as if it is their duty to die. But there is no right or duty to take any human life including one's own. It will be the church's duty to express in word and deed its patience, tenderness, and love for those nearing death. They will be comforted, supported, and offered the hope of the Christian gospel, not driven to despair.

A community must be more than a winner-take-all clash of individual interests.[5]

Reflections on Will Willimon's Sermon

Willimon's sermon presented the topic of suicide in a non-funeral context. Here Willimon focuses on assisted suicide and critiques it theologically. This sermon is not intended to be a complete ethical discussion on the subject. It cannot answer all questions, but it boldly takes a stance. Obviously when challenging a congregation in a sermon or public address, one cannot deal with every important point in a complete way. There is not enough time. For example, Willimon did not have opportunity to point out that he was not condemning natural deaths, in which a person has refused the use of artificial life support and entrusted the timing of death to God.

There are medical treatments that may be rejected without the moral burden of committing suicide. As Gilbert Meilaender affirms, "Treatments that are useful and perhaps even lifesaving may sometimes be *excessively burdensome*. Because life is not our god, we need not accept all burdens—no matter how great—in order to stay alive."[6] To reject or withdraw from a form of medical treatment involves a rejection of that treatment, and its consequent burdens, not necessarily a rejection of the gift of life. Meilaender explains,

> From among the various lives still available to a suffering patient—some longer than others; some filled with more burdens than others—we choose one life in particular. Just as the soldier going on a suicidal mission does not choose to die but, rather, to live in a certain way, recognizing that to live in this way may mean not to live as long, so also the patient refusing an excessively burdensome treatment still chooses life—one particular life from among the several still available.[7]

---

5. Lutheran Church–Missouri Synod, *They May Have Life*, which primarily deals with abortion. For the full statement on euthanasia, see Lutheran Church–Missouri Synod, *That They May Live*.

6. Meilaender, *Bioethics*, 70. Moltmann's discussion (above) has some overlap with Meilaender's concern. See also Nancy Duff, *Making Faithful Decisions at the End of Life*, who distinguishes between assisted suicide and assisted dying.

7. Meilaender, *Bioethics*, 70. He also states that this criterion can be abused. "It guides us in our decision making, but it does not make decisions for us. It trains us to

Sometimes the suffering patient asks to be allowed to "die naturally." Allowing someone to die according to the winding down of one's own natural biological clock and intentional "mercy" killing are not the same thing. They are two different ethical choices.

But Willimon could not go into all possible objections, questions, and side issues to show the thoroughness of his position, not in one sermon. He took the ethical stance he did and boldly proclaimed it within a short time-frame, giving enough food for thought so that, whether his listeners fully agreed with him or not, they were challenged to think through the ramifications of the acceptance of euthanasia. Their own private conversations were meant to follow.

Further Thoughts on Euthanasia

People prone to be guided by their feelings will often settle the issue based on anecdotes that seem relevant, instead of sustained reasoning and argumentation. Certainly many anecdotes or frightening scenarios can be found. I will confess that I can imagine situations which I would rather die to avoid than endure. Most active ministers have observed unforgettable situations where someone's physical suffering was immense. Yet, though we live in a time when medical advances can alleviate sensations of pain more than any previous age, Willimon notes that the discussion often moves into the realm called "quality of life." This is a dangerous term because it is amorphous, like slithering jelly that will not stay in place, and can easily mean something different to you than to me. As with modern abstract art, it can be subject to private interpretation rather than have an obvious public meaning that is the same for everyone. This is a real danger because we live in an age when too many people are encouraged to elevate subjective criteria and personal preferences above other important considerations.[8]

As Willimon says, for some people the phrase "quality of life" means the ability to live without depending on other people for assistance. For others, quality of life means usefulness to self or family or society, the ability to contribute to your own good or that of others. Is value to be based on self-recognition of your own contribution or also on the recognition

---

distinguish between the burdens of treatment and the burden of life, a distinction we are often tempted to pass by." Meilander, *Bioethics*, 71. Also see the pastoral reflections on related questions in Davies, *Not Uninformed*, 29–58, especially 46–55.

8. Copan, *True for You*, reviews and critiques current arguments.

of other people about your particular contribution? Either way, Dietrich Bonhoeffer argued that it is a false assumption that a human life is only valued if it is "useful." God can use the weak to prompt "the strong to new tasks that develop their own social value."[9] Ultimately, God will take beggars and victims like Lazarus, people who serve no recognizably useful social purpose, and count them worthy of receiving eternal life. "Where, other than in God, should the measure for the ultimate worth of a life lie?"[10]

Bonhoeffer knew that some are very sick and very unhappy. But his concern is that whatever misery and suffering is involved, the sufferer is a human being and cannot be treated as though his or her humanity had already ended. Respect for the full range of humanity has to be taught and practiced at all times, otherwise the bond that connects people can be weakened in times of stressful chaos and societal breakdown.

Bonhoeffer wrote his book on ethics as he faced the quandary of how to guide a confused church while struggling against the Nazi movement, which advocated that both the handicapped and elderly infirm should be eliminated. On Hitler's orders, many of these helpless people were brought to an early death. Initially, however, Hitler thought this process of destroying the infirm should be hidden from the German people, even though there were some public advocates within the medical community. The history of that atrocity is not completely told, however, if we fail to remember that, once it became known, there were physicians, nurses, and clergy who opposed the Nazi policy or hid patients. Bishop Clemens August Graf von Galen, Father Bernhard Lichtenberg, Pastors Paul-Gerhard Braune and Friedrich von Bodelschwingh Jr., made very vocal and courageous stands in public opposition.[11] Their stories are reminders that it is important to oppose trends that debase human life before a time of extreme societal chaos or war, after which it becomes more difficult to be effective. As we live today in a new context, what influences our valuation of human persons?

9. Bonhoeffer, *Ethics* (2005), 193.
10. Bonhoeffer, *Ethics* (2005), 193.
11. I owe this information on von Bodelschwingh to Karlfried Froehlich, whose father was a member of the Confessing Church; Froehlich lectured on German resistance to National Socialism at the Theological Students' Fellowship forum at Princeton Theological Seminary, 1990. See also Gilbert, *Second World War*, 11–12, 20, 39, 105, 109, 224, 336, 379, 395. Gilbert demonstrates how much of this program had to be hidden from the general public when first enacted. For a personal account of facing this tragedy, see Hong, *Bright Valley of Love*.

Richard John Neuhaus pointed out that human beings are weakest at the entrance and exit doors of life. If you weaken respect for life at either end of the spectrum then you weaken it at the other end as well. This is why the euthanasia movement drew strength after the advent of federally legalized abortion. But Neuhaus's additional concern also needs to be remembered. If respect for human life is weakened at the entrance and exit doors, it devalues human beings across the full range of life. What we do with the weak involves all of us, not just the weak.

May we never see again the face of evil which Bonhoeffer beheld! Yet there are many masks. Great expressions of evil and the outworking of dehumanization do not generally develop overnight, but often require a preceding process whereby societal norms are shifted and changed, and legal hindrances removed, however much those preparations seem inadvertent and undirected. In considering this, we need to remember that nothing is inevitable, and the course of history may be changed by the decisions and actions of particular men and women.[12] Unfortunately it is not always clear to good people which societal problem needs our most immediate attention and full devotion of time and energy. In all that we do with the time given us, we need the guidance and direction of the Holy Spirit.

Concern About Suffering and the Right to Die

In paying close attention to these areas of concern, we are right to distrust those who say that the right to die will never become the obligation to die, because we cannot trust that public attitudes in the future will be guided by our current moral vision and ethical constraints, not when more and more elements of our Christian cultural heritage are discarded in North America and Europe. Furthermore, sadly, we cannot trust the ethical practice and good conduct of all physicians, but must hold them to high standards as we remain vigilant on behalf of the weak. Professor Kalman Kaplan and other professional clinicians reviewed the medical records of patients who were deemed terminally ill and "assisted" into death by Dr. Jack Kevorkian. These physicians and psychiatrists testified at one of his trials, pointing out that some of the people he killed were not diagnosed as terminally ill. Some were very lonely, or fearful of disability, but not necessarily in physical pain or suffering from any terminal

---

12. This theme is demonstrated in Johnson, *Modern Times*.

disease. The evidence has recently been updated and made accessible to the wider public.[13]

The thought of someone we know suffering tugs at our hearts, yet we cannot speak for those who do suffer. C. S. Lewis learned from a physician that not all who suffer are in a hurry to die. Lewis remembered,

> Once I said to a doctor that I didn't see why the incurably sick shouldn't be given release from pain; and I remember what he said: 'You've had no clinical experience, Lewis. Like most of the people who talk like that you're in robust health. You'll find it's hardly ever the incurably sick who want to be released, whatever the pain is like. It's their families, who hate to see them suffer, and can't stand the emotional strain (or, of course, the worry and expense), that start saying, "Doctor, he mustn't be allowed to suffer—far better to put him out of his misery."[14]

This physician's experience with dying patients came from a time when modern advances in medicating pain were not as advanced as today, and his observation is important as a testimony to the way the human spirit often clings to physical life in particular examples of suffering. Yet I doubt the physician Lewis spoke with worked at a major trauma center. In some circumstances, we find such horrific pain that people do beg to die. For example, in a major burn center, a physician or nurse is more likely to hear a patient request help to die before a first or second skin graft. It is always heart-wrenching to work with someone in this condition. Advances in medicine, however, allow many to survive longer by inducing a coma until appropriate surgeries and a greater depth of healing can take place.

We need to be very cautious about thinking we *know* the incurably sick want to die. If they do request death, does that give us the moral ground we need for terminating their life? If so, under what conditions? Which are the most appropriate safeguards? Simultaneously, we can ask whether an unnatural prolongation of life is also morally wrong, because

---

13. Kaplan, *Right to Die*, 109–63, offers evaluations of the first forty-seven cases of Kevorkian's physician-assisted suicides, by means of both a physical autopsy and a preliminary psychological autopsy. It was revealed that no more than 32 percent of these patients were terminal. The abstract of the essay says, "While 73.9 percent were described as reporting pain, only 42.6 percent were revealed at autopsy to have a specific anatomical basis for their pain. However, 36 percent were described as depressed, 66 percent as having some disability, and perhaps of key importance, 90 percent expressed a fear of dependency."

14. Qtd. in Wrong, "Meeting," 111.

it increases the time of suffering. A lot of hard work is required as we face these questions.

Recommended Reading

Paul Copan, *True for You, But Not For Me.*
Jennifer Michael Hecht, *Stay.*
Gilbert Meilaender, *Bioethics.*

25

Searching for Words on Occasions When People Weep

by Mark Koonz

THERE ARE SO MANY books on sermon preparation that I will not repeat good general advice here.[1] Rather, I will look at options for how the sermon functions in the context of the memorial service—from the perspective of both preacher and attendees—as well as how biblical texts may function in the context of the sermon.

It is important to personalize the service and message in some way, using life stories or vignettes that bring the deceased person to mind, with gentleness and integrity. However, there is no magic formula for getting the length of time and content right, because "too short" can be as offensive as "too long." This all takes discernment. Some of the people who attend may be sensitized to spiritual realities to a greater degree than usual, especially in tragic circumstances, perhaps only for a short window of time, so prayer is needed for the preacher to organize carefully

---

1. Croft and Newton, *Conduct Gospel-Centered Funerals*; Gibson, *Preaching for Special Services*; cf. Long and Lynch, *Good Funeral*. In the overall approach to the service for a death by suicide, preachers should be sensitive to the power of anger mixed with grief in the family and congregation. For a father's story of seeking hope in sorrow, see Bayly, *Last Thing*. This is a reminder of the passionate depths of grieving people, with a short chapter on suicide. Also important is Kim, *Preaching to People*. Kim's focus is not primarily the funeral service, but is a necessary reminder that suffering listeners attend on Sunday as well.

and speak as well as possible. We also pray for the people who attend to hear well, with softened hearts and opened ears.

There are boundaries that are necessary. On the one hand, something informal may be soothing and help create an open receptivity to spiritual matters. On the other hand, some people are offended by a message that is too short, especially one that sounds simplistic or formulaic. People who attend want to hear something meaningful with respect shown to the family. Preachers who have solid content with one or two good illustrations usually find receptive hearers because the people listening feel they are taken seriously. In addition, family and friends want personal references and true words spoken about the person who died. It is generally not helpful to whitewash over all problems or to exaggerate the good. When people feel the preacher is not being honest it does not help their receptivity.

Not all preachers use the same approach for funerals and memorial services. One noted preacher does not even offer a regular sermon for funerals. He studies the life of the person, and presents different aspects of that life in a conversational style, while weaving highlights together with the content of biblical passages. These either connect in some personal way with the person's life or express the Christian hope we celebrate together. Both aspects form part of his running message, but it is rarely recognized as a homily because it is so informal. On the other hand, he practices a very different approach when the congregation gathers for worship on Sunday. He takes a biblical text and preaches an expository message before thousands. He has the mental power and giftedness to hold an audience spellbound, week in and week out, but he sets aside his normal preaching method for funerals and gives much shorter messages.

Why does this noted preacher choose not to give a formal sermon? Because he does not want to weigh down grieving people with too many words. To give a formal and heavy message during a time of mourning is the opposite of putting salve on a wound. Thus he weaves biblical truths together with personal remarks in an easy-to-listen-to conversational style. This model serves as a reminder that pastoral care involves humane, practical expressions of concern, and funeral/memorial services are something other than opportunities to demonstrate one's preaching prowess. In a grieving context, there will always be opportunities to speak about our hope in Christ without making it a command performance.

A Short Word on Pastoral Self-Care

The time after the service is also significant. Every preacher who does the best that can be done will expend a great deal of energy, and needs prayer for the hours following the service of a suicide victim. There will often be a drop of energy or mood, a feeling that it could have been done better. It is common that any adrenalin rush that carries one through the public service will be followed by a letdown, sometimes leading to a mild depression. In the memoirs of world political leaders, there is often considerable space given to the details of a great crisis, telling how they survived a threat, turning it around to their advantage and accomplishing their goals. One former president recalled the sense of euphoria when a crisis was successfully navigated, but went on to say that that very moment was also the most dangerous time to relax, because as an exhausted leader his guard was down. At such times, he was more apt to make an unnecessary mistake in another direction.

We can learn a lot from this observation. Pastoral care requires personal self-care before a funeral service, so that one can prepare with as much freshness and strength as possible. But special care is also needed for the hours and days afterwards. If you do not answer the phone for the rest of the day, you may avoid snapping at someone in a conversation that grates on your nerves. Don't bounce back like Superman the next day either. Sometimes a delayed-stress reaction catches up with you after serving others in crisis. Physical exercise is needed as well as a change of focus. Going fishing, hiking in the hills, binging on movies, tilling the garden are good options. Taking time for self and getting away from people may help recharge one's batteries. Self-imposed renewal is strategic immediately after a tragic crisis and funeral. Jesus searched for a quiet place after a hard day of ministry (Mark 6:31), and so must we. Rest is necessary in order to recover our inner balance, and our decision to be proactive about rest is based on love and respect for the entire congregation. Allowing time for immediate renewal brings us back to God's people more quickly, as more completely ourselves, than pretending that we are stronger than we are or untouched by the tragedy. Therefore, self-care must be practiced as an intentional discipline. When this is quietly done, there will be an on-going gift of love given to the whole congregation.

When Selecting a Text, Look in Familiar Places

Regardless of preaching style, at every funeral the truth of our hope should be read from the Scriptures or woven into our remarks. This is most often the vehicle chosen by the Holy Spirit to minister to human hearts. "Faith comes by hearing the word of God" (Rom 10:17). There are a multitude of verses a preacher can use to address ultimate concerns about forgiveness, tragic circumstances, sin and grace, death and the hope of resurrection to eternal life. Are the familiar and expected verses inadequate for a suicide? We may fear so, but my advice is that the biblical verses you have in mind are not inadequate. However, they need to be spoken in a way that does not present them as a pat answer, but in a way that acknowledges how hard it is to grasp their significance when we are in deep pain.

The passages that give comfort when people die of old age or in a sudden tragedy are also the passages that generally give comfort when people die by suicide. This statement is based on the observations of many pastors. The gospel message meets various human needs in many different contexts, and is always one and the same gospel. Just as people need to be reminded that Jesus defeated death at the funeral of a child or beloved grandmother, so they need to be reminded that Jesus defeated the power of sin and death at the funeral of a suicide. Just as those who bury a spouse who died in an automobile wreck need to hear that Jesus promised to prepare a place for them (John 14:1–3), so too those who bury a spouse who died by suicide need to hear the same promise. The good news that brings hope needs to be spoken in different funeral contexts. The degrees of tension and grief may vary on the part of those listening, but everyone present needs to know that God's promises do not shift and change.

The gospel has many aspects, like a great diamond with many facets and light moving through it to cheer the viewer's eye, constantly refracted and transmitted whichever way it is turned. One message cannot contain all the good news or say everything helpful. We do not have to cram our message full of additional verses in order to preach the multifaceted gospel. One message from the Scripture can be offered as good news for the day, if properly oriented to our hope in Christ. One message can be true to the gospel and say important things that need to be said, without saying everything. We do not need to put every profound thought into one funeral message. Finally, we must rely on the Holy Spirit to use the small bit we share and multiply its impact (John 6:8–13).

There is freedom in selecting texts and finding the right avenue of approach. The power of God to speak through a biblical passage to engage with grieving hearts is not limited by the way a person dies. You may preach on the forgiveness and love of God at a suicide service, or a passage on the resurrection hope, with every confidence that the Holy Spirit can use it efficaciously.

There Is an Opportunity to Include Passages Touching on Great Doctrines of the Faith

When I was preaching for several years in a small town in Montana, I constantly spoke at funerals of the triumph of Jesus over sin and death, presenting this as the basis for our hope in forgiveness and resurrection, when God will give us glorified immortal bodies. Time and again I saw evidence that messages highlighting the resurrection of Christ were meaningful to a number of people, though I varied my messages and did not re-use old sermons verbatim, focusing on a different angle as often as possible. I also worked hard to make the funeral sermon personal by communicating stories about the person who died, always leaving plenty of time for remembrances. These often touched the hearts of those who attended. While I never reached a comfort level in funerals, I found a basic pattern that was meaningful. However, the day came when I sensed I could not build on the same doctrinal theme at every funeral.

When our community was shaken because a man in his twenties committed suicide, born and raised in his hometown, I knew there would be a large crowd at his service. I also knew most of those people had already heard several of my funeral messages. In small rural communities neighbors come from far and near to give support in times of tragedy. So I had a hard choice to make as I searched for a biblical text to use. If people anticipated most of my content, they would likely allow their attention to wander.

As I asked God to show me what to do, my mind turned to the second chapter of James Torrance's book *Worship, Community, and the Triune God of Grace*. The opening pages of this chapter are worth their weight in gold. Torrance once met a man at the ocean whose wife was dying. He wanted to pray because he had been raised in a Christian home, but he could not pray. He had not worshipped or prayed in years, and could not do it now no matter what was at stake. Did Professor Torrance throw him back on himself and tell him to try harder? No. Rather he said, "You have been walking up and down this beach, wanting to pray, trying to pray, but not knowing how to pray. In Jesus Christ we have someone who is praying for you. He has heard your groans and is interceding for you and with you and in you."[2] He proceeded to tell him about the mediation of Jesus in God's presence, where he prays for each one of us, where he intercedes on our behalf when we cannot pray, when we cannot trust, when we cannot hope.

Torrance then told the man about Luke 22:31 and the promise that Peter would be upheld by the prayers of Jesus. Even though Peter denied three times that he knew Jesus, he was not rejected or turned away, but remained with the disciples. The risen Jesus gave Peter three opportunities to affirm his love for him (John 21:15ff). Peter had been upheld, even in his denial, by the intercessory prayers of Jesus. Then Torrance reminded him of Rom 8:26-27, which promises that "the Spirit helps us in our weakness. We do not know how to pray as we ought, but the Spirit himself intercedes for us with groans that words cannot express." Torrance tied this verse to the man's problem, saying, "None of us knows how to pray, but the Spirit knows all about us. He knows all about you and is interpreting your desires and groans and your longing to know how to pray. He is interceding for you and leading you to the Father."[3] As they talked he affirmed the great promise at the end of Rom 8, that nothing in life or death can separate us from the love of God. Soon afterwards, he met the man's wife and prayed with both of them.

As I reread these pages, I was guided to speak on the mediation of Christ at the service. At the funeral, I acknowledged the pain family and friends were enduring in the aftermath of this suicide, but near the beginning I also said something like the following: "Although we cannot honor his final choice, we can remember and honor his life as a whole. We give thanks to God for the gift of his life, for the time that we shared with him, for the person we knew and welcomed into our homes. There were aspects of his life that were good and can be lifted up today without shame." We reviewed some of these positive memories in detail. Next I acknowledged the real grief felt by his mother and other mourners, saying something like, "During a time of grief we can barely function. There is no joy or inner strength. We cannot sing, we cannot laugh, and we

---

2. Torrance, *Worship*, 33–34.
3. Torrance, *Worship*, 34–35.

cannot pretend that things are normal. For some people here, the grief is so hurtful and deep that you cannot pray. You cannot even think about God. You feel you cannot connect with the spiritual resources you need." Then I shared the story of the man who could not pray, as James Torrance told it in his book, and connected it to both Rom 8 and the passages in Hebrews that speak of the ongoing ministry of intercession which Jesus continues in heaven (Heb 6:20; 7:25–28; 8:1–6). I highlighted the theme that when we cannot pray Jesus is praying for us, and sending the Holy Spirit to share in the ministry of strengthening us by divine intercession.

> In times like this God does not ask you to do more good deeds, not even pray more. Just as an apple tree does not produce apples in a time of drought, you cannot produce anything like spiritual fruit when your spirit is dry, wrung out and exhausted. God does not expect that you pray at this time, God does not expect or demand anything of you. Right now, God is upholding you and taking care of you. You are upheld by the prayers of Jesus, who understands your weakness in time of grief. He knows all about your pain. He stands in for you and represents you before God the Father. Whenever you can pray, he always takes your prayer, places it on his own holy lips, and brings it to the Father.[4]
> The same happens when you cannot pray. When you can only sigh or groan, he places those sighs and groans on his own holy

---

4. This is not based on a naïve picture-model (Jesus kneeling in prayer) that can only portray one conversation at a time, but by recognition that the mind of the Creator is that of the triune God who can track all the particulars and contours of our space-time universe without being contained within it. As our ascended mediator between heaven and earth, as both Son of God and son of Mary, Christ Jesus participates in the triune fellowship in the heavenly dimension wherein the limitations of time cannot encroach. In eternity, the mediator can bring each prayer before God the Father without fail, so that what is true for one person on earth can simultaneously be true for billions. Your prayer is not heard the less because someone else has God's attention. This is one model but not the only one. We do not know exactly how or to what extent the human Jesus in his heavenly ascension interacts with each person on earth. Traditionally, Lutherans have held that there is a communication of attributes between the divine nature and the human nature of Jesus, gifting more than we can imagine to his human mind. For those theologians who think the attribute of divine omniscience is not entirely communicated to the human mind of Jesus, neither in his earthly ministry nor in his ascension, his ongoing worldwide mediation is not necessarily excluded. Jesus's heavenly prayers on behalf of the world could still be formed in such a way that he offers an encompassing prayer of mediation, the eschatological fulfillment of which will include the fulfillment of all human prayers directed to God. First John 2:1 says Christ is our advocate, yet words are not necessary for his advocacy to be effective. His very presence in the holy place is the enduring reminder of his redemptive achievement on our behalf. The ongoing ministry of the Holy Spirit can embrace our longings and prayers and connect them always to the mediation of Christ and the future which God promises.

lips, and prays for you in the right way in communion with the Father. As he stands in for you, he offers a perfect and complete prayer to the Father on your behalf. You are represented and upheld by this mediator, just as he once upheld Peter with his intercessions. Whether you can pray or cannot pray, he will never turn away from you. So do not fear if you cannot pray today, because Jesus is praying for you.

This message pointed to an important doctrine which is not often used at funeral services, and so it came as a fresh word. Several listeners said it made God seem closer and less remote. The passages in Hebrews about having a mediator in heaven who sympathizes with us in our weaknesses (infirmities can be physical, mental, or spiritual) is especially meaningful to people bent under a great weight of sorrow. If there is a common concern surrounding suicides, it is fear of God's judgment and condemnation. It is not for any preacher to intrude on the prerogative of God in regards to judgment, but the affirmation that God provides a mediator who sympathizes with us in our weaknesses is a truth about God that fills out the biblical picture of God. This mediator is God's gift to all and serves God's redeeming purpose. As we recognize the fullness of this divine sympathy, an expanded idea of God is made possible, one that can help people receive the comfort of the Holy Spirit. This is a comfort that enhances reverential awe.

In this review, my intention is only to highlight how many options the funeral preacher actually has when it comes to presenting the content of our faith. Whether the doctrine is the mediation of Christ or something else that is biblical, central doctrines can strike a chord with people when brought to bear upon heartfelt problems. Hugh Ross Mackintosh, a noted preacher in Scotland, saw greater attendance at Sunday worship and more positive responses when preaching on the great doctrines of the faith.[5] The great doctrines of the Bible can be woven into suicide

---

5. In the essay "The Heart of the Gospel and the Preacher," which T. F. Torrance highly recommended to pastors, Hugh Ross Mackintosh said there was a longing for the right kind of doctrinal preaching. "In the first place, it has been the experience of many preachers to receive more earnest thanks for sermons on great Christian doctrines than at any other time; second, it is noticeable that in churches where the pastor believes in preaching of this sort, and does his best to furnish it, the proportion of men in the audience is larger than usual." Mackintosh, *God In Experience*, 85. He also stressed the need felt by both men and women to hear Christian truth presented in worthy and intelligent ways. In this regard, James S. Stewart cautioned that preaching on doctrines can be done in a dull and mistaken way, as though Christ died for the church in order to leave a depository of doctrine. It can be done in an empty way, as when truths are unfelt by the

funeral messages in multiple ways. What I presented above is only one example. Following Mackintosh's lead opens up many biblical passages for consideration, far more than can be discussed here. For example, one preacher took a text about creation and focused on the Holy Spirit's work of bringing order into chaos, then talked about the chaos that can unravel our lives, and moved into prayers for God to bring the Spirit's healing into the family's pain. In addition, he talked about the doctrine of resurrection that promises a renewing of human life and order in the created realm. The passages that express these truths are plentiful, therefore we can look far beyond the sections of Scripture mentioned in this chapter to find the right texts.

The Psalms

Many of the psalms in the Bible were originally meant for public worship in ancient Israel, songs to be sung by a choir or assembly as part of communal worship at Solomon's Temple. Some older ones may have been originally presented as personal songs to God, worshipful expressions that arose in private prayer, such as the songs attributed to Miriam or King David. But more often than not psalms served a public purpose, and this may have been the composer's intention from the start. Later, during the Second Temple period, when diaspora synagogues first came into use in Jewish communities far from Jerusalem, the psalms were spoken or sung in weekly synagogue gatherings or used at home for Sabbath prayer, and thus became formative in developing the prayer language for numerous generations. It is possible that in his youth Jesus committed most or all of the book of Psalms to memory (along with Deuteronomy and Isaiah), which was probably quite a common feat rather than an exceptional one, a central part of a Jewish boy's education in his day.

The Psalms were Jesus's prayer book, and for that reason we cannot underestimate their importance as a spiritual resource. In the agony of

---

preacher, as though no joy or strength can be derived from them. It is done in the best way when people know they have been offered Christ himself in and through the words of the sermon, so they may receive the strong, bracing comfort of New Testament hope. As Stewart so often emphasized, people today do not need a description of Christianity, rather they need Christ. The preacher must preach as one who believes that if the gospel message is fantasy, then there is no hope for humanity anywhere. For him preaching doctrine in the best sense was "heralding the wonderful works of God." These emphases are found throughout Stewart's published sermons as well as his valuable books on preaching, *Heralds of God* and *A Faith to Proclaim*.

his crucifixion Ps 22 formed his cry to God. It is possible he attempted to pray it to the end, even if broken by pain and lack of breath, for this psalm begins in despair but ends in hope. If Jesus used these psalms throughout his life then we should not neglect their formative power. There will be parts that are strange to us, as can only be expected with anything written twenty-five hundred or three thousand years before our time, but they are worth working through on our part.

The Presence or Absence of the Psalms in Public Worship Services

The psalms are a holy trysting place where God returns repeatedly to minister to broken people, though not in a way that we can control. The removal of the psalms from Christian life leaves a void. For decades prior to the Nazi's rise to power, church leadership throughout Germany had removed the public readings of the psalms from Sunday services.[6] This was not done with any foresight of the rise of Nazism, and we cannot blame them for not knowing the future. They participated in "the spirit of the age" without understanding the consequences that were to follow, which we are all in danger of doing in our own time. Yet, had these ancient Jewish prayers been read consistently in the churches, then there would have been a countering force at work in the hearts and minds of the general populace during Hitler's rise to power. By countering force, I mean that the Jewish roots of the Christian understanding of God could not be denied, nor could Jesus's Jewishness have been ignored, and a more responsible ethic affirmed.

During the Reformation, Martin Luther knew that, as a preacher and teacher, he could never ignore the psalms. Yet the historic Lutheran witness to Christ became subverted in Germany in the centuries following Luther under the impact of German Idealism, and petitionary prayer was devalued since the time of Friedrich Schleiermacher, removing a vital spiritual connection with the psalms. In this development, the psalms were not held before the general public on a regular basis. Given this historic negative example, together with the positive example of our Lord (consider the frequent use the New Testament writers made of Ps 110), it seems we should not neglect to pray the psalms and reflect on them in our daily lives. Yet as with everywhere else in the Bible, the Holy Spirit

---

6. Conversation with Karlfried and Ricarda Froehlich, 1990.

must breathe life into these words and apply them to our hearts. They are dead and with no effect apart from the work of the Spirit.

The Private Appeal of the Psalms

Over the course of centuries the book of Psalms has not lost appeal to Christians. Since the advent of the printing press and wide distribution of Bibles, many who read the Bible in their homes frequently return to the psalms. Especially favored is the twenty-third psalm, a concise poetical affirmation of God's faithfulness. Whether this psalm originally referred to God's care for David as an individual, or for the ancient kingdom of Israel, does not really matter to readers who resonate with these words. They gravitate to this psalm because they sense the same Shepherd has been at work in their own lives too. They sense an underlying promise that includes them. They welcome the spiritual fellowship David sang about. This is an indication, repeated across many generations, of how people are hungry for God's nearness, open to the same divine guidance, praying for their own protection, and hoping for the gift of everlasting life as they face death.

People return to select verses in other psalms again and again. Every conceivable emotion is expressed somewhere in this collection of ancient poetry, showing us what it means to call on God in prayer from a variety of moods and circumstances. Pastors in past generations knew of people in their congregations who suffered great adversity and withdrew into themselves. Some quit reading the Bible altogether in the aftermath of personal tragedy—with the singular exception of verses in Psalms. While serving in a congregation committed to reading four lessons each Sunday, I once heard a lady say, "The only part of the Bible I can relate to is the psalms." This comment does not stand alone. Devout Jews and Christians have often sensed there is spiritual depth and power in these verses. Without denying that the Holy Spirit can speak into our minds and hearts through any part of Scripture, we should ask why the psalter has such enduring appeal.

Part of the reason must be that the psalms are steeped in expressions which show all the range of human emotions. One poet laughs in joy over a surprising deliverance from danger, while another screams in anger at some terrible injustice. We feel their humanity come through to us in these vivid expressions. If David is cherished long after his day, it is not just because we like the story of the young hero who challenged Goliath with his sling. We also remember the story of his moral failure with Bathsheba and his scheme to destroy her husband, Uriah. Yet when rebuked by Nathan he repented from the depths of his being. In knowing this sordid story, we are drawn to the way he prayed for mercy in Ps 51. Putting it all together, we feel we are in contact with someone like ourselves, a real human with a mix of good and bad qualities. We take this to mean that God does have spiritual relationships with people just like us, and this gracious possibility gives us renewed hope. In overhearing part of these ancient conversations, we realize we can have our own conversation with God.

Propinquity, When Expressions of Mood or Thought Resonate

At times there may be a deep communication of mood between the words of a psalm and the modern reader, which naturally varies from person to person. The idea of "propinquity" may apply. Propinquity is an old word which meant "nearness" in Shakespeare. When used today by psychologists of music, this word refers to the way a selection of notes (usually three) within a short measure of time affects the mood of the listener. In some cases, it is possible the music helps create or enhance a certain feeling, while in other cases it taps into something already deeply felt inside the listener. There may be a proximate communication, a match between the mood of the music and the current mood of the listener. When this happens, the result can be dynamic as well as subtle. If a person is sad and the musical sound matches her emotion, then it can bring a sense of release, some uplift of spirit and renewed energy. This is one reason why some sad music may help depressed people, while happy music has little power to lift their mood. It is almost the emotional equivalent of meeting someone who understands you and thinks like you, of meeting a friend who shares your strongest interest or your most heartfelt pleasure (or, in this case, your heartfelt pain). This comes as close as you can get to the feeling of being understood without being in a live conversation with another person.

Something like the principle of propinquity may work through great literature as well, though in a different way than audio music, and is part of the reason why people can resonate with a favorite book, ranging from *Pride and Prejudice* to *The Lord of the Rings*, or favorite type of story (romance or thriller), or favorite character in a story. Reading or hearing the psalms brings the possibility of spiritual and emotional resonance with aspects of the human experience. This is why a careful selection of psalms used in a memorial service may be helpful in a time of grief, though individual responses will vary. My purpose is not to point to any particular text for a suicide funeral, but to highlight this section of Scripture as a rich resource that may be mined continually.[7]

The Psalms and Pastoral Care

There is nothing new in turning to the psalms for spiritual guidance, nor is there anything new in the recognition that wounded humans can find personal healing and help in these sacred verses. Long ago, the biblical teacher at Antioch, Diodore of Tarsus (who died before AD 394), highlighted the importance of the psalms for pastoral care. Diodore said,

> Of course, those who need only the psalms of thanksgiving because life has been exceedingly kind to them are very fortunate. But we are human, and it is impossible for us not to experience difficulties and encounter the forces of necessity rising both from without and from within ourselves. Thus, when our souls find in the psalms the most ready formulation of the concerns they wish to bring before God, they recognize them as a wonderfully appropriate remedy. For the Holy Spirit anticipated all kinds of human situations, setting forth through the most blessed David the proper words for our sufferings through which the afflicted may find healing.[8]

The power of a particular psalm to minister to an individual is real, as Diodore of Tarsus advised, but the context of preaching brings together a very diverse group of people. Each member of the congregation has different life experiences and personal needs. The one psalm that matches one person's needs may not match another's. Even so, perhaps one particular verse comes very close to expressing what many people feel in that critical hour and need to hear acknowledged. Even when we cannot address every concern, giving acknowledgment can provide an opening for spiritual ministry.

---

7. A very readable commentary is Goldingay, *Psalms for Everyone*. In addition to standard commentaries, insightful books include: Bonhoeffer, *Psalms*; Brueggemann, *Message of the Psalms*; Lewis, *Reflections on the Psalms*; Peterson, *Long Obedience*; and Wright, *Case for the Psalms*.

8. Froehlich, *Biblical Interpretation*, 82–83.

Difficulties with Preaching from Psalms

It is helpful to remember that these psalms generally do not present the voice of God speaking a word directly to people, like a message given through a prophet. These are generally human prayers offered to God. They are also songs sung to educate people about God, telling a congregation why they should praise the creator of heaven and earth. And they can serve both purposes at the same time.

Public prayers and songs may have both a vertical and a horizontal direction, with some words directed towards God and some words directed towards the congregation in the very same passage. In certain texts, the voice of God breaks through, as in Ps 32:8, "I will guide you." But most of the time the direction of words moves from humanity to God or from a single song leader towards the gathered people. Cumulatively, the horizontal message of these psalms, that is, the thought that moves from human speaker to human listener, affirms honoring God's name in daily living and ethical behavior, as well as trusting in God's provision and protection. Cumulatively, the vertical message of these psalms, where thought moves from human speaker to our creator, is praise which recounts or alludes to great moments of deliverance, particularly the exodus from Egypt. These are affirmations that God is lord of creation, provider of good, protector or deliverer of Israel. These praises affirm God's involvement in Israel's history, and by implication remind us that God is still involved in human history even when we cannot see this clearly (the table of nations in Genesis implies it, as does the Great Commission).

Some psalms contain outbursts of joyous praise, while a few express fear and cries for deliverance from danger. In Ps 137, God is not the one speaking outrageously or promoting vengeance—that is the expression of the person praying in pain and rage because of injustice. Underneath is a cry for God to bring justice. This shows why we have to attend to the question of who is speaking and the direction the expression is meant to go. Does the thought move from the human speaker towards God or from God to the people? These passages display a great variety of emotion and experience, giving us permission to call on God in every kind of circumstance, which does not mean that every expression contained in a lament is the most appropriate way to pray.[9] Jesus taught the most appropriate way to pray, and every ancient prayer can only be measured against his standard. He himself used the psalms as his own prayer book, to be

---

9. Froehlich, "Discerning the Voices," 75–90.

sure, but the prayer he taught his disciples summarizes the key elements of appropriate prayer and must serve as our chief guide. This is popularly known as "The Lord's Prayer."[10] The "prayer of Jabez" in 1 Chr 4:10, for example, is not the standard for Christian prayer, nor is every isolated verse taken from the Psalter. But the God who heard cries from broken hearts, and many inadequate prayers, is also willing to hear our prayers. Genuine cries from the human heart, disorganized as well as orderly prayers, are heard because the relationality is honored.

Gaps that Have to be Bridged by Life Experiences in Fellowship with God

It is also helpful to remember that the language of the Psalter is not ours. It comes from a very ancient time and a culture very different from any modern technological society. So there is work for the preacher because we cannot assume that each image or reference will readily translate. And there is another concern because of the large time gap between then and now. If we make the experience of the psalmist seem objective as something back there in history, but yet outside the experience of the people listening to the sermon, then we lose an important opportunity. The goal is to connect what happened to the psalm-singer so long ago in Israel with what is happening to people today. As Elizabeth Achtemeier says, "The point of a sermon from the psalms is so to appropriate the language of the psalm for the congregation that what happened long ago for the psalmist happens in the immediate now for the congregation."[11] How do I help the people to find themselves in the psalmist's words or world? That is a key question because we are relating a spiritual journey in the present to a spiritual journey in the past. We are seeking to discover whether we can make the link and affirm the same thing about God, finding the same hope in times of pain or fear.

When considering a passage from Psalms, the idea of propinquity does not just apply to moods or feelings, but to life experiences (including harsh ones) that make us reflect on God's presence and faithfulness (or make us fear God's absence). So the connection is not just about how one feels emotionally, but also includes how one thinks about God. If someone living nearly three thousand years ago came to a conclusion

---

10. Matt 6:11–15; Luke 11:1–4.
11. Achtemeier, *Preaching from the Old Testament*, 148.

about God that seems honest in your own estimation, the intellectual and spiritual connection is remarkable. Eugene Peterson puts his finger on this in his focus on Ps 124.

> Subjected to our most relentless and searching criticism, Ps 124 will, I think, finally convince us of its honesty. There is no literature in all the world that is more true to life and more honest than Psalms, for here we have warts-and-all religion. Every skeptical thought, every disappointing venture, every pain, every despair that we can face is lived through and integrated into a personal, saving relationship with God—a relationship that also has in it acts of praise, blessing, peace, security, trust and love. Good poetry survives not when it is pretty or beautiful or nice but when it is true: accurate and honest. The psalms are great poetry and have lasted not because they appeal to our fantasies and our wishes but because they are confirmed in the intensities of honest and hazardous living.[12]

The only people who can test a psalm like this are people who have lived through hard times and still found they could sing praises to God. Bloodied and bruised, Paul and Silas were given a song "in the night season." Can anyone today relate to their experience? No psalm will minister to everyone in the same way, because there are not subjective resonances to every expression. So there is no quick and easy comfort that comes automatically. However, when personal experiences match with an affirmation expressed in biblical poetry the power of confirmation through propinquity can minister. There will be times of trial when people sense the faithfulness of God, either throughout a crisis or after surviving one.

Long ago, at the center of human history, it was Jesus who tested the truth of Ps 22 when he was broken and humbled. The opening verse was the voice of despair, but then moved towards affirming hope in God. By enduring despair Jesus's ability to hope in God was tested to the extreme limit. We too may suffer, in various ways, but not without the hope of God's final deliverance. For us, there is no promise of immediate rescue, but there is a promise of God's ultimate rescue from death. This is part of the painful tension we live with in this age. We have the promises now, but the fulfillment is yet to come.

---

12. Peterson, *Long Obedience*, 75.

Bibliography

Abelson, Kassel. "Suicide," 1–11. *The Rabbinical Assembly*, 2005. https://www.rabbinicalassembly.org/sites/default/files/public/halakhah/teshuvot/20052010/abelson_suicide.pdf.
Achtemeier, Elizabeth. *Preaching from the Old Testament*. Louisville: Westminster John Knox, 1989.
Acolatse, Esther. *Powers, Principalities, and the Spirit: Biblical Realism in Africa and the West*. Grand Rapids: Eerdmans, 2018.
Allen, Diogenes. *Philosophy for Understanding Theology*. Atlanta: John Knox, 1985.
Allison, Dale C., Jr. *Encountering Mystery: Religious Experience in a Secular Age*. Grand Rapids: Eerdmans, 2022.
———. *The Resurrection of Jesus: Apologetics, Polemics, History*. Edinburgh: T&T Clark, 2021.
Amundsen, Darrel W. "The Anguish and Agonies of Charles Spurgeon." *Christian History*, 1991. https://christianhistoryinstitute.org/magazine/article/anguish-and-agonies-of-charles-spurgeon.
———. "Did Early Christians 'Lust after Death'? A New Wrinkle in the Doctor-Assisted Suicide Debate." In *Suicide: A Christian Response: Crucial Considerations for Choosing Life*, edited by Timothy J. Demy and Gary P. Stewart, 285–95. Grand Rapids: Kregel, 1998.
Anderson, Ray S. *Dancing with Wolves While Feeding the Sheep: The Musings of a Maverick Theologian*. Eugene, OR: Wipf & Stock, 2001.
———. *The Gospel According to Judas*. Colorado Springs: Helmers & Howard, 1991.
Aquinas, Thomas. *The Summa Theologica of St. Thomas Aquinas, Volume III*. Westminster: Christian Classics, 1981.
Augustine. *The City of God*. Translated by Marcus Dods. New York: The Modern Library, 1950.
———. *On Free Choice of the Will*. Translated by Anna S. Benjamin and L. H. Hackstaff. New York: Macmillan, 1964.
Bailey, Kenneth E. *Through Peasant Eyes*. Grand Rapids: Eerdmans, 1983.
Baldwin, Joyce G. *1 and 2 Samuel: An Introduction and Commentary*. Downers Grove, IL: InterVarsity, 1988.
Bales, James D. "The Relevance of Scriptural Interpretation to Scientific Thought." *Bulletin of the Evangelical Theological Society* 4 (1961)129–35.
Bar, Shaul. *God's First King: The Story of Saul*. Eugene, OR: Wipf & Stock, 2013.
Barclay, John M. G. *Paul and the Gift*. Grand Rapids: Eerdmans, 2015.

Barlow, Dominic, producer. *Garrow's Law.* Aired November 1, 2009 to December 4, 2011, on BBC One.

Barth, Karl. *Church Dogmatics.* 2/2. Edited by G. W. Bromiley and T. F. Torrance. Translated by G. W. Bromiley et al. Edinburgh: T&T Clark, 1957.

———. *Church Dogmatics.* 3/3. Edited by G. W. Bromiley and T. F. Torrance. Translated by G. W. Bromiley and R. Ehrlich. Edinburgh: T&T Clark, 1960.

———. *Church Dogmatics.* 3/4. Edited by G. W. Bromiley and T. F. Torrance. Translated by A. T. Mackay et al. Edinburgh: T&T Clark, 1961.

———. *Deliverance to the Captives.* Translated by Marguerite Wieser. New York: Harper & Brothers, 1961.

Battenhouse, Roy. "The Tragedy of Absalom: A Literary Analysis (2 Samuel 13–18)." *Christianity and Literature* 31 (1982) 53–57.

Bayly, Joe. *The Last Thing We Talk About: A Christian View of Death.* Bloomington, IL: Clearnote, 2014.

Becker, Ernest. *The Denial of Death.* New York: Simon and Schuster, 1973.

Beker, J. Christian. *Paul the Apostle: The Triumph of God in Life and Thought.* Philadelphia: Fortress, 1987.

Bennett, Arnold. *Clayhanger.* New York: E. P. Dutton, 1910.

Berman, Alan L., et al. *Adolescent Suicide: Assessment and Intervention.* 2nd ed. Washington, DC: American Psychological Association, 2006.

Binswanger, Ludwig. *Sigmund Freud: Reminiscences of a Friendship.* New York: Grune & Stratton, 1957.

Bliss, Kathleen. "Michael Foster." *Frontier* 2 (1959) 258.

Bloesch, Donald G. *Essentials of Evangelical Theology.* Volume 2: *Life, Ministry, and Hope.* San Francisco: HarperCollins, 1982.

———. *Freedom for Obedience: Evangelical Ethics for Contemporary Times.* San Francisco: Harper & Row, 1987.

———. *The Holy Spirit: Works and Gifts.* Downers Grove, IL: InterVarsity, 2000.

Bock, Darrell. *The Missing Gospels: Unearthing the Truth Behind Alternative Christianities.* Nashville: Nelson, 2006.

Bolt, Peter G. "'With a View to the Forgiveness of Sins': Jesus and Forgiveness in Mark's Gospel." *Reformed Theological Review* 57 (1998) 53–69.

Bonhoeffer, Dietrich. *Ethics.* Edited by Eberhard Bethge and translated by Neville Horton Smith. New York: Macmillan, 1962.

———. *Ethics.* Works of Dietrich Bonhoeffer 6. Translated by Reinhard Krauss et al. Edited by Clifford Green. Minneapolis: Fortress, 2005.

———. *Psalms: The Prayer Book of the Bible.* Minneapolis: Augsburg Fortress, 1974.

———. *Temptation.* Edited by Eberhard Bethge and translated by Kathleen Downham. London: The Camelot Press, 1955.

Boswell, James. *Boswell's Life of Johnson.* Volume 2: *1776–1784.* New York: Oxford University Press, 1948.

Brown, Peter. *Augustine of Hippo: A Biography.* Berkeley: University of California Press, 2000.

Bruce, F. F. *The Gospel of John.* Basingstoke: Pickering & Inglis, 1983.

———. *The Hard Sayings of Jesus.* Downers Grove, IL: InterVarsity, 1983.

Brueggemann, Walter. *The Message of the Psalms.* Minneapolis: Augsburg Fortress, 1984.

Brusselmans, Christaine, et al. *Toward Moral and Religious Maturity: The First International Conference on Moral and Religious Development*. Morristown: Silver Burdett, 1980.
Buechner, Frederick. *Telling Secrets*. San Francisco: HarperOne, 2000.
Burnett, Richard, ed. *The Westminster Handbook to Karl Barth*. Louisville: Westminster John Knox, 2013.
Burton, Bryan. "Universalism." In *The Westminster Handbook to Karl Barth*, edited by Richard Burnett, 217–18. Louisville: Westminster John Knox, 2013.
Bush, Michael D., ed. *This Incomplete One: Words Occasioned by the Death of a Young Person*. Grand Rapids: Eerdmans, 2006.
Caird, G. B. *The Truth of the Gospel*. London: Oxford University Press, 1950.
Calvin, John. *Calvin's Commentaries*. Vol. 12, *Commentaries on the Book of the Prophet Daniel*. Translated by Thomas Myers. Grand Rapids: Baker, 2005.
———. *Commentary on a Harmony of the Evangelists Matthew, Mark, and Luke*, Vol. 3. Translated by William Pringle. Grand Rapids: Baker, 2005.
———. *Institutes of the Christian Religion*. Vols. 1 and 2. Edited by John T. McNeill. Translated by Ford Lewis Battles. Philadelphia: Westminster, 1960.
Cameron, Nigel M. de S., ed. *Universalism and the Doctrine of Hell: Papers Presented at the Fourth Edinburgh Conference on Christian Dogmatics, 1991*. Grand Rapids: Baker Books, 1992.
Carlsen, Mary Baird. *Creative Aging: A Meaning-Making Perspective*. New York: Norton, 1996.
Carnell, Edward J. *The Kingdom of Love and the Pride of Life*. Eugene, OR: Wipf & Stock, 2007.
Carter, Tom, ed. *2200 Quotations from the Writings of Charles H. Spurgeon*. Grand Rapids: Baker Books, 1988.
Cassuto, Umberto. *A Commentary on the Book of Genesis Part II: From Noah to Abraham*. Translated by Israel Abrahams. Jerusalem: Hebrew University, 1984.
Catechism of the Catholic Church. Second edition. Washington, DC: United States Catholic Conference, 1997.
Chapell, Bryan, ed. *The Hardest Sermons You'll Ever Have to Preach: Help from Trusted Preachers for Tragic Times*. Grand Rapids: Zondervan, 2011.
Chesterton, G. K. *Orthodoxy*. Mineola, NY: Dover, 2004.
Clark, Chap. *Hurt 2.0: Inside the World of Today's Teenager*. Grand Rapids: Baker Academic, 2011.
Clebsch, William A. "Editor's Introduction." In *Suicide: Biathanatos* by John Donne, vii-xvii. Chico, CA: Scholars Press, 1983.
Clemons, James T., ed. *Sermons on Suicide*. Louisville: Westminster John Knox, 1989.
Clinton, Tim, et al. *The Quick-Reference Guide to Counseling Teenagers*. Grand Rapids: Baker, 2010.
Colwell, John. "The Contemporaneity of the Divine Decision: Reflections on Barth's Denial of 'Universalism.'" In *Universalism and the Doctrine of Hell*, edited by Nigel M. de S. Cameron, 139–60. Grand Rapids: Baker, 1992.
Como, James T. *C. S. Lewis at the Breakfast Table and Other Reminiscences*. San Diego: Harcourt Brace, 1992.
Copan, Paul. *Is God a Moral Monster? Making Sense of the Old Testament God*. Baker, 2011.

———. *True for You, But Not for Me: Deflating the Slogans That Leave Christians Speechless*. Minneapolis: Bethany House, 1998.
Cottrell, Jack. "Suicide and Forgiveness." In *God's Amazing Salvation: The Collected Writings of Jack Cottrell*, vol. 13, 157–59. Mason, OH: Christian Restoration Association.
Colyer, Elmer M. *How to Read T. F. Torrance: Understanding His Trinitarian and Scientific Theology*. Downers Grove: InterVarsity, 2001.
Craig, William Lane. "Dale Allison on Jesus' Empty Tomb, his Postmortem Appearances, and the Origin of the Disciples' Belief in his Resurrection." *Philosophia Christi* 10 (2008) 293–301.
———. *The Only Wise God: The Compatibility of Divine Foreknowledge and Human Freedom*. Grand Rapids: Baker Books, 1987.
———. *Reasonable Faith*. Wheaton, IL: Crossway, 1994.
Cranfield, C. E. B. *The Gospel According to Saint Mark*. Cambridge: Cambridge University Press, 1989.
———. *Romans: A Shorter Commentary*. Grand Rapids: Eerdmans, 1988.
Crews, Frederick, ed. *Unauthorized Freud: Doubters Confront a Legend*. New York: Penguin, 1999.
Crisp, Oliver D. "On the Vicarious Humanity of Christ." *International Journal of Systematic Theology* 21 (2019) 235–50.
Croft, Brian, and Phil Newton. *Conduct Gospel-Centered Funerals: Applying the Gospel at the Unique Challenges of Death*. Grand Rapids: Zondervan, 2014.
Cullmann, Oscar. *Prayer in the New Testament*. Translated by John Bowden. Minneapolis: Fortress, 1995.
Davies, D. Eryl. *Not Uninformed: Sure and Certain Hope for Death and Dying*. Fearn: Christian Focus, 2020.
Demy, Timothy J., and Gary P. Stewart, eds. *Suicide: A Christian Response: Crucial Considerations for Choosing Life*. Grand Rapids: Kregel, 1998.
Denker, Rolf. *Angst und Aggression*. Stuttgart: Kohlhammer, 1974.
Donne, John. *Suicide: Biathanatos*. Edited by William A. Clebsch. Chico, CA: Scholars Press, 1983.
Droge, Arthur J., and James D. Taber. *A Noble Death: Suicide and Martyrdom Among Christians and Jews in Antiquity*. San Francisco: HarperCollins, 1992.
Duff, Nancy. *Making Faithful Decisions at the End of Life*. Louisville: Westminster John Knox Press, 2018.
Durkheim, Emile. *Suicide: A Study in Sociology*. Translated by John. A. Spaulding and George Simpson. Glencoe, IL: Free Press, 1951.
Earman, John. *Hume's Abject Failure: The Argument Against Miracles*. New York: Oxford University Press, 2000.
Eddy, Paul Rhodes, and Gregory A. Boyd. *The Jesus Legend: A Case for the Historical Reliability of the Synoptic Jesus Tradition*. Grand Rapids: Baker Academic, 2007.
Erler, Rolf Joachim, and Reiner Marquard, eds. *A Karl Barth Reader*. Translated by Geoffrey W. Bromiley. Grand Rapids: Eerdmans, 1986.
Evans, C. Stephen. *Kierkegaard's "Fragments" and "Postscript": The Religious Philosophy of Johannes Climacus*. Atlantic Highlands, NJ: Humanities Press International, 1983.
Fee, Gordon D. *The Disease of the Health and Wealth Gospels*. Vancouver: Regent College, 2006.

———. *Jesus the Lord According to Paul the Apostle: A Concise Introduction.* Grand Rapids: Baker Academic, 2018.
Fest, Joachim. *Plotting Hitler's Death: The German Resistance to Hitler 1933–1945.* Translated by Bruce Little. New York: Metropolitan Books, 1996.
Fitzgerald, Percy Hetherington. *An Examination of Dr. George Birkbeck Hill's "Johnsonian" Editions.* London: Bliss, Sands, 1898.
Foster, Michael. "The Christian Doctrine of Creation and the Rise of Modern Natural Science." *Mind* 43 (1934) 446–68.
———. "Christian Theology and Modern Science of Nature I." *Mind* 44 (1935) 439–66.
———. "Christian Theology and Modern Science of Nature II." *Mind* 45 (1936) 1–27.
———. *The Political Philosophies of Plato and Hegel.* Oxford: Clarendon, 1935.
Foster, Michael B. *Mystery and Philosophy.* London: SCM, 1957.
Fowl, Stephen E. *Philippians.* Grand Rapids: Eerdmans, 2005.
France, R. T. *The Gospel According to Matthew: An Introduction and Commentary.* Grand Rapids: Eerdmans, 1985.
Frankl, Victor. *Man's Search for Meaning.* New York: Touchstone Books, 1970.
Freud, Sigmund. *The Ego and the Id.* Translated by Joan Riviere. Edited by James Strachey. New York: Norton, 1962.
Froehlich, Karlfried, trans and ed. *Biblical Interpretation in the Early Church.* Philadelphia: Fortress, 1984.
———. "Discerning the Voices: Praise and Lament in the Tradition of the Christian Psalter." *Calvin Theological Journal* 36 (2001) 75–90.
———. *Sensing the Scriptures: Aminadab's Chariot and the Predicament of Biblical Interpretation.* Grand Rapids: Eerdmans, 2014.
———. "'Take Up and Read': Basics of Augustine's Biblical Interpretation." *Interpretation* 58 (2004), 5–16.
Gaventa, Beverly. *When In Romans: An Invitation to Linger with the Gospel According to Paul.* Grand Rapids: Baker Academic, 2016.
Geach, Peter. *Providence and Evil.* London: Cambridge University Press, 1977.
Geisler, Norman. *Christian Ethics: Options and Issues.* Grand Rapids: Baker, 1989.
Geivett, R. Douglas, and Gary R. Habermas, eds. *In Defense of Miracles: A Comprehensive Case for God's Action in History.* Downers Grove, IL: InterVarsity, 1997.
Gerali, Steven. *What Do I Do When Teenagers are Depressed and Contemplate Suicide?* Grand Rapids: Zondervan, 2009.
Gibson, Scott M. *Preaching for Special Services.* Baker Books, 2001.
Gibson, Scott M., and Karen Mason. *Preaching Hope in Darkness: Help for Pastors in Addressing Suicide from the Pulpit.* Bellingham: Lexham, 2020.
Gilbert, Martin. *The Second World War: A Complete History.* New York: Holt, 1989.
Goldingay, John. *Psalms for Everyone, Part 1: Psalms 1–72.* Louisville: Westminster John Knox, 2013.
———. *Psalms for Everyone, Part 2: Psalms 73–150.* Louisville: Westminster John Knox, 2014.
Green, Michael. *Matthew for Today.* Dallas: Word, 1988.
Gunn, David M. *The Fate of King Saul: An Interpretation of a Biblical Story.* Sheffield: JSOT Press, 1984.
Habermas, Gary R., and Michael R. Licona. *The Case for the Resurrection of Jesus.* Grand Rapids: Kregel, 2004.

Hauer, Christian E. "The Shape of Saulide Strategy." *Catholic Biblical Quarterly* 31 (1969) 153–67.
Hecht, Jennifer. *Stay: A History of Suicide and the Philosophies Against It*. New Haven: Yale University Press, 2013.
Hong, Edna. *Bright Valley of Love*. Minneapolis: Augsburg, 1976.
Hordern, William. *Living by Grace*. Philadelphia: Westminster, 1975.
Houston, James, and Michael Parker. *A Vision for the Aging Church: Renewing Ministry for and by Seniors*. Downers' Grove: IVP Academic, 2011.
Hsu, Albert Y. *Grieving a Suicide: A Loved One's Search for Comfort, Answers, and Hope*. Downers Grove, IL: InterVarsity, 2017.
Hurtado, Larry W. *Why On Earth Did Anyone Become a Christian in the First Three Centuries?* Milwaukee: Marquette University Press, 2016.
Jenson, Philip. *Reading Jonah*. Cambridge: Grove, 1999.
Johnson, Paul. *Modern Times: The World from the Twenties to the Nineties*. New York: HarperCollins, 1991.
Jones, Clay. "Killing the Canaanites: A Response to the New Atheism's 'Divine Genocide' Claims," *Christian Research Journal* 33 (2010) 28–35.
Kaplan, Kalman J., ed. *Right to Die Versus Sacredness of Life*. New York: Routledge, 2018.
Kaplan, Kalman J., and Matthew B. Schwartz, *A Psychology of Hope: A Biblical Response to Tragedy and Suicide*. Grand Rapids: Eerdmans, 2008.
Kaplan, Kalmon J., and Paul Cantz. *Biblical Psychotherapy: Reclaiming Scriptural Narratives for Positive Psychological and Suicide Prevention*. Lanham: Lexington, 2017.
Kegan, Robert. *The Evolving Self: Problem and Process in Human Development*. Cambridge: Harvard University Press, 1982.
———. "There the Dance Is: Religious Dimensions of a Developmental Framework." In *Toward Moral and Religious Maturity: The First International Conference on Moral and Religious Development*, edited by Christaine Brusselmans et al., 403–40. Morristown: Silver Burdett, 1980.
Kierkegaard, Søren. *The Sickness unto Death*. Translated and edited by Howard V. Hong and Edna H. Hong. Princeton: Princeton University Press, 1980.
———. *Søren Kierkegaard's Journals and Papers*. Vol. 4: S–Z. Translated and edited by Howard V. Hong et al. Bloomington: Indiana University Press, 1975.
———. *Stages on Life's Way: Studies by Various Persons*. Translated and edited by Howard V. Hong and Edna H. Hong. Princeton: Princeton University Press, 1988.
Kim, Matthew D. *Preaching to People in Pain: How Suffering Can Shape Your Sermons and Connect with Your Congregation*. Grand Rapids: Baker Academic, 2021.
Klenicki, Leon, and Richard John Neuhaus. *Believing Today: Jew and Christian in Conversation*. Grand Rapids: Eerdmans, 1989.
Koonz, Mark. "Matters of the Heart: James E. Loder on Homosexuality and the Possibility of Transformation." In *Embracing Truth: Homosexuality and the Word of God*, edited by David W. Torrance and Jock Stein, 196–217. Edinburgh: Handsel, 2012.
———. "The Old Question of Barth's Universalism: An Examination with Reference to Tom Greggs and T. F. Torrance." In *Theology in Scotland* 18 (2011) 33–46.
———. "Prayer and the Cure of Souls in James E. Loder's Counseling Ministry." In *Edification: The Interdisciplinary Journal of Christian Psychology* 5 (2011) 66–74.
Kourdakov, Sergei. *The Persecutor*. New York: Revell, 1973.

Krych, Margaret. *Teaching the Gospel Today: A Guide for Education in the Congregation*. Minneapolis: Augsburg, 1987.

Kurosawa, Akira, dir. *The Seven Samurai*. 1954. Criterion Collection, 2006. DVD.

Lane, Tony. "The Wrath of God as an Aspect of the Love of God." In *Nothing Greater, Nothing Better: Theological Essays on the Love of God*, edited by Kevin J. Vanhoozer, 138–67. Grand Rapids: Eerdmans, 2001.

Leder, Jane Mersky. *Dead Serious*. New York: Macmillan, 1989.

Leventhal, Barry R. "The Masada Suicides: The Making and Breaking of a Cultural Icon." In *Suicide: A Christian Response*, edited by Timothy J. Demy and Gary P. Stewart, 269–83. Grand Rapids: Kregel, 1998.

Lewis, C. S. *Christian Reflections*. Edited by Walter Hooper. Grand Rapids: Eerdmans, 1982.

———. *George MacDonald: An Anthology*. New York: HarperCollins, 2001.

———. *Mere Christianity*. San Francisco: HarperCollins, 2001.

———. *The Problem of Pain*. New York: Macmillan, 1978.

———. *Reflections on the Psalms*. San Francisco: HarperCollins, 2017.

Licona, Michael R. *The Resurrection of Jesus: A New Historiographical Approach*. Downers Grove, IL: InterVarsity, 2010.

Loder, James E., Jr. *Educational Ministry in the Logic of the Spirit*. Edited by Dana R. Wright. Eugene, OR: Cascade, 2018.

Loder, James E. *The Logic of the Spirit: Human Development in Theological Perspective*. San Francisco: Jossey-Bass, 1998.

———. *The Transforming Moment*. 2nd ed. Colorado Springs: Helmers & Howard, 1989.

Long, Thomas G., and Thomas Lynch. *The Good Funeral: Death, Grief, and the Community of Care*. Louisville: Westminster John Knox, 2013.

Luther, Martin. *Commentary on Galatians*. Translated by Erasmus Middleton. Grand Rapids: Kregel, 1979.

———. *The Large Catechism*. Translated by Robert H. Fischer. Philadelphia: Fortress, 1959.

———. *Luther: Letters of Spiritual Counsel*. Edited and translated by Theodore G. Tappert. Vancouver: Regent College, 2003.

———. *Luther's Works, Volume 19: Lectures on the Minor Prophets*. Edited by Hilton C. Oswald. Saint Louis: Concordia, 1974.

———. *Table Talk*. Translated and edited by Theodore G. Tappert. Philadelphia: Fortress, 1967.

The Lutheran Church–Missouri Synod. *That They May Have Life*. St. Louis: Concordia, 2024.

The Lutheran Church–Missouri Synod. *That They May Live*. St. Louis: Concordia, 2024.

MacDonald, George. *Unspoken Sermons*. Whitethorn: Johannesen, 1997.

———. *What's Mine's Mine*. Whitethorn: Johannesen, 2000.

MacDonald, Grenville. *George MacDonald and His Wife*. Whitethorn, CA: Johannesen, 1998.

MacKay, Donald M. *Science, Chance, and Providence*. Oxford: Oxford University Press, 1978.

Mackintosh, Hugh Ross. *God In Experience: Essays of Hugh Ross Mackintosh*. Edited by Paul K. Moser and Benjamin Nasmith. Eugene, OR: Pickwick, 2018.

MacLaren, Alexander. "The Last Pleading of Love." In *Expositions of Holy Scripture: Matthew 9–28*, 270–85. Grand Rapids: Baker Books, 1974.

———. "'See Thou to That!'" In *Expositions of Holy Scripture: Matthew 9–28*, 299–310. Grand Rapids: Baker Books, 1974.

McGee, J. Vernon. *Questions and Answers*. Nashville: Nelson, 1990.

McGrath, Alister E. *Intellectuals Don't Need God and Other Modern Myths: Building Bridges to Faith Through Apologetics*. Grand Rapids: Zondervan, 1993.

Meilander, Gilbert. *Bioethics: A Primer for Christians*. 2nd ed. Grand Rapids: Eerdmans, 2005.

Menninger, Karl. *Man Against Himself*. New York: Harcourt Brace, 1966.

———. *Whatever Became of Sin?* New York: Hawthorne Books, 1973.

Metzger, Bruce M. "The Lord's Prayer." Presentation. Quachita Baptist University Chapel, December 1996.

Midelfort, H. C. Erik. "Religious Melancholy and Suicide: On the Reformation Origins of a Sociological Stereotype." In *Madness, Melancholy, and the Limits of the Self: Studies in Culture, Law, and the Sacred*, edited by Andrew D. Weiner et al., 41–56. Madison: University of Wisconsin Law School, 1996.

Moltmann, Jürgen. *Ethics of Hope*. Translated by Margaret Kohl. Minneapolis: Fortress, 2012.

Montgomery, John Warwick, host. *Christianity on Trial*. KYMS California, March 11, 1984.

———. *Defending the Faith in a Messy World: A Christian Apologetics Primer*. Irvine: 1517 Publishing, 2017.

———. *History, Law, and Christianity*. Edmonton: Canadian Institute for Law, Theology, and Public Policy, 2002.

Moser, Paul K., and Benjamin Nasmith. Editors. *God In Experience: Essays of Hugh Ross Mackintosh*. Eugene, OR: Pickwick, 2018.

Nicholi, Armand M. *The Question of God: C. S. Lewis and Sigmund Freud Debate God, Love, Sex, and the Meaning of Life*. New York: Free Press, 2002.

Niditch, Susan. "Samson as Culture Hero, Trickster, and Bandit: The Empowerment of the Weak." *Catholic Biblical Quarterly* 52 (1990) 608–24.

Novak, David. "Suicide Is Not a Private Choice." *First Things* 75 (1997) 31–34.

Oberman, Heiko A. *Luther: Man Between God and the Devil*. Translated by Eileen Walliser-Schwarzbart. New Haven: Yale University Press, 2006.

Oden, Thomas C. *Classical Pastoral Care: Volume Four: Crisis Ministries*. Grand Rapids: Baker Books, 1994.

O'Mathuna, Donal P. "But the Bible Doesn't Say They Were Wrong to Commit Suicide, Does It?" In *Suicide: A Christian Response*, Timothy J. Demy & Gary P. Stewart, eds., 349–66. Grand Rapids: Kregel, 1998.

Packer, James I. *Finishing Our Course with Joy: Guidance from God on Engaging with Our Aging*. Wheaton, IL: Crossway, 2014.

Pannenberg, Wolfhart. *Anthropology in Theological Perspective*. Translated by Matthew J. O'Connell. Philadelphia: Westminster, 1985.

Parrott, Les, III. *Helping the Struggling Adolescent: A Guide to Thirty Common Problems for Parents, Counselors, and Youth Workers*. Grand Rapids: Zondervan, 1993.

Parsons, Mike. *Suicide and the Church: A Pastoral Theology*. Cambridge: Grove, 2010.

Patton, John. *Is Human Forgiveness Possible? A Pastoral Care Perspective*. Nashville: Abingdon, 1985.

Peterson, Eugene. *A Long Obedience in the Same Direction*. Downers Grove, IL: InterVarsity, 2000.

Pinnock, Clark H. *The Flame of Love: A Theology of the Holy Spirit.* Downer's Grove: InterVarsity, 1996.
Plantinga, Alvin. *Knowledge and Christian Belief.* Grand Rapids: Eerdmans, 2015.
Plass, Ewald M., ed. *What Luther Says.* St. Louis: Concordia, 1986.
Polkinghorne, John. *Science and Providence: God's Interaction With the World.* Boston: Shambhala Publications, 1989.
Pollard, William G. *Transcendence and Providence: Reflections of a Physicist and Priest.* Edinburgh: Scottish Academic, 1987.
Ramm, Bernard. *Offense to Reason: A Theology of Sin.* San Francisco: Harper & Row, 1985.
Russell, Bertrand. *A History of Western Philosophy.* New York: Simon & Schuster, 1972.
Rutledge, Fleming. *The Crucifixion: Understanding the Death of Jesus Christ.* Grand Rapids: Eerdmans, 2015.
———. *Three Hours: Sermons for Good Friday.* Grand Rapids: Eerdmans, 2019.
Sayer, George. "C. S. Lewis and George MacDonald." In *The Canadian C. S. Lewis Journal* 91 (1997) 24–33.
———. *Jack: A Life of C. S. Lewis.* Wheaton: Crossway, 1994.
Schmidt, Alvin J. "Hospitals and Health Care: Their Christian Roots." In *How Christianity Changed the World,* 151–69. Grand Rapids: Zondervan, 2004.
Schmidt, Wilhelm. *The Origin and Growth of Religion: Facts and Theories.* Translated by H. J. Rose. Proctorville, OH: Wythe-North Publishing, 2014.
Schwartz, Matthew B., and Kalmon Kaplan. *Biblical Stories for Psychotherapy and Counseling: A Sourcebook.* New York: Routledge, 2004.
Scully, Matthew. "Victor Frankl at Ninety: An Interview." *First Things* 52 (1995) 39–43.
Seamands, David A. *Redeeming the Past.* Colorado Springs: David C. Cook, 2002.
Shemesh, Yael. "Suicide in the Bible." *Jewish Bible Quarterly* 37 (2009) 157–68.
Shuster, Marguerite. *Power, Pathology, Paradox: The Dynamics of Evil and Good.* Grand Rapids: Zondervan, 1987.
Spitz, René A. *The First Year of Life: A Pschoanalytic Study of Normal and Deviant Development of Object Relations.* New York: International Universities Press, 1965.
Sproul, R. C. *Now, That's a Good Question!* Carol Stream, IL: Tyndale House, 1996.
Spurgeon, C. H. *C. H. Spurgeon's Sermons.* Vol. 22. Pasadena, TX: Pilgrim Publications, 2005.
———. "Fear of Death." *The Spurgeon Center.* https://www.spurgeon.org/resource-library/sermons/fear-of-death.
———. *Lectures to My Students.* Grand Rapids: Zondervan, 1954.
Standing Conference of the Canonical Orthodox Bishops in the Americas. "A Pastoral Letter on Suicide." Crestwood, NY: St. Vladimir's Seminary, 2007.
Stauffer, Richard. *The Humanness of John Calvin: The Reformer as a Husband, Father, Reformer, and Friend.* Translated by George Shriver. Nashville: Abingdon, 1971.
Stendahl, Krister. *Paul Among Jews and Gentiles.* Philadelphia: Fortress, 1976.
Stewart, James S. *A Faith to Proclaim.* Grand Rapids: Baker Books, 1976.
———. *Heralds of God.* New York: Scribner's Sons, 1946.
Sturges, John, dir. *The Magnificent Seven,* 1960. 20th Century Fox, 2016. DVD.
ten Boom, Corrie, et al. *The Hiding Place.* Translated by John E. Meeter. Washington Depot, CT: Chosen, 1971.
Thompson, Marianne Meye. "Committing the Unforgivable Sin." *Christianity Today,* 43 (1999) 82.

Tillich, Paul. *Systematic Theology, Volume II: Existence and the Christ.* Chicago: University of Chicago Press, 1957.

———. *Systematic Theology, Volume III: Life and the Spirit: History and the Kingdom of God.* Chicago: University of Chicago Press, 1963.

Torrance, David W., and Jock Stein, eds. *Embracing Truth: Homosexuality and the Word of God.* Edinburgh: Handsel, 2012.

Torrance, James B. "The Vicarious Humanity of Christ." In *The Incarnation: Ecumenical Studies in the Nicene-Constantinopolitan Creed A.D. 381*, edited by Thomas F. Torrance, 127–47. Eugene, OR: Wipf & Stock, 1998.

———. *Worship, Community and the Triune God of Grace.* Downers Grove, IL: InterVarsity, 1996.

Torrance, Thomas F. *Atonement: The Person and Work of Christ.* Edited by Robert T. Walker. Downers Grove: IVP Academic, 2009.

———. *The Doctrine of Grace in the Apostolic Fathers.* Eugene, OR: Wipf & Stock, 1996.

———, ed. *The Incarnation: Ecumenical Studies in the Nicene-Constantinopolitan Creed A.D. 381.* Eugene, OR: Wipf & Stock, 1998.

———. *Incarnation: The Person and Life of Christ.* Edited by Robert T. Walker. Downers Grove: IVP Academic, 2008.

———. *Karl Barth, Biblical and Evangelical Theologian.* Edinburgh: T&T Clark, 1990.

———. *The Mediation of Christ.* Colorado Springs: Helmers & Howard, 1992.

———. *Preaching Christ Today: The Gospel and Scientific Thinking.* Grand Rapids: Eerdmans, 1994.

———. *Space, Time and Resurrection.* Edinburgh: Handsel, 1976.

Tubb, Amy. "Suicide Still a Leading Cause of Maternal Death." *Maternal Mental Health Alliance*, October 12, 2023. https://maternalmentalhealthalliance.org/news/mbrrace-2023-suicide-still-leading-cause-maternal-death.

van Unnik, W. C. "The Death of Judas in Saint Matthew's Gospel." In *Sparsa Collecta: The Collected Essays of W. C. van Unnik Part Four*, edited by Cilliers Breytenback and Pieter W. van der Horst, 3–16. Leiden: Brill, 2014.

Vaughan, Joy L. *Phenomenal Phenomena: Biblical and Multicultural Accounts of Spirits and Exorcism.* Waco: Baylor University Press, 2023.

Vanauken, Sheldon. *A Severe Mercy.* New York: Bantam, 1981.

Vanhoozer, Kevin J. *Nothing Greater, Nothing Better: Theological Essays on the Love of God.* Grand Rapids: Eerdmans, 2001.

Vitz, Paul C. *Sigmund Freud's Christian Unconscious.* New York: Guilford, 1988.

Walton, John H., and J. Harvey Walton. *The Lost World of the Israelite Conquest: Covenant, Retribution, and the Fate of the Canaanites.* Downers Grove: IVP Academic, 2017.

Warfield, Benjamin B. *Studies in Tertullian and Augustine.* Oxford: Oxford University Press, 1932; Grand Rapids: Baker, 2003.

Watt, Jeffrey R. "Calvin on Suicide." *Church History* 66 (1997) 463–76.

———. *Choosing Death: Suicide and Calvinism in Early Modern Geneva.* Kirksville: Truman State University Press, 2001.

Waugh, Alexander. *The House of Wittgenstein: A Family at War.* New York: Anchor, 2010.

Wead, Douglas. *The Compassionate Touch.* Minneapolis: Bethany, 1980.

Webster, Richard. *Why Freud Was Wrong: Sin, Science, and Psychoanalysis.* New York: BasicBooks, 1995.

Weiner, Andrew D., et al. *Madness, Melancholy, and the Limits of the Self: Studies in Culture, Law, and the Sacred*. Madison: University of Wisconsin Law School, 1996.
Welker, Michael. *God the Spirit*. Translated by John F. Hoffmeyer. Minneapolis: Fortress, 1994.
Wesley, Charles. *Sacred Poetry: Selected From the Works of the Rev. Charles Wesley*. New York: Protestant Episcopal Society, 1864.
Wesley, John. *Wesley's Notes on the Bible*. 1765. Online Christian Library. http://www.ccel.org/ccel/wesley/notes.html.
———. *The Works of John Wesley, Complete and Unabridged, Volume VII: Sermons, III*. 3rd ed. Peabody: Hendrickson, 1991.
———. *The Works of John Wesley, Volume XIII: Letters*. Peabody: Hendrickson, 1872, 1991.
Wesley, John, and Charles Wesley. *The Poetical Works of John and Charles Wesley, Volume IX*. Edited by G. Osborn. London: Wesleyan–Methodist Conference, 1870.
West, John G. "Richard Baxter and the Origin of 'Mere Christianity.'" *Discovery Institute*, January 1, 1996. https://www.discovery.org/a/460/.
Wiersbe, Warren, and David Wiersbe. *Ministering to the Mourning: A Practical Guide to Pastors, Church Leaders, and Other Caregivers*. Chicago: Moody, 2006.
Wiesel, Elie. *Five Biblical Portraits*. Notre Dame: University of Notre Dame Press, 1981.
Willimon, Will. *Aging: Growing Old in Church*. Grand Rapids: Baker Academic, 2020.
Wolpe, David. *David: The Divided Heart*. New Haven: Yale University Press, 2014.
Wright, N. T. *The Case for the Psalms: Why They Are Essential*. New York: HarperCollins, 2013.
———. *Judas and the Gospel of Jesus: Have We Missed the Truth about Christianity?* Grand Rapids: Baker, 2006.
———. *The Resurrection of the Son of God*. Minneapolis: Fortress, 2003.
———. *Surprised by Hope: Rethinking Heaven, the Resurrection, and the Mission of the Church*. HarperCollins Publishers, 2008.
Wrong, Charles. "A Chance Meeting." In *C. S. Lewis at the Breakfast Table and Other Reminiscences*, edited by James T. Como, 107–14. San Diego: Harcourt Brace, 1992.
Younger, K. Lawson. *Ancient Conquest Accounts: A Study in Ancient Near Eastern and Biblical History*. Sheffield Academic, 2009.
Ziegler, Philip G. *God's Adversary and Ours: A Brief Theology of the Devil*. Forthcoming.

Index

Index of biblical characters (excluding references to Christ, Jesus of Nazareth, Satan), many without commentary

Abel, 144
Abimelech, 33
Absalom, 42–43, 123
Ahithophel, 42–43, 46, 53–54, 101, 123, 184
Amnon, 43

Bathsheba, 269

Cain, 144, 249
Caiphas, 52

David, king of Israel, 39–43, 53–54, 61, 101, 122–23, 266, 268–69
Delilah, 38
Doeg, 43

Elijah, 38, 57
Elisha, 57
Esther, 57

Goliath, 269

Hushai, 41–42

Jeremiah, 44, 161
Job, 35–37, 73, 179, 248
Jonah, 44–46
Joseph, 73

Judas, 34, 39, 46–54, 112–13, 123–24, 184

Lazarus, 179

Martha, 179
Mary, 179
Miriam, 266
Moses, 44, 61

Nathan, 269
Nebuchadnezzar, 103

Paul/Saul of Tarsus, 50–51, 67, 76, 85n21, 160–61
Pilate, 52

Samson, 37–39, 120–21
Samuel, 40, 122
Saul, king of Israel, 33–34, 39–42, 53, 101, 121–23,
Simon Peter, 47, 50–52, 124

Tamar, 43

Uriah, 269

Zimri, 33

Index of authors, ancient and modern

Abelson, Kassel, 62n9
Achtemeier, Elizabeth, 272

INDEX

Acolatse, Esther, 109n19
Albright, William F., 51n30
Allen, Diogenes, 14n1, 216n4
Allison, Dale, 97n17, 152n12
Ambrose, of Milan, 79
Amundsen, Darrel, 87n26, 145n14
Anderson, Ray, 6, 47–48, 51, 106n15
Aquinas, Thomas, 23, 87–90, 103, 113, 200–201
Aristotle, 248
Athanasius, of Alexandria, 23, 106n15
Augustine, of Hippo, 23, 59, 72, 75, 78–87, 103, 113, 191, 200–201

Bailey, Kenneth, 70n16
Baldwin, Joyce, 41
Bales, James, 109n20
Bar, Shaul, 39n7
Barclay, John M. G., 161n11
Barnhouse, Donald, 2
Barth, Karl, 19–20, 22–23, 39n7, 52–54, 74, 142, 169–76, 180, 183, 188n4, 204
Battenhouse, Roy, 43n15
Bauckham, Richard, 51n30
Baxter, Christina, xiii-xv, 148n3, 153n14
Baxter, Richard, 128–29
Bayly, Joe, 258n1
Beasley, Alan, 60n6
Beker, J. Christiaan, 87n25
Benedict XVI, Pope (see Ratzinger), 201
Bennett, Arnold, 159
Berman, Alan, 28n18
Bethge, Eberhard, 186
Binswanger, Ludwig, 164n17
Blackmun, Justice Harry, 247
Bliss, Kathleen, 216
Bloesch, Donald, 38–39, 57–58, 97n17, 203
Blomberg, Craig, 51n30
Bock, Darrell, 48n21
Bodelschwingh, Friedrich von, 254
Bolt, Peter, 66n12
Bonhoeffer, Dietrich, 16, 19–20, 73–74, 129, 142, 181–86, 188n4, 204, 219, 254–55, 270n7
Boros, Ladislaus, 203

Boswell, James, 24, 127–28
Boyd, Gregory, 152n12
Brandeis, Justice Louis, 247
Braune, Paul-Gerhard, 254
Bronson, Charles, 134
Brown, Peter, 79n7
Bruce, F. F., 50–51
Brueggemann, Walter, 270n7
Buechner, Frederick, 26n15
Buntain, Mark, 154
Burton, Bryan, 52n31
Bush, Michael, 6

Caird, George, 2n2
Calvin, John, 23, 101–13, 244
Camus, Albert, 163
Canaris, Wilhelm, 182
Cantz, Paul, 36n3, 55
Carlsen, Mary Baird, 174–75, 213n1
Carnell, Edward John, 214
Carroll, Lewis (see Dodgson), 139
Carter, Tom, 145n13
Cassuto, Umberto, 62
Chapell, Bryan, 12
Chesterton, G. K., 139, 146–51, 201
Christie, Agatha, 161–62
Clark, Chap, 28n18
Clebsch, William, 86, 115
Clement, of Alexandria, 78, 118
Clemons, James, 126, 245–46
Clinton, Tim, 28n18
Colwell, John, 52n31
Colyer, Elmer, 106n15
Copan, Paul, 57n3, 253n8, 257
Cottrell, Jack, 197–99
Craig, William Lane, 21n13, 49n25, 57n3, 152n12
Cranfield, Charles, 50, 161n11
Crews, Frederick, 165n19
Crisp, Oliver, 106n15
Croft, Brian, 258n1
Cullmann, Oscar, 97n17

Davidson, Lucy, 245
Davies, D. Eryl, 253n7
Demant, Vigo A., 214–22
Denker, Rolf, 190n10
Dietrich, Veit, 94

Diodore, of Tarsus, 270
Dodgson, Charles, 139
Donne, John, 115–19
Donne, John, the son, 116
Droge, Arthur, 76n6, 87n26
Duff, Nancy, 252n6
Durkheim, Emile, 249

Earman, John, 152n13
Eddy, Paul Rhodes, 152n12
Erler, Rolf Joachim, 170n2
Eusebius, of Caesarea, 78
Evans, Craig, 51n30
Evans, C. Stephan, 135n9

Fee, Gordon, 36n2, 109n18
Fest, Joachim, 182n3
Fielding, Henry, 126n11
Fitzgerald, Percy, 128
Foster, Michael Beresford, 215–22
Fowl, Stephen, 76n6
Frankl, Victor, 134
France, Richard, 46
Froehlich, Karlfried, 86n23, 254n11, 267n6, 270n8, 271n9
Froehlich, Ricarda, 267n6
Freud, Sigmund, 159–60, 163–67

Garrow, William, 126
Gaventa, Beverly, 18n6
Geach, Peter, 21n13, 49n25
Geisler, Norman, 73
Geivett, R. Douglas, 152n13
Gerali, Steven, 28n18
Gibson, Scott, 12, 28n18, 258n1
Gilbert, Martin, 254n11
Goldingay, John, 270n7
Gore, Charles, 218
Green, Clifford, 182n7
Green, Michael, 67
Gregory, of Nazianzus, 78
Grimm, Brothers (Jacob and Wilhelm), 163
Gunn, David, 39n7

Habermas, Gary, 152n12, 152n13
Hauer, Christian, 39n8
Hecht, Jennifer, 149n7, 257

Hegel, Georg, 163
Henry, Matthew, 123
Hitler, Adolf, 254, 267
Hobbes, Thomas, 163
Homer, 72
Hong, Edna, 254n11
Hooykaas, Reijer, 220n12
Hordern, William, 54n38
Houston, James, 174–75
Hsu, Albert, 6, 26n15
Hugo, Victor, 161
Hurtado, Larry, 149n5

Jaki, Stanley, 220n12
John Paul II, Pope, 201
Johnson, Paul, 255n12
Johnson, Samuel, 24, 127–30, 183
Jones, Clay, 57n3

Kaiser, Christopher, 220n12
Kant, Immanuel, 163
Kaplan, Kalman, 36n3, 55, 62, 255–56
Käsemann, Ernst, 97n17
Kegan, Robert, 166n21
Keith, Scott, 63n10
Kettler, Christian, 106n15
Kevorkian, Murad (Jack), 249, 255–56
Kierkegaard, Søren, 131–37, 189–90
Kim, Matthew, 258n1
Klenicki, Leon, 181
Koonz, Nancy, 3
Koonz, Mark, 52n31, 98n20, 172n3
Kourdakov, Sergei, 64–65
Krych, Margaret, 55
Kurosawa, Akira, 134

Lane, Tony, 57n2
Leder, Jane Mersky, 28n18
Lee, Bruce, 100
Leventhal, Barry, 62n9
Lewis, C. S., 22, 33, 36n3, 72–74, 78, 108, 110, 129n16, 138–39, 162n14, 167, 176n14, 177–80, 256, 270n7
Lichtenberg, Bernhard, 254
Licona, Michael, 152n12
Lindvall, Terry, 167n24

290　INDEX

Loder, James, 98–99, 148n4, 164n18, 174–75, 179, 208–9, 213n1
Long, Thomas, 258n1
Lucy, of Syracuse, 89n33
Luther, Martin, 23–24, 45–46, 85, 91–100, 103, 110, 113, 186, 204–5, 243–44, 267
Lynch, Thomas, 258n1

McCarthy, Cormack, 161
McGee, J. Vernon, 193–94, 199
McGrath, Alister, 166n23
McLaughlin, Jarrett, 224–31
McLaughlin, Meg Peery, 224–31
MacDonald, George, 138–40, 158, 179
MacDonald, Grenville, 139
MacDonald, Philip, 139
MacDonald, Ronald, 139
MacKay, Donald, 152n13
MacLaren, Alexander, 47, 49n26
Mackintosh, Hugh Ross, 14–15, 136, 265–66
Manson, William, 51n30
Marquard, Reiner, 170n2
Marx, Karl, 163
Mason, Karen, 12, 28n18
Meilander, Gilbert, 252–53, 257
Menninger, Karl, 27, 160
Metzger, Bruce, 97n17
Midelfort, Erik, 91, 94
Miller, Arthur, 111
Miller, Dennis, 249
Moltmann, Jürgen, 187–89, 252n6
Montgomery, John Warwick, 21n13, 183, 194–96, 199

Nebelsick, Harold, 220n12
Neuhaus, Richard, 181, 255
Newman, John Henry, 218
Newton, Phil, 258n1
Nicholi, Armand, 167
Niditch, Susan, 37n5
Niebuhr, Reinhold, 156
Nissiotis, Nikos, 208
Novak, David, 250
Novatian, 87n25

Oberman, Heiko, 96

Oden, Thomas, 93
Olsen, Dan, 1
Osborn, George, 122
O'Mathuna, Donal, 40

Packer, James, 174–75
Palmer, Earl, 147n2
Paley, William, 179
Pannenberg, Wolfhart, 160n9, 168, 189–92
Parker, Michael, 174–75
Parrott III, Les, 28n18
Parsons, Mike, 245–46n1
Patton, John, 27n16
Paulinus, of Nola, 118n7
Peterson, Eric, 232–43
Peterson, Eugene, 270n7, 273
Pinnock, Clark, 67–68
Plantinga, Alvin, 166n23
Plass, Ewald, 92n2 and n3
Plato, 72, 74–75, 78, 164
Polkinghorne, John, 152n13
Pollard, William, 152n13
Pythagoras, 75

Ramm, Bernard, 97n17, 163
Ratzinger, Cardinal Joseph, 201
Ridgeway, General Matthew, 41n11
Rousseau, Jean-Jacques, 163
Russell, Bertrand, 75n5
Rutledge, Fleming, 6

Sayer, George, 139n2
Schall, James, 150n9
Schleiermacher, Friedrich, 267
Schmidt, Alvin, 174n9, 220n12
Schmidt, Wilhelm, 166n23
Schwartz, Matthew, 36n3, 55, 62
Seamands, David, 148n4, 164n18
Shakespeare, William, 269
Shelley, Percy, 179
Shemesh, Yael, 33n1, 42n13
Shuster, Marguerite, 36, 111
Skinner, B. F., 163
Socrates, 75
Spinoza, Baruch, 163
Spitz, René, 190
Sproul, R. C., 197, 199

Spurgeon, Charles, 141–45
Stalin, Joseph, 110
Stark, Rodney, 220n12
Stendahl, Krister, 87n25
Stewart, James S., 136, 265–66n5
Story, Cullen, 51n30
Sturges, John, 134n7

Taber, James, 76n6, 87n26,
Tappert, Theodore, 94
Temple, William, 217
ten Boom, Betsy, 173–74
ten Boom, Casper, 173
ten Boom, Corrie, 173
Teresa, Mother, 153–54
Thompson, Marianne Meye, 67
Thompson, Silouan, 206n10
Tillich, Paul, 156–65
Tolkien, J. R. R., 139, 163
Torrance, James, 106n15, 262–64
Torrance, Thomas F., 19n7, 52n31, 54n38, 87n25, 136, 148n3, 152n12, 220n12, 265n5
Tubb, Amy, xivn1

van Unnik, W. C., 52n32
Vanauken, Jean "Davy," 177–78, 180
Vanauken, Sheldon, 73, 177–78, 180
Vaughan, Joy, 109n19

Vitz, Paul, 166n23
Voltaire, 163
von Galen, Clemens August Graf, 254

Walton, J. Harvey, 57n3
Walton, John H., 57n3
Warfield, Benjamin, 80
Watt, Jeffrey, 101–3
Waugh, Alexander, 96n12
Webster, Richard, 165n19
Welker, Michael, 97n17
Wentworth, Patricia, 161–62
Wesley, Charles, 121–22
Wesley, John, 120–26, 217
West, John, 129n16
Wiersbe, David, 12
Wiersbe, Warren, 12
Wiesel, Elie, 40–41
Willimon, Will, 174–75, 223–31, 246–54
Wittgenstein, Ludwig, 95–96
Wolpe, David, 42–43
Wrong, Charles, 72–73, 75, 256n14
Wright, N. T. (Tom), 48n21, 152n12, 210n14, 270n7

Younger, K. Lawson, 57n3

Ziegler, Philip, 109n19

www.ingramcontent.com/pod-product-compliance
Lightning Source LLC
Chambersburg PA
CBHW071233230426
43668CB00011B/1422